CAPITALISM
IN CRISIS

CAPITALISM IN CRISIS

Globalization and World Politics Today

FIDEL CASTRO

Edited by David Deutschmann

OCEAN PRESS
Melbourne • New York

in association with

EDITORA POLITICA
Havana

Cover design by David Spratt

Copyright © 2000 Ocean Press
Copyright © 2000 Editora Politica
Copyright © 2000 Fidel Castro

All rights reserved. No part of this publication may be reproduced, stored in a
retrieval system or transmitted in any form or by any means, electronic,
mechanical, photocopying, recording or otherwise, without the prior permission
of the publisher.

ISBN 1-876175-18-4

First printed 2000

Printed in Australia

Published by Ocean Press
Australia: GPO Box 3279, Melbourne, Victoria 3001, Australia
   • Fax: (61-3) 9329 5040 • E-mail: edit@oceanpress.com.au
USA: PO Box 834, Hoboken, NJ 07030 • Fax: 201-617 0203

Website: www.oceanpress.com.au

Library of Congress Card No: 99-070353

OCEAN PRESS DISTRIBUTORS
United States: LPC/InBook,
      1436 West Randolph St, Chicago, IL 60607, USA
Canada: Login Brothers,
      324 Salteaux Cres, Winnipeg, Manitoba R3J 3T2, Canada
Britain and Europe: Global Book Marketing,
      38 King Street, London, WC2E 8JT, UK
Australia and New Zealand: Astam Books,
      57-61 John Street, Leichhardt, NSW 2040, Australia
Cuba and Latin America: Ocean Press,
      Calle 21 #406, Vedado, Havana, Cuba
Southern Africa: Phambili Agencies,
      PO Box 28680, Kensington 2101, Johannesburg, South Africa

Table of contents

Editor's Preface

GLOBALIZATION IS AN OBJECTIVE REALITY underlining the fact that we are all passengers on the same vessel — this planet where we all live. But passengers on this vessel are traveling in very different conditions.

A trifling minority is traveling in luxurious cabins furnished with the internet, cell phones and access to global communication networks. They enjoy a nutritional, abundant and balanced diet as well as clean water supplies. They have access to sophisticated medical care and culture.

The overwhelming and suffering majority is traveling in conditions that resemble the terrible slave trade from Africa to America in our colonial past. That is, 85 percent of the passengers on this ship are crowded together in its dirty hold, suffering hunger, disease and helplessness.

Obviously, this vessel is carrying too much injustice to remain afloat, pursuing such an irrational and senseless route ...

It is our duty to take our rightful place at the helm and ensure that all passengers can travel in conditions of solidarity, equity and justice.

Fidel Castro's opening speech to the South Summit, April 12, 2000

Many books have been written on the subject of globalization. Many conferences have debated its meaning and direction. Voices from the Third World have been allowed little space in this debate. Among the strongest of these voices — and it must be said, among the most radical — has been Cuba's Fidel Castro.

In this book Fidel Castro adds his voice to the growing international chorus against neoliberalism and the globalization of privilege and exploitation. He denounces a system which colonized, enslaved and plundered the peoples of the globe for centuries and which continues to do so today in the name of "free market economics."

The Cuban leader bluntly describes the world today as "one giant casino" and asks: "Why not seek other formulas and admit that humankind is able to organize its life and its destiny in a more rational and humane manner?" Fidel Castro asks what kind of globalization is needed:

> It cannot but be supportive, socialist, communist or whatever you want to call it. Does nature, and the human species with it, have much time left to survive in the absence of such change? Very little time. Who will be the builders of that new world? The men and women who inhabit our planet. What will be their basic weapons? Ideas will be, and consciousness. Who will sow them, cultivate them and make them invincible? You will. Is it a utopia, just one more dream among so many others? No, because it is objectively inevitable and there is no alternative to it. It has been dreamed of before, only perhaps too early. As the most visionary of the sons of this island, José Martí, said: "Today's dreams will be tomorrow's realities."

If there is a singular theme that emerges from this volume it is the role of ideas. Fidel Castro thrives in the intellectual and moral challenge that now faces not only the oppressed of the world in seeking solutions that will benefit the immense majority, but also the forces for social change. This book reflects his never-ceasing drive to "sow and cultivate" these ideas of hope and struggle, providing them with a content that creates their invincibility. He lives and breathes this belief in the dreams of today and the realities of tomorrow.

⌘

This book is published by Ocean Press in association with Editora Politica of Havana. The director of Editora Politica, Santiago Dorques, provided support and encouragement for the project, as did Mirta Muñiz of Ocean Press in Havana.

The items contained in this selection are from May 1998 to April 2000. They include speeches and written messages by Fidel Castro. Among the speeches are those given in the Dominican Republic, Venezuela, Brazil and South Africa. During these last two years, Fidel Castro has been outspoken on the need to find an alternative to globalized plunder, poverty and despair.

The items have been excerpted for this volume, which has sought to feature the contributions of Fidel Castro on not only the subject of globalization but also on some of the central issues of world politics at the beginning of a new century.

This selection contains a distinct voice from the Third World that deserves to be heard. It is a radical alternative to the neoliberal "models" of social development promoted by the World Bank and the IMF.

David Deutschmann
Melbourne, Australia
June 2000

1

There are No Economic Miracles

World Trade Organization, Geneva

L ast March, the U.S. government made public the "1998 Trade Policy Agenda of the United States" where it was literally indicated that it is set to be "aggressive, directed globally and at all key regions of the world"; that "as the most important and successful economy in the global trading system, the United States is in a strong position to use its powers of persuasion and influence to pursue this Agenda"; and that "despite the substantial market openings that have been achieved in recent years, there remain too many barriers to U.S. goods and services exports throughout the world." Such language is distressing.

Together with this, on September 1995 following a U.S. initiative, discussions began in the Organization of Economic Cooperation and Development (OECD) — an exclusive First World club — to work out a Multilateral Agreement on Investments. This was so, even though the World Trade Organization already existed with 132 member countries in different stages of development.

Due to problems obviously related to the sovereignty of states, the subsequent idea to negotiate that agreement in the World Trade Organization was strongly opposed by numerous members at the Ministerial Conference held in Singapore on December 1996. However, the agreements reached there did not prevent the OECD — made up, as I said, by developed countries — from proceeding with the

---

Speech at the special session of the World Trade Organization commemorating the 50th anniversary of the multilateral trade system, held in Geneva, May 19, 1998.

elaboration of the Multilateral Agreement on Investments.

Attempts by the United States to introduce key aspects of the Helms-Burton Act in the said agreement led the negotiations to a standstill, leaving only the United States and Europe involved while the other 13 OECD member nations were left out.

The above-mentioned act illustrates U.S. behavior in its economic war against Cuba. The extraterritorial nature of these and other measures led the European Union to request from the WTO the establishment of a Special Panel which was then approved on November 20, 1996.

Later on, by 11 April, 1997, an understanding was reached on the basis of certain U.S. pledges associated with the implementation of, and amendments to, the Helms-Burton Act. The European Union, to avoid weakening the WTO, agreed to temporarily suspend the beginning of the Special Panel activities.

An amazing and shrewd maneuver had allowed the United States to leave the dock at the WTO and undertake the laying down of new rules in international law within the framework of the OECD in an attempt to retroactively insert in the Multilateral Agreement on Investments the supposed illegality of the nationalizations conducted in the late 1950s — a date exactly coinciding with the triumph of the revolution in Cuba. It is a principle that can also be applied to nationalizations in other countries after 1959, the intention being to internationalize the principles of the infamous Helms-Burton Act under the umbrella of a multilateral agreement. That act, which has not been amended at all, has arbitrarily turned people who were Cuban citizens at the time of the expropriations into expropriated Americans.

Actually, the extraterritorial principle of the blockade [of Cuba] had been in force long before that shameful act came into existence. The U.S. Administration prevents every U.S. company, wherever it is based, from trading with Cuba. That constitutes a violation of sovereignty and is extraterritorial by nature. There are plenty of reasons for the world to feel humiliated and be concerned, and the WTO should be capable of preventing an economic genocide. Disputes between the United States and the European Union about this law should not be settled at the expense of Cuba. That would be an inconceivable dishonor to Europe. The agreements announced in London yesterday are unclear, contradictory and threatening for many countries, as they are unethical. The economic blockade has already cost Cuba $60 billion.

In the last few years, the United States has approved over 40 laws and executive decisions to apply unilateral economic sanctions against 75 nations representing 42 percent of the world population.

The United States obtained practically everything it wanted from the agreements leading to the establishment of the WTO, and particularly the General Agreement on Services, its old dream. The same applies to the Agreement on Trade-Related Aspects of Intellectual Property Rights, a field it controls thanks to its technological development and systematic plundering of the best minds in the world. Some of its patents have received up to 50 years of exclusive rights and it has additionally obtained other highly beneficial agreements.

The United States also has the peculiar privilege of issuing the currency in which the central banks and the trade bank deposits worldwide keep most of their hard currency reserves. The transnational companies of the nation whose citizens have the lowest saving rates are purchasing the world's riches with the money saved by people in other countries and the money printed without the gold backing agreed upon in Bretton Woods, and unilaterally ended in 1971.

Therefore, if the European currency emerges as a strong and prestigious currency, the euro would be welcome! It would benefit the world economy!

New issues introduced in the WTO's agenda by the wealthy countries are threatening a reduction of the developing countries' competitive possibilities — in the midst of already difficult conditions fraught with inequalities — which will certainly be used as pretexts for non-tariff barriers or to prevent their commodities access to the markets.

The Third World countries have been losing everything: custom tariffs that protected their emerging industries and produced revenues; agreements on basic commodities; producers associations; price indexation; preferential treatment; any instrument protecting their exports value and contributing to their development. What are we being offered?

Why isn't the unfair and unbalanced trade mentioned? Why is the appalling burden of the external debt no longer being discussed? Why is the official development aid being reduced? If every developed country did like Norway, there would be $200 billion available to the Third World for its development. Norway should be imitated!

How are we supposed to make a living? What goods and services shall we export? What industrial production will be left to us? Only those with a technology gap and a high input of human labor and which are highly pollutant? Might this be an attempt to turn a large part of the Third World into an immense free-trade zone full of assembly plants that do not even pay taxes?

Why is the strongest economic power in the world obstructing

China's access to the WTO when that country shelters one fifth of the world population? Why does it jeopardize the admission of Russia and other countries? No nation, big or small, can be left out of this important institution, nor should it; and its admission must not be subjected to humiliating conditions.

The developing countries must fend off divisions. Unity is our only asset, the only guarantee in the defense of our legitimate aspirations.

Those of us who were colonies yesterday and are still today enduring the consequences of backwardness, poverty and underdevelopment, we are the majority in this organization. Every one of us has the right to a vote and no one has the right to veto. We should turn this organization into an instrument of the struggle for a more just and better world. We should also appeal to those responsible statesmen, sensitive to our realities, who can undoubtedly be found in many developed countries.

Despite so much euphoria no one can be sure of how long the U.S. economic system, ruled by the blind laws of the market economy, will be able to prevent a financial meltdown. There are no economic miracles. That is clear now. The absurdly inflated stock prices in the stock markets of that economy — unquestionably the strongest in the world — cannot be sustained. In similar situations history is not known to have made exceptions. The problem is that now a big crisis would be global and have unforeseeable consequences. Not even the adversaries of the prevailing system could wish that to happen.

It would be worthwhile for the WTO to assess these risks and include among the so-called "new issues" another one: "Global Economic Crisis: What to do?"

2

For a Just, Globalized World

Economia 98 International Conference, Havana

I have deep convictions about the course the world is taking, about that globalization we have talked about and which we have baptized; just to give an idea and to synthesize in one phrase what we designate as neoliberal globalization. This does not deny the globalization process, which is inevitable, which is inexorable, and which has to be deeply studied.

I exhorted you to meditate on this topic, to research, delve deeply into it; to help, advise, disseminate, as an essential thing, truthfully, without any dogmas; I repeat, without any kind of dogmas, and with broadmindedness, listening to every one, without thinking that we are the owners of the absolute truth. On the contrary, if we believe something, we're interested in enriching and substantiating what we believe.

There will no longer be one single thinker. Hundreds of thousands, millions of thinkers can make up the thinker our times need. Names do not matter. There were times in which humankind was limited to one tenth of what it is today, and people wrote for the few millions who knew how to read and write, of which only a part was able to get to know their work.

Humankind today reaches the figure of six billion people, and, as I was saying this morning, many millions know how to read and write, and there is a lot of media to disseminate ideas. Given the struggle of ideas at a world level, oftentimes there is no access to the mass media

Speech at the Economia 98 International Conference in Havana, July 3, 1998.

controlled by the big transnationals, or there is no access to the large television or information networks. But there is always a way to make the message reach the world, there is always a possibility, and the more communications develop, the more this will be possible.

New ideas to prepare the peoples for the future are needed and we must start struggling right now. Beginning today, we must start building awareness — a new awareness, I would say. It is not that the world lacks awareness today; but such a new and complex era as this one requires principles more than ever. It requires a lot more awareness, and that awareness will be built, by adding together, we might say, the awareness of what is happening and the awareness of what is going to happen. It has to be built by adding together more than just one revolutionary thought and the best ethical and humane ideas of more than one religion, of all authentic religions, I would say — I am not thinking of sects, which of course are created for political ends and for the purpose of creating confusion and division— the sum total of the preaching of many political thinkers, of many schools and of many religions.

We have even spoken here of some of the eminent theoreticians of this century who have played a role and whose ideas may have certain validity; but we must bring together the ethical and humane sense of many ideas, some of which emerged in very remote times of human history: Christ's ideas with the scientifically founded socialist ideas, so just and profoundly humane, of Karl Marx, the ideas of Engels, the ideas of Lenin, the ideas of Martí, the ideas of the European Encyclopedists who preceded the French Revolution and those of the forefathers of the independence of this hemisphere, whose most outstanding. symbol was Simón Bolívar, who was capable, two centuries ago, to dream of a united Latin America. This was at a time when the horse was the fastest existing means of land transportation, on which a messenger might very well take three months to get from Caracas to Lima, or to Ayacucho, or to Bolivia. What primitive means they used in their struggle! There were no telephones, or communications, or radio, and they had the impetus and energy to travel all over a continent and dream of a united Latin America. Yes, those sentiments, that projection, those ideas, must also be taken up in our ideas of today.

When Bolívar spoke about the unity of the continent, what today is the United States was a nation located near the Atlantic coast, very far east from the Mississippi River, a nation which later would extend west at the expense of the Indians' lands and the lands of the Spanish and Indian descendants that inhabited them — that story is well known. That is why he spoke about the hemisphere, he did not exclude the United States, of course; but the United States then was not the United States that we know today: it was the 13 colonies that had recently freed themselves from British colonialism.

An important part of the territory of the America that Bolívar knew is missing today. Hardly anybody lived in Canada. He envisioned the union of that America so early. But others after him also dreamed of a united world, and we ourselves will have to think of a united world, because humankind is inexorably moving in that direction. Globalization is creating the conditions for that united world.

That was a great idea of Bolívar's; but really, when one analyzes the conditions, one can see that the united America he dreamed of was impossible in those times. The minimum cultural and material conditions did not exist for bringing about that union he partly achieved in Great Colombia before his death. But he was a visionary, in the same way Miranda was a visionary of independence.

I was saying that this world marches toward unity today. This is not a dream, but an objective reality, which gradually begins to take place and begins to take shape as a necessity for human survival.

I went further this morning when I was audacious enough to say something bolder concerning this planet's natural resources, which some powers selfishly want to preserve in order to sustain their so-called welfare societies. In a globalized world, those resources must be at the service of humankind. Many countries of the Third World were forced to build their economies based on resources that are becoming exhausted for the exclusive benefit of the developed societies. What will be left for them later?

In fact, when one sees that, for example, just in perfecting and developing nuclear weapons, the United States spends $5 billion every year; when one reads that it spends $27 billion in espionage and intelligence work every year, and in manufacturing new, modern weapons — known as intelligent weapons — and planes invisible to radar, has millions of men ready for war, hundreds of the most modern warships, lots of aircraft carriers and submarines and bases all over the world, one wonders why and what for. There has to be elaborate forethought for this, a culture of domination and an instinct for appropriation.

That is why [the United States] is not very concerned with the environment and other things, like reducing their gas emissions. It always opposes every international agreement aimed at preserving nature based on a universal sense of the common heritage of humanity. It raises objections of all kinds, because it does not want to commit itself to anything that may limit its lust for domination and enjoyment of the world's natural resources.

We could also ask ourselves another question: What good will all those weapons do them, when the peoples, a lot more cultivated and aware, learn the truth? What good will those weapons do them, when they have to suffer a deep economic crisis? That crisis will inevitably come when that gigantic balloon of the stock markets, which have absurdly multiplied their real values, deflates. They are imaginary values, without any material foundation, artificially created thanks to the privileged conditions of a state that, due to peculiar historical circumstances, has become the issuer of the main reserve currency accepted and circulated in the world, turning paper into gold, something which alchemists dreamed of accomplishing as far back as the Middle Ages.

They buy everything they can in the world, the main industries and services, and even promising, fertile lands. There are countries, like Argentina, where everything has been privatized, even important highways and streets — not only electricity, oil, gas, airports, airlines, railroads. There are advertisements abroad so that big transnationals from the United States and Europe can buy immense tracts of land in the fertile Argentine plains. There are some foreign investors there who own 200,000, 300,000 or 400,000 hectares of land. Not only industries and services are handed over to foreign capital, also resources like land, the lands of our peoples that will have to produce for the peoples, in exchange for a plate of lentils. That is why we maintain, based on mathematical facts, that such a neoliberal globalization is not sustainable; that the crisis is inevitable. And these crises, due to the increasingly globalized character of the world economy, will also be global, universal.

For a moment, I will try to imagine what would happen in the United States itself with the tens of millions of owners of inflated stocks, those families who deposited their savings in those stocks, if all of a sudden the stock markets collapse and with them those absurdly multiplied values.

They cannot avoid this, it is congenital; it is in the genes of the system that begot it, in the laws that govern its development. There is no way they can avoid it, unless they do what they will never do: renounce that system. No matter how much they preach and how much they propagate their ideology, their lies and their deceits, they cannot avoid it. The objective factors for change will present themselves as such; the factors to be prepared are the subjective ones.

I didn't come here, really, to draw up a plan and assign tasks to anybody. I came here as a guest the same as you did, among the many national and international congresses and activities I'm invited to.

The imperialists, in their propaganda against Cuba, can't stop talking about Castro: "Castro did or undid this and that." They individualize policies, they individualize processes: "Castro's revolution, Castro's communism." Everything is Castro's work, Castro's action, what really corresponds to millions of citizens in this country, first of all, to those who are carrying out the most arduous tasks.

While we are here speaking, at night already, there are hospitals attending patients, doctors on duty, and there are the family doctors a few steps away from whoever might need them as our system of family medicine has made possible. And at this time, there might even be many compatriots working, preparing the land for planting cane, or getting ready for the work that they will begin at 2:00 or 3:00 a.m., or after sunrise, under the tropical sun, a sun that is felt more and more, in an ever-changing climate.

We don't work with air-conditioning the way they work in the privileged temperate climates, over there where very often they don't even have mosquitoes. We, the vast majority of this planet's inhabitants, work in the part of the world where every day there are more fungi, more bacteria, more vectors, more insects, more mosquitoes, more global warming, more natural disasters, cyclones, floods or prolonged droughts. These are the conditions under which our peoples work and under which Cuban people work today.

If we are here before this microphone and the lights are on, it is because through the length and breadth of the country, at this very hour, there are thousands of workers attending the power lines and the boilers of the thermoelectric plants producing electricity to give us this light. And in this same way, there are others working on the railroads, others in transports that cannot stop, others loading and unloading at the docks, others even building, others on merchant ships. There are millions of people working or resting to go back to work tomorrow, although, on this occasion, being a Saturday, many will have the day off, but not all of them, because in order for part of them to have a free day, there are hundreds of thousands working and attending to the services that the rest need, the families, the children and other workers.

Yes, this is not Castro's revolution, it is the revolution of a people, it is the revolution of millions of workers. It is not a revolution of the bourgeoisie, nor of oligarchs, nor of transnationals; it is a revolution of workers, and of working people who have managed to keep united, to confront the giant, to confront the colossus. And when a Cuban says this, he must never say it out of vanity; our revolutionary comrades will never say it out of vanity, or out of chauvinism, or out of pride.

When we say this, we do so with satisfaction, of course; but that satisfaction stems from a sense of responsibility and of duty, the idea that by resisting here we are helping the fraternal peoples in this hemisphere and elsewhere. Demonstrating that it is possible to resist, and to resist even under the most incredible circumstances, we are proving what a human being is capable of, what values are capable of and what ideas are capable of.

Our enemies try to strike at our truths, and they slander that work of a whole people by every means possible, they plot and try to subvert it, they try to kill hope, to sow pessimism; if not, what is it they want to achieve with that indecent blockade? To break the morale of our people, who, almost uniquely in the world, suffers the harassment, the economic war and also the non-economic war, the political war and the ideological war of the greatest power that has ever existed in history — for the first time a hegemonic world power.

The United States is today the basis of globalized imperialism and the fight against that form of dominion has to be globalized, too.

[The empire] has its theories, its theoreticians and the media to disseminate them. The peoples dominated by that global empire must also have their theoreticians among the ranks of the intellectuals; first of all, economists — those with a political sense, not economists to serve the transnationals. Economists must develop ideas based on profoundly scientific foundations and human experience and convey them to their people.

Today, economists of the people must be political economists; and politicians must be politicians with — if it is possible — a maximum of knowledge. Today that is really the basis on which the fate of humanity depends, the basis on which our struggles are being carried out. And the politicians who do not understand, or do not want to understand, or who do not strive to understand economics, are not worthy of exercising their duty.

It is not a matter of saying nice things because the elections are near, or because you want your party to win a few more votes. It is not a matter of expressing things to obtain support with a multitude of reporters behind you. We have closely followed the so-called Summit of the Americas summoned by the United States.

I don't want to offend anyone but I have observed the politicians at those summits, under the domineering presence and the pressure of the heads of the empire. In those hemispheric summits there are usually two types of meetings, some are public and others are private. The politicians act one way in the public meetings and another in the private ones; when the press is no longer there, they can express some of their concerns, and they do.

As a rule, there is a lot of play-acting in those meetings, I won't say by everyone. I must admit there are serious politicians, even under those conditions; some who are even courageous. But one can see how demagogy prevails, along with a submission that sometimes borders on slimy flattery and weakness in many Latin American politicians. The leaders from the group of Caribbean countries that were colonies until after the Cuban Revolution's triumph behave differently. They express themselves and tell the truth in pure English, even to the president of the United States. We feel great respect for all of them and we have stood by those who are an inseparable part of the political life of our America.

As you know, Cuba is banned from participating in those so-called summit meetings. Actually, they can't imagine the great honor they're doing us, because that's where the demagogic masters go to set down the guidelines for the demagogic servants, or for those who, without being demagogues or servants or accepting guidelines, have no other choice but to bear the humiliation.

[The United States] greatly underestimated the Cuban people. They thought there would never be a revolution here, that there could never be organizations or parties or people who would not sell out, who would not give in, who would not be corrupted. That underestimation did us a lot of good, because by the time they realized it, we had beaten their army; we had disarmed their 80,000 men and had given the weapons to the people.

Arbenz could not do that in Guatemala, neither could other progressive, revolutionary men, like Allende, who also obtained power wishing to transform his country. How long did his noble effort last, achieved through the purest electoral means? Did it perhaps help to keep the CIA from conspiring with the most reactionary and con-servative elements to overthrow him? All this has been written, it is there for all to see, a lot has been published, and it is already a confessed crime of those who give themselves the luxury of breaking the law everywhere and even publishing, after a few years, the crimes they have committed.

They underestimated Cuba. They considered it to be its most faithful colony, its most secure domain, and they got careless. When they got around to realizing it, the people were already in power, and there were revolutionary laws, a people with ideas, a people with fighting traditions, who for the first time enjoyed justice, true freedom and equality, who for the first time felt respect for their dignity and their human condition. And when an individual comes to realize, or to absorb, or to live with those values, he or she is capable of anything. It becomes possible to send 500,000 sons and daughters within a few years to many parts of the world, to shed their blood even. More than all the Peace Corps, which the great empire organized, in fact, *after* the triumph of the revolution — don't forget that.

The defeat at the Bay of Pigs, or let us say, the Cuban victory at the

Bay of Pigs, was what [also] led to the establishment of the Alliance for Progress. During the first year of the revolution, we had been at an OAS meeting in Argentina — we had not been expelled yet — and we stated that Latin America, which at the time didn't owe a single penny, had to develop. Its population was a lot less than it is now, and we stated that $20 billion were needed to further that development.

Who would have thought then that a little later, right after the Bay of Pigs, afraid that the fire might spread throughout the hemisphere, they would establish the Alliance for Progress, offer $20 billion and press for agrarian and other reforms. Just look at how times change! Before that, any Latin American government would have been overthrown for an agrarian reform, considering it a communist measure. Later, they themselves were praising agrarian reform, tax reforms, abundant money, as an aid to all those economic and social programs, Peace Corps, etc.

Our sugar quota, most of it, was divided among Latin American countries. It was a quota of more than four million tons.

So the very existence of the revolution forced them to concern themselves with the situation in Latin America and to propose reforms to buffer, to alleviate the conditions it found itself in. All this comes about after the Cuban Revolution.

That is why Cuba is here. You needn't look for many explanations, because this revolution put its trust in humankind, in the people.

We can, of course, speak of satisfaction: it satisfies us that our people not only was able to help other peoples one way or another, but that it can, through its struggle, continue to be example and continue to cooperate with the cause of humanity.

We are not nationalistic — nationalism is not our basic idea, although we deeply love our country. We consider ourselves internationalists and internationalism is not at odds with the love of one's homeland, for the land where a human being is born or where millions of human beings are born. That's why I spoke about identity. Neither is the love for the land where one was born incompatible with a united world and with a globalization of another character, which I called socialist. The culture and the identity of a country is not incompatible with a united, completely globalized world.

More dangerous for the culture of each of our countries is the ideological poison that they spread every day through their powerful communication resources, their television chains, their cinema chains. They are the owners, they control everything. The films are made there, the canned culture with which they try to feed our spirits every day — not bread, but canned culture, yes. Food for the soul in the form of cultural poison.

What they invest in espionage alone or what they invest in the resources they use to poison the minds of the peoples would be enough for the health standards of the Third World to rise to those of the developed countries; the infant mortality, the mortality of women during childbirth, of people who die from infectious diseases that could be saved. It would suffice with a vaccine that can cost pennies. These are the realities.

That's where the danger lies: threatening our cultures, our identities and our aspirations that each of our brothers can live a decent life and have all that is necessary for a proper life, and, as we said, be immensely rich spiritually.

A just, globalized world, globalized under another conception, would not only save the physical space we must live in, but would create millions, hundreds of millions, thousands of millions of millionaires. Not the type of millionaires as are vulgarly conceived today, in material goods that should be distributed in an equitable and just manner. They would be millionaires in human spirit, which only under another system and under other conceptions can be infinitely enriched.

Why must there be unemployment? Why must there be surplus production crises? Why don't machines and technology work to serve humankind so that everyone has the opportunity to work? And not 70 or 80 hours as when the Industrial Revolution began in England, and not 60 or 70, as many still work today with two or three jobs to be able to live, but working perhaps 20 hours a week, perhaps 15, using that productivity, so that the citizens of this planet have the necessary material goods: housing, food, health care, recreation, culture; true culture that uplifts human being instead of debasing them; culture that does not turn children into murderers. Such a culture can only be reached by other roads.

There are many comrades — some are here among us today — working and spending countless hours of the day and the night not only working as much as necessary, but also studying and developing themselves. For my part, I enjoy the privilege of having a little more time than I had 20 or 30 years ago, due to the need that we all have to delve deeply into and understand the complex problems of today. Our revolution is the work of a people and of thousands of cadres and leaders. It is not and could never be the work of a single individual.

3

Global Economic Crisis

Autonomous University of Santo Domingo

I was wondering what I should say to you. There are many topics, an endless number of topics. I could speak about Cuba but we speak about Cuba every day, and when we do not, others do it for us and against us. I could perhaps then, in a few words, say that Cuba is still there and it will continue to be there.

Every now and then they publish that Castro is no longer there, or that Castro's days are numbered. They are such fools and such idiots that they do not realize that this is the least important factor. What would be the worth of a revolution if it depended on Castro or on any single individual? Poor idiots who for so long have applied that concept and believed in it!

From the very beginning, in their infinite plans to eliminate leaders of the Cuban Revolution, I was awarded the honor of being the first on their list. I once jokingly said that I had the undesirable record, or the inglorious record — well, perhaps it is glorious; but it would be best to call it the undesirable or unusual record — of being the primary target of assassination attempts against personalities and politicians, at least in this century, and perhaps in many others. They believed in the idea that the end of Castro would be the end of everything. They keep asking about Castro's health, or disseminating news, almost weekly or every two weeks, of his demise, or predicting diseases, or calculating his age.

From August 20-24, 1998, Fidel Castro visited the Dominican Republic to attend a meeting of CARIFORUM, a special meeting of Caribbean heads of state and government. This speech was delivered on August 24, 1998.

It is said a lady should never be asked about her age. We politicians might be considered like those who do not like to be reminded of their age. It is not out of vanity, no. It is simply upsetting not to be able to continue fighting and annoying them for a much longer period of time.

But these are matters of personal choice that have nothing to do with the philosophy of life, politics and history. That is why I said that, of all the predictions, that was least important.

They have little time to turn back the pages of history and recall the past. The march of history is adamant. We have had so many setbacks since last century. So many leaders died! However, that did not stop our country's historical struggle.

I concede that at a certain time, certain people can play a certain role. However, I hold this as a relative truth. Actually, I believe the role that any individual has played at any time has always depended on circum-stances that had nothing to do with the individual.

If Bolívar had been born in 1650 or 1700 no one would know the name Bolívar. Only a century later, and when new ideas keep emerging as a result of serious problems that have been accumulating for a long time, are big changes and their protagonists possible. If it had not been for the historical process that preceded the French Revolution, who would have ever heard of Danton, Robespierre, Mirabeau and all those individuals with an intense but short life because, according to Saturn's legend, the revolution devoured its own children. There was an abbot who became famous because when someone asked him what he had done during the revolution, he answered, "Stayed alive."

The role an individual can play depends completely on events that have nothing to do with their personal ability that can only manifest itself under certain circumstances. That is what happened with the fore-fathers of our independence movement and all personalities throughout history. Previous conditions are required for which no individual can take credit.

Martí, when was he born? At the right moment, the right day, the right hour, the right minute, the right second; had he been born a century before, perhaps Martí's name would have never been heard of. That is also the case with Máximo Gómez, to whom we paid a well-deserved tribute, but still short of the enormous tribute he deserves.

The association of historical events with specific people has long been rooted in the propaganda and even in the minds of reactionaries, imperialists and enemies of the revolution. Thus they speak about Castro's revolution, they personalize it: Castro did this, Castro did that. The person who least believes that — and really I am being completely honest — is me. I think that I am one of those who have never felt that way. It's a matter of life perception and of watching history in a philosophic way. People are a different thing. One day we used this phrase: Men die, but the people are immortal.

We do not mind their predictions, their concerns. Presently, when all their plans have failed, when all their lies and wishful thinking have been ridiculed, they are trying to figure out what lies ahead for Cuba as the laws of biology take their toll. We are not worried about what will happen in Cuba, because we shelter no doubts about what will happen in Cuba. What we are asking ourselves, and it is what these wishful thinkers should be asking themselves, is what will happen in the world.

Cuba's modest work will live on with the revolutionary spirit that made it possible. But the history of our country, just like your history, your future, will depend on the future of the world. Even the future of the United States will very much depend on that other future.

In strictly national terms, I can simply say that our country has resisted, when everyone, everywhere, was predicting the opposite. After the collapse of the socialist bloc and the demise of the Soviet Union, where we had our markets and our main supplies of fuel, raw material, etc., those trade relations we had managed to establish on equitable bases were lost overnight. They had enabled us to confront the U.S. blockade for many years, and not only confront it, but advance in many fields.

The demise of the socialist camp had them dreaming that the demise of the Cuban Revolution was a matter of days, or weeks at the most. They saw the European socialist countries collapse one after the other and they were expecting to read in the papers the news of Cuba's collapse, which was not a baseless assumption.

They did not need those countries to collapse, but they needed the collapse of Cuba. Those countries were a lot more developed, with a lot more resources than we have; nevertheless, when they renounced socialism the West immediately lifted the blockade and other restrictions, offering them loans, assistance and, above all, recipes. They got the worst poison.

When we saw this and analyzed the whole process, the fundamental elements and causes and the way things were unfolding, we foresaw the disappearance of the Soviet Union. Two years before it happened, at a July 26 rally, in Camagüey province, I said something that left everyone somewhat amazed and confused. I said, "And if one day we wake up to find that the Soviet Union has disappeared, we will continue fighting, and we will continue building socialism."

Yes, that immense, rich and powerful country collapsed and an economy comprehensively built in over 70 years was dismantled. It had been a country where one republic produced certain things while others produced other things, they exchanged products and produced many things in cooperation.

Overnight, we lost the market for many million tons of sugar that enjoyed a preferential price. We had discovered that the prices of products exported by the more developed countries did not stop increasing while those of the products exported by our countries kept falling. If we signed for the volumes and prices of the goods to be exchanged in a five year period, for the imported products we did so on the basis of prices close to those of the world market; the purchasing power of our products after five years was a lot less than it had been at the beginning of the five year period.

Meanwhile, the price of every machine, every piece of equipment, every product that we imported was higher and the price of our sugar — our main export item — was still that of the world market plus a preferential premium, and the price of other commodities remained the same they had been the first year of the agreement.

Added to this, one day the price of oil surged, it jumped to huge figures. By then, however, we had reached an agreement based on sliding prices. We said that if we were talking proletarian internationalism then the prices of our products, especially sugar, must increase as the prices of your export products increase.

How far did the price of sugar then climb? It was between 25 and 30 cents a pound. Theirs, which was beet sugar, cost even more and with that we were able to pay for the oil and other products. But it was mainly with sugar that we could pay for the oil whose price had increased 12 to 14 times. After the oil price boom, less than a barrel of oil could be bought with what could buy a ton of oil before the revolution's triumph.

Imagine what it means for a country to lose such fair and reasonable trade relations, plus the market. All the machinery, or the vast majority of the tractors, trucks and equipment we had, originated there. It is true they used up a lot more fuel than others from the West, but that was not a big problem because the ships with the fuel followed right behind the equipment. And when there was a hurricane or a pest plague — like those introduced in our country that more than once damaged sugarcane or other crops — the agreed products never failed to reach our country. The agreements were rigorously observed as if protected by a guarantee clause.

We received credits. And mark my words: with one hectare of well-cultivated cane, we could buy up to 30 tons of rice. It was an excellent exchange, because they had some rice surpluses and they sold it at the international price. Our export prices basically fluctuated in conjunction with the oil prices, and with a 10 tons of sugar yield from one hectare of sugarcane, we could buy up to 30 tons of rice, wheat or other important foods.

That revenue enabled the country to advance its economic and social development program.

There is much talk outside our country about our education system, health care and even sports. Yes, that is true but there is no talk about the tens of thousands of kilometers of highways that have been built. No one speaks about the many dams built all over the country and that, from the 35 million cubic meters of water capacity we started out with, we now have over 10 billion. We were applying the most advanced technical programs in sugarcane and rice cultivation because not all the rice came from the Soviet Union, a significant part we produced ourselves and we were planning to grow all of the rice we needed by using flat terraces, increasing yields, cutting costs and using water more efficiently.

It is never mentioned that we mechanized the sugarcane harvest, where more than 300,000 workers worked before the revolution, if only for three or four months a year, and that after the revolution they found permanent jobs. The cane-cutting work force disappeared, replaced first, by the mechanical cane haulers, and then by the harvesting machines, which cut and hauled the cane really raising productivity.

It is not said that many trades in our country were mechanized: rice was cut with the famous sickle when the revolution triumphed, but later it was all cut with machines. Construction work was manual; it was all mechanized afterwards. Transportation was done with oxen — a good deal of it — all of it was subsequently mechanized. Electric energy reached only 50 percent of the population, electrification now benefits over 90 percent. Sugar was hauled on people's backs in 250 pound bags, which at a time weighed 300 pounds. No one knows the number of people who later developed back problems. All sugar shipments, millions of tons per year, were mechanized, except for those destined to small countries that do not have facilities to receive bulk sugar, in which case, a certain number of bags, a minimum amount, had to be hauled manually.

Work was extraordinarily humanized thanks to the revolution. Electrical energy capacity was multiplied ten-fold or more than ten-fold while, new mechanical industries were created. We now manufacture our sugarcane harvesting machines. We were even manufacturing bulldozers, although some of the components were imported, but it considerably reduced costs. We were producing forklifts and other equipment, creating jobs and reducing the country's hard currency spending. We manufacture the main components for the sugar factories. We were already manufacturing up to 70 percent of components for the sugar factories, even if we had to import 30 percent in centrifuges and certain equipment and components that we were not able to produce in our country.

We developed science at a very rapid pace, and there is hardly any talk about this. Today we have thousands of scientists, because, aware of that sector's importance, even under the "special period," we have continued to carry out scientific research. At this moment, research is proceeding on potential vaccines against AIDS, even against cancer. This is in addition to a great number of new medicines and vaccines, some of them solely made and developed in our country.

I am not going to refer to the number of houses we built. Foremost, we had already achieved four million tons per year in cement production capacity and enough building materials to build 100,000 houses per year when, unfortunately, the "special period" set in.

We had not been wasting our time. I must honestly say though, that the abundance of available resources did not help develop our thrifty habits. I cannot deny that there were even some who rode the tractor to go visit a girlfriend. This might be great for romance, but from the economic viewpoint is disastrous. Our domestic consumption was then 13 million tons of fuel per year.

The degree of development we had reached became a terrible liability with the collapse of the socialist camp, especially the Soviet Union.

The Soviet Union had resisted the first intervention after the World War I, which had turned the country into a wrecked piece of land. Then, it was again destroyed before 20 years had passed, totally destroyed, sustaining the loss of 20 million people, a country that had defeated Nazism.

[The Soviet Union's war effort was based on] the will of a people who had lived under a certain social regime, regardless of the enormous mistakes that were made, mainly subjective mistakes — we do not need to name them, they are well known. It was a people who for the first time had been the owner of all the riches, peasants who became owners of the land and workers who became owners of the factories, because there had been a social change and that people had developed a great capacity for struggle and a great selflessness.

When every other country in Europe surrendered to the first shots, the Soviet Union — despite huge political errors committed before that war, and huge military errors, such as having the defense forces totally demobilized while three million troops and tens of thousands of tanks were being concentrated next to their border — was the only country which resisted, on and on. The other countries, as soon as their lines were broken by a few divisions, sat down to negotiate. But that is another story.

Thus, it seemed impossible that that country which, despite so much destruction, had attained nuclear parity in a short period of 20 to 25 years and that could not be conquered by Hitler with his millions of soldiers, could be destroyed by the West without firing a single shot, conquered without firing a single shot. We could foresee what was going to happen and, unfortunately, it did.

I said that the recipes were the worst. As a result of those recipes Russia's GDP — no longer the Soviet Union — has been dropping yearly to 45 percent of what it produced in 1989, before the Soviet Union's dissolution and the beginning of the capitalist construction. The Russian Federation produced between 400 and 500 million tons of oil per year, all the gas they wanted to meet their demand and export a considerable volume to the West, steel, raw materials, which Cuba would have to do without. They kept the factories of spare parts for trucks, machinery, all kinds of equipment, which Cuba was left without.

Our production, which dropped to 65 percent, began to recover despite lacking all those things. Today we are up to around 76 percent, it is not 45 percent, and we are making progress, although it will take some time before we can make a comeback. Ours is a blockaded country, a doubly blockaded country: the old [U.S.] blockade tightened and the new unexpected blockade which left us with the fuel-wasting equipment but without the oil tankers coming from the Soviet Union, nor the food that used to arrive, nor the prices for our sugar, not even the markets for that sugar. We were left without something as vital as fuel, when over 90 percent of the country had been electrified. If electrification had only been 50 percent it would have been less difficult. All the achievements of more than 30 years became an additional liability in those circumstances. When people get used to certain services like electricity, considered essential, there is no going back. You can serve it by quotas, do other things — you have gone through this — blackouts and similar things which had ceased to exist in our country a long time ago.

A significant merchant fleet had been created in the country, also a deep sea fishing fleet and for transportation. Practically all manual work had been mechanized. The hard physical work that our workers used to do no longer existed.

How could the country be saved under such circumstances? Those in the North tightened the screws when they perceived these objective realities. A building resting on two pillars had lost one. The other pillar, however, was the people, our people's consciousness, its ability to struggle, to resist, its heroism.

Our revolution was not an imported product. It was created by our people. Ninety percent of the weapons we used in our war had been seized from the enemy. Nobody supplied us with weapons, and only now and then we got a few. It was a genuine revolution, an authentic revolution, our people's revolution; it wasn't exported to us or waged for us. We had no relations with the Soviet Union, not because we were prejudiced, rather because we took into account the international situation with the Cold War.

We tried to purchase the first weapons from a country in Western Europe, Belgium. They were the weapons we used to defend ourselves, using our experience in guerrilla warfare, since it would not have being possible to resist a U.S. attack with conventional methods. The first ship arrived and there were no problems; but when the second ship arrived and it was being unloaded by hundreds of workers and soldiers, there was a terrible explosion. Then, when people surged to rescue the victims, there was another explosion: more than 100 people died, hundreds were injured.

Those were the first weapons we bought in the West, in order not to give a pretext to the gentlemen in the North. Some cannons were bought in Italy with their corresponding ammunition. Pressure began and the cannons arrived but with hardly any ammunition. As we had received only a small amount of ammunition, the deliveries were cut off. This was the same time that the threat of aggression increased and the very moment we enacted the land reform law.

The Bay of Pigs invasion was not conceived in the United States because we had proclaimed the socialist nature of revolution. It was conceived immediately after we passed the land reform law in May 1959. There were large U.S. estates comprising tens of thousands of hectares each, and some of them even up to 200,000 hectares held by one single transnational company. The revolution had to be destroyed. What's this about letting land reform hurt the interests of U.S. companies? Haven't these guys learned the Guatemala lesson?

Today we know very well the cost of that lesson for Guatemala: over 100,000 people disappeared, around 150,000 dead, mostly as a result of repression. One hundred and fifty thousand lives was the toll of that expedition against Jacobo Arbenz. We knew that story well. We were trying to get weapons for the people because we knew the recipe. They were the ones who could not tell the difference between the situation in Guatemala and in Cuba, where there had been a victorious revolution against forces organized, supplied and trained by the United States, where 80,000 troops were finally defeated with just 3,000 weapons, 25 months after the *Granma* landing.

They did not realize that the people were in command. There is the historic experience of what the people can do. You know this because if there has been a country in this hemisphere with a difficult and hazardous history it is this fraternal Dominican country.

You have even gone through the experience of fighting against 40,000 U.S. troops landing in your own territory, and you were not defeated. They could not defeat the people and the military who took sides with the people, whose most outstanding figure I mentioned in the decoration ceremony and whom we will always remember — the figure of Francisco Caamaño. They could not crush you. They had to negotiate, to find a way out, one way or another, through an inevitable compromise. There were some Latin American countries that even joined the aggression, that invasion of the Dominican Republic. First, there was the invasion and then the sanctioning of the invasion by the very famous OAS. It is not possible to forget that.

So aggressions against Cuba began due to a land reform law. Of course, for every measure the United States took, Cuba responded with a countermeasure: suspension of the sugar quota, nationalization of certain companies, total suspension, total nationalization. Many landlords and very rich Cubans believed it would be a matter of days, because people have theirs beliefs, right? The belief then was that it was impossible: A revolution right next to the United States? Oh, forget it! Many of them practically took a vacation waiting for our neighbors to do away with us. The big mansions were left empty. What did we do? We brought 100,000 scholarship students into the vacationists' houses! We did not take anybody's house, not at all! They went on vacation, and since their vacations were extended indefinitely... The houses are there, preserved and kept at the service of the nation.

Now the Helms-Burton Act says that the owners of those houses are Americans, therefore, the law applies also to those properties and other vacationists' properties. It is incredible, for the first time in history they achieve the status of citizens and the benefit of the law. Even Clinton himself once said that it was madness.

What the Helms-Burton Act claims is that before they lift the blockade, it would cost Cuba $100 billion. Listen, if only we had the machine they have in the U.S. Treasury to print their green bills! It is preposterous, a law with extraterritorial reach to prevent investment in Cuba. Then we look at the United States in amazement and say: "Hey, who are the main advocates of socialism in Cuba today?" The United States is, because they don't want people to invest [in Cuba]. As for us, every time we can, we invest in something: another piece of socialism.

Where does this irrationality or this inconsistency of doing everything possible to prevent investment in our country lead to? How could our country get the resources under such circumstances? I repeat, how could our country get the resources under such circumstances? Just like the vast majority of the Third World countries that are not swimming in a sea of oil, which need technology, and capital. We are not an exception to that rule.

Before the "special period," before the Soviet Union collapsed, we realized that some sectors of the economy could not develop with the support of the socialist camp alone, because they did not have the technology for it. Actually, eight or nine years before the collapse of the socialist camp we had made the decision to create joint ventures in some sectors as a complement to the socialist development of our country. We had been meditating, delving deeply into the problem.

They are trying to suffocate us at all costs when everything they have tried has failed. But they wanted to take advantage of the special moment. Their other calculations, their other plans had failed, including the mercenary invasion, which lasted less than 72 hours, because we knew we could not permit the consolidation of a beachhead. They had a government ready on an airplane.

A big surprise, a new underestimation that was punished. The government stayed waiting in Miami. They are still waiting!

It was a dirty war like the one they waged in Nicaragua. They managed to organize bandits in every province and mainly in the area of the Escambray Mountains, which was the zone they were preparing for their projected invasion. But we cleaned up the Escambray Mountains and reduced their forces to a minimum.

There was a time when they had around 1,000 counterrevolutionaries there, supplied by airdrops. But some of the weapons fell into our hands because we had also organized "our bandits" or had infiltrated their forces, or had formed our own "counterrevolutionary" organizations. Anyway, the infiltrated revolutionaries ended up being the leaders of the organizations. That was when we had to tell them: Listen, don't overdo it! They were really outstanding.

The forces that defended the revolution learned the ability to fight those bandits. Do you know why? Because they never used physical violence. I am pleased to say here that they never used violence. We did not use it in war and we have never used it in peace times. We did not use it in the first years that were the most difficult and we have never used it during the time of the revolution, no matter what they say, no matter how much they lie and how much they slander. Cuba and our people know very well how things are over there and what our ethical rules are. We will never resort to such methods. Those who use torture to seek information never learn anything.

Since our forces followed that rule they developed the ability to infiltrate the enemy groups. There was a moment when the CIA and their enthusiastic followers had organized 300 counterrevolutionary organizations, some of them better known, more important. Thus, it was a long battle.

After that came pirate attacks, plans for direct invasion of Cuba. This is known today thanks to certain documents. At the time we denounced the plans that the government had ordered the Pentagon to elaborate, to fabricate a pretext for a direct invasion against Cuba. This was after the Bay of Pigs.

All this laid the ground for the Soviet-Cuban agreement to deploy strategic missiles in our country. This is a lengthy subject which I recently talked about with CNN, a major U.S. TV network, in a program where I was asked many questions and, with the support of documents, I answered them all: What was the origin of the conflict? What happened? Finally, it was proven that they were preparing a direct invasion. That was the origin of the October [Missile] Crisis.

After the crisis, there were more pirate attacks and sabotage throughout all these years; there were also assassination plans, not only those which were institutionally organized but also those organized by the groups that were trained, very well trained, and let loose to carry out assassination attempts and personal actions, covering up U.S. responsibility.

All those groups are made up by the same people who blew up the plane over Barbados, who participated in the dirty war against Nicaragua supplying weapons mainly from El Salvador and Honduras, weapons obtained through the scandalous connection called Irangate which ended up in Central America. It is these same groups that carried out those apparently independent assassination attempts, but there is proof that they were tolerated for many years.

There is no doubt that the terrorist actions in our capital aimed at sabotaging tourism and further suffocating our country's economy were known and tolerated. It was absolutely impossible to carry them out without those whose duty it was to prevent them knowing about them, since they were organized from the United States with Central American mercenaries. It would have been impossible, and we have recent proof of that. A system of terrorism against Cuba was deliberately created in which everyone was responsible but no one was guilty. In other words, the most devilish mechanisms of dispersing responsibility were created, pursuing the same policy of harassment to try to annihilate our revolution.

We have lots of information about this, but I do not want to talk about this subject now. I did not really intend to. I simply want to emphasize that the main thing for Cuba is our people. The question is, how is it possible that in such difficult conditions, which I have described, our people have been able to resist?

IT IS IN THIS CONTEXT that we appraise those feelings of support and solidarity that you have shown so generously and extraordinarily in the last few days. And you cannot imagine how much this helps us. The same way the Caribbean people helped us in Jamaica when they greeted us with mass rallies where we spoke Spanish to English-speaking crowds. They showed such awareness and such knowledge! Such a demonstration of their understanding of Cuba's policy of solidarity with Africa, and of our struggle against apartheid and its army, one of the most sophisticated and technically advanced, which was in possession of seven nuclear weapons when we were fighting against them, at the Angolans' side, in Cuito Cuanavale and close to the Namibian border. [The South Africans] could not take up this challenge and were forced to negotiate. These negotiations put an end to colonialism in Namibia and stepped up the demise of apartheid.

Today, many in the West speak of apartheid: it's great that it disappeared! They speak of that apartheid of which many of them were accomplices, the same apartheid they never blockaded, the same apartheid that wrote some of the most shameful, revolting and humiliating pages in modern history. They speak about it, but they never mention the Cuban fighters involved in that struggle, the Cuban fighters who died in those battles. They never mention a Caribbean country that sent up to 55,000 volunteer fighters at the most decisive and critical moments of that war.

The people of Africa do know and do not forget. The people of South Africa and their African leaders do know and do not forget. Others now go to Africa — to countries we helped liberate from the colonial yoke and defend from apartheid with our blood — to invest millions and billions. Cuba has not gone there, and will not go there, to invest a single penny. We invested what we had to invest, what is worth much more than money, much more than all the transnationals put together: our sweat, our blood and our lives! Such is the country they want to destroy.

During the final stage of that battle I'm talking about, since part of our forces were stationed elsewhere, 40,000 Cuban troops and 30,000 Angolans were involved with all their gear, the tanks, the antiaircraft means — 1,000 antiaircraft pieces — against a country that could have used any of the seven nuclear weapons it had. In this august center I ask myself, did the Americans know that South Africa had seven nuclear weapons?

Those who know everything — or almost everything — in matters of espionage. Those who invest more than $27 billion a year in the Central Intelligence Agency alone, plus whatever they invest in the National Intelligence System — it could be between $30 billion and $40 billion.

I ask myself if they really did not know that South Africa had seven nuclear weapons. If they didn't know, how could South Africa obtain those weapons? But the fact remains that the Cubans were there fighting. They would have perhaps rejoiced if the racists had used any of those weapons against the Cuban troops!

Of course, we had taken all measures in case that happened. Our tactic was to arrange our forces in groups no larger than 1,000 heavily armed men.

We are absolutely convinced that they did know [about South Africa's nuclear weapons] but that did not help them prevent the defeat of the powerful apartheid army.

Yesterday, I spoke about the airport in Grenada that has proven to be vital for the quick economic development that island is having. They had excellent conditions for tourism, but they did not have an airport. The Cuban designers prepared the plans; it was almost built over the sea. We recently had the opportunity to see it.

It was almost complete when the well-known invasion took place. There, with great fanfare to humiliate us, the gentleman who ordered the invasion also landed. Not much time has passed, just a few years, and the Grenadians received us there, recently, with extraordinary affection. In that same airport, they have placed a plaque dedicated upon our arrival, to the memory of the builders who worked at that airport, some of whom died when that unjustifiable, treacherous attack was launched against Grenada.

One must have faith in history. One must have faith in the peoples. That encourages us in this fight, and teaches us. Do not think those are simply signs that can be erased, or simple slogans or words blown away by the wind. No, they are like hurricanes that can fell the biggest obstacles. They are like hurricanes in the conscience of the U.S. people. They are like hurricanes of universal conscience. They are like lie-sweeping hurricanes. Because people who act like that and people who, under a deluge of lies and slanders, dare to support a country like Cuba, they make an impression. This is evident in the way international agencies present it and, curiously enough, in the way certain U.S. television networks have broadcast the message.

They realize that their efforts are pointless, that time passes and their campaigns are weaker instead of stronger; time passes and the peoples' consciousness grow; time passes and the peoples come closer together; time passes and the peoples with modest resources available to them are organizing themselves to act, to speak up and to make others listen.

What I am saying here is what all Cubans feel. It is also proof that we are aware of the great value of your solidarity, as an effective means of defense, of protection even — as you yourselves said — against insane plans.

This is a people that I really love, that I really admire, to whom I am grateful. The first thing we learn about in the history of Cuba is the participation of this fraternal Dominican people in our independence struggle. We learn of Martí's deep affection for this country. We know that the Montecristi Manifesto was written here. And, we cannot forget that Gómez and Maceo set off from here for that epic war of 1895. And, it is not only what they did but also the example they set for us, the ideas they left us as a legacy.

I was trying to show yesterday the most intimate thoughts of Martí, his ideas on the world, his ideas on Latin America. And he expressed them little by little, especially as the war came nearer, and he expressed them more and more clearly.

Although he said that it had to be done in silence, he could no longer keep silent. Anyone can follow his writings and see how he referred to the mighty power that was emerging without naming it, expressing his anguish and his determination to prevent this hemisphere from being devoured by that power. Finally, the day before his death, 24 hours before his death, Martí names that power as the United States, which he says must be prevented "from spreading through the Antilles, as Cuba gains its independence, and from overpowering with that additional strength our lands of America. All I have done so far, and all I will do, is for this purpose."

He was very clear that final day before his death when he spoke from his heart what he felt deep inside, and said: "It has had to be done in silence." He was so intelligent; he understood that if he revealed such ideas before the time was ripe, it would be impossible to realize them. He was organizing the expedition, buying weapons; but at that moment he says it clearly.

He knew that it was crucial to organize the fight for independence, to organize the forces, coordinate them all, provide them with weapons and begin the struggle for a short war, as bloodless as possible. He proclaimed this in the Montecristi Manifesto, although as he wrote it the ships with almost all of the weapons had already been seized. He set out with his bare chest full of his ideas. He set out full of faith in his people. He set out full of faith in those heroic warriors, especially in that extraordinary commander who was Máximo Gómez.

Yesterday, I wanted to highlight the ideas those men fought for, the ideas for which they sacrificed so much, the broad scope of their cause. And how sad when an amendment was imposed, after dismissing the soldiers of the Liberation Army and liquidating, in the context of a Constitutional Assembly, the party created by Martí.

An amendment — not even a law, something they usually do — was attached to a law, an appendix that gave them the right to intervene in Cuba's internal affairs. It was a right they printed in the constitution of our alleged sovereign republic, plus a naval base in one of the country's best harbors. That military base is still there and nothing has been said about when it will be returned.

Since madness cannot last forever, and imperialism will not last forever either, not a single drop of blood will be shed for that base.

It has always been clear to us that blood need not be shed for a piece of territory that sooner or later will be returned to the homeland or to humankind. In any event, if a drop of blood is shed, it should be shed for the good of humankind and for the planet on which the human family must live. And, it will live one day under principles other than ruthless exploitation and selfishness, inequality and injustice; they will be fraternity, true fraternity, fraternity and justice among all human beings on this planet. That is really worth any sacrifice.

Since we believe in that future, we might say like Allende: "Rather sooner than later," that world will come.

That was the intervention. That was the trick they played on our country. Then they bought up everything, they took possession of everything. By distorting our history, they began by creating an anti-national attitude. We owed everything to the "generosity" of the United States, they said.

They had showed up after 30 years of heroic struggle by our people, which had sacrificed the lives of hundreds of thousands of its children. It was only after Spain had been defeated, because Spain could not keep up the fight, that they intervened and occupied our island. Following the occupation of our island, they occupied the Philippines, and then, our beloved sister, the island of Puerto Rico.

We are very happy to remember Puerto Rico here. They have just given the world an impressive lesson. What the Puerto Rican people have just done, a hundred years later will have to be recorded with golden letters in the annals of neoliberalism.

We are talking about commemorations and, that unanimous movement, that Puerto Rican strike... See how, after 100 years of English, the Puerto Rican people stand up to defend its culture, its language and its patriotic feelings that cannot be destroyed. There is something behind that attitude and that is a feeling of national pride. What were they fighting against? Against what is most fashionable in the world now: the privatization of a telephone company.

Everybody is selling everything everywhere. We also have had to sell part of our telephone system to keep it from becoming a museum piece, and to expand communications and modernize them. This is something for which we do not have any capital. We have had to sell a piece of the enterprise, as part of a carefully analyzed and well calculated plan, due to our need for technology and capital that we cannot easily obtain right now. They have organized a national strike. At an economists meeting, I first heard the news from a Puerto Rican economist about the idea of a general strike and I was really amazed because a general strike has never occurred in any Latin American country.

Every day an enterprise is auctioned off and they, who live there under the dominion of the neoliberal power par excellence, have opposed the privatization of an enterprise. It is an example, and I would say that it is the best tribute, or the best reminder, the best warning and message that the Puerto Rican people could have conveyed 100 years after the island's occupation by U.S. troops.

They used more subtle methods in our country. They took hold of the entire economy, the best lands, the factories. They imposed a constitution and an amendment to it. It must have been a source of deep suffering for Máximo Gómez and others!

Martí, Maceo, Agramonte and hundreds of heroes were already dead. They were spared that anguish, that suffering. They had had faith in their people and its ability to overcome all the obstacles, all the setbacks.

Those who had fallen before were well aware of the stumbling blocks that could appear. More than one of those fighters, like Máximo Gómez, had been through the terrible Zanjón Pact when divisions within the Cuban forces — as Martí said — caused the demoralization that led the army to surrender before the full independence of the country had been attained.

Every time something like this happens, it pleases us to remember those who gave their lives to achieve these objectives. That is why we oppose the individualization of merits. We always remember — particularly in my case, for the many years I have had the privilege of participating in this struggle — many comrades who were killed since the very first days of the revolutionary struggle. We also cherish the sacred memory of those who, since last century, have fought and fell so that there might be today an independent country called Cuba.

I SAID A LONG TIME ago that the important question is not what will happen in Cuba But what will happen in the world. I cannot give you a categorical, accurate response, but I can affirm a few things. The so-called new order — every now and then a new order appears — this neoliberal order they are trying to impose on the world is not sustainable. To be exact, the neoliberal globalization is not sustainable.

This is a major starting point and an encouraging element to us all in this struggle, because the fight is not pointless, the fight is not for a single country. Today, the struggle of any country, any people, especially the Third World peoples, is forced to become a struggle for the whole world, a universal struggle. Any contribution to the struggle counts, however modest. Some can do more, some less, depending on certain factors and circumstances.

I was saying, and I have said it in Geneva and in many other places, something that cannot be denied: globalization is inevitable. It is a product of history, of the development of productive forces, as Marx said in his times. Those were times, of course, when many of today's problems were not known and could not be known. He had great foresight. He perceived a law in the development of human society and he devoted much of his life to study this law, and to study capitalism which he knew better than Friedman and better than those in the World Bank, the International Monetary Fund and all others.

The man who best knew capitalism was Karl Marx. Marx knew more about capitalism than he did about socialism, because Marx conceived socialism as a society that would come afterwards. He did not try to describe how a socialist system would be, and even less to say how a socialist constitution should be. He was well aware it was not his task. His task was to thoroughly study a social system, a historical law. He was absolutely certain that that society would inevitably have to be replaced by another, not because of anybody's whim, nor because of anybody's wish, but as a real and objective need of human development.

He criticized the utopian socialists. I count myself among those he criticized, and rightly so. Before I read my first Marxist text, by myself I reached the conclusion that this system was chaotic, absolutely chaotic. That is the reason why I became sort of a utopian communist, someone who begins to imagine a different, more just society. Of course, I knew about justice and injustice, although I did not grow up as a proletarian. I grew as the son of a landowner.

Marx talked about the utopian socialists, but he basically studied the elements I mentioned. Others had to do that, because he did not like to play the prophet of socialist construction. This opens up a whole new angle, another field.

Another very important thing: he did not conceive socialism in one single country. Until the end of World War I, none of the Marxist authors and theoreticians conceived the idea of socialism in only one country. They felt it was absolutely impossible, as they were thinking of the development of England, Germany and the United States. Even after the famous October Revolution, they did not conceive of socialism in that backward country of Europe, the most backward country of Europe. It was a country with an 80 percent rural population and a limited intelligentsia, although very knowledgeable in theory and brilliant thinkers who were familiar with all the political ideas of the times.

Socialism emerged after a war that destroyed the few industries they had, some of them important. They tried to build socialism with an emerging, though very militant, working class and the 80 percent of rural workers. Another option was to surrender, but they preferred to attempt to build socialism in that country, a task undertaken when the hopes for revolutions in Germany and other industrialized countries had been lost. That is the historical truth.

I remember reading that at one point Lenin thought of building capitalism under the workers' leadership, a workers' government. He said: We have to build capitalism; we have to develop the productive forces. But harassment, aggression, isolation and the critical situation were such that he had no other choice but to accept the challenge. Marx would have held his head in despair, really.

I am not saying they were wrong. I honestly say that if I had found myself in such a predicament, I would have done just that. It was really more irrational to believe in the possibility that our revolution would stand after the socialist camp collapsed, the unipolar world emerged and the sworn enemy of our country had become more powerful and stronger than ever, when we could not even count on any help from abroad. Nevertheless, we said: Let's go ahead. This was eight years ago, or so, because the problems were evident before 1990.

It is not that we are building socialism. Right now, we are basically defending the sovereignty and independence of our country and the achievements of socialism. If we can build a little bit of socialism we do it, but mainly we want to improve what we have done, to achieve excellence — that our more than 60,000 medical doctors are better doctors.

Just think that under the "special period," we have been able to continue reducing infant mortality rate to 7.2 [per 1,000 live births]. Our doctors are certainly better.

Our 250,000 to 300,000 teachers are gaining knowledge every day. We continue to graduate teachers because some of them retire and we have a reserve of them so the rest can study. Thousands of teachers have the opportunity to study full time receiving their salary, which is modest, given our present economic difficulties. But they are paid their salaries and can dedicate full time to studying and upgrading. We are improving our teachers' excellence. A better selection is made for admission to teachers' schools and colleges and we are improving their training. We are doing the same with all of our professionals.

The revolution has graduated 600,000 university professionals, and we find jobs for all of them. If they want to do a different job, they do some retraining.

After our development lost its momentum and the economy declined, we could not ensure the best possible job to every graduate. But still the universities were not closed down. A considerable number of students enroll in the universities every year, now more rigorously selected according to their school records, vocation and abilities. However, we are not using all the capacity available in our universities. There are more than 20,000 university professors. Their number has not declined. They are still there, studying and upgrading themselves.

We are using some of the available capacity in our universities for students of certain countries, not to the extent we would really wish. There was a moment when our country had 22,000 scholarship students. That figure was unsurpassed by any country, a very high per capita of scholarship students per citizens of the country. Now, for example, we have some plans for students of CARICOM countries who have difficulties to study in their countries. These are very small, geographically isolated countries that cannot have university faculties, and we have offered them all the scholarships they want.

That will not ruin us. They will have the same professors who are already there, so there will not be additional costs on that account. They will use the facilities that already exist, so there will not be any additional costs on that account, either. There will be costs, however, for their accommodation. We do this free of charge but we do recommend the countries to send their students some aid, for their personal expenses, to compensate for the scarcities that even our students suffer in this period we are living through.

So we are improving our quality. Our researchers, who are very young, have more experience and increasingly ambitious programs.

We have downsized the administration as much as possible, and we are trying to achieve efficiency with better controls. Since we have opened our country to entrance and exit by hundreds of thousands and millions of people, we are running all sorts of risks: security risks when terrorist plans are organized abroad to conspire, scheme, introduce explosives. All this becomes easier, but it is not only that. Our concern is not only related to security, it is habits and a way of life.

Tipping had ceased to exist in our country. Now, based on the practice established in international tourist services and the need for an incentive for the people who work in this sector, additional to their good will, we have accepted it. It would also be impossible not to, it is a habit, everybody tips — more or less generously — for a service. That is inevitable.

We have had to accept the free circulation of hard currency. It came from abroad through different channels and we could not spend time chasing people who had hard currency. So, we made it legal to have and use hard currency. It helps in a given situation. We never did this before the "special period." Of course, those who receive it spend it, they buy certain products, and part of the value is like an aggregated value to help meet the needs for food, medicine, etc., of those who do not have the privilege of a remittance from abroad.

We have had to do many things, taking risks we never had to take before. We have to be a lot more careful, and we have a lot of trained dogs that had to learn two things. Dogs, in the special case of our country, need to have two trades: they have to be experts in detecting drugs and explosives. You do not need dogs to detect explosives, only a small group for a situation like this of an international meeting. You do not have groups running around, very well motivated and trained, desperate because the revolution has not collapsed, unsatisfied with a tightened blockade plus an additional blockade when those who were the pillars of our trade collapsed. Desperate with the revolution's resistance, they intensify their plans. You do not have that problem; practically no other country has it. They want to hurt tourism, they want to hurt and discourage foreign investment so as not to give our country the slightest chance.

That is the reason for all the efforts we need to make, for all the measures that must be taken, since it is not only with dogs that their plans are discovered. If there is anything we have learned, it is how to discover plots. Dogs help, of course. Tourism brings all of these dangers, and foreign investment too, by creating differences. It undoubtedly promotes corruption. There is the practice of a commission so that a company is given preference over another — all of that. All this forces us to strive for a more efficient organization, for more efficient audits, and auditors to audit the auditors.

You cannot imagine what this struggle is like. It is the struggle against all that comes along with the historical social system that has prevailed in the last few centuries. I should avoid generalities because there are many strictly honorable, strictly honest investors who do not get involved in such activities, but some do.

The country has opened up. It is no longer a country in a glass case. We have put forward the thesis that virtue should be cultivated in contact with vice; if not, virtue exists in a pure glass case, totally aseptic, without any pathogenic germs, with a thousand filters that prevent the contaminated air from entering.

This is what I said: Virtue is cultivated in the struggle against vice. If you are pure in the glass case, when the germs appear, you might not have enough antibodies.

Our people have a lot of moral antibodies and a consciousness. But there are always a number of people who are prone to become ill, ideologically ill. The enemy encourages them, offering its super consumer society — the U.S. society is not only a consumer society but a super consumer society — as a model, as a dream, promoted through the media. They themselves proclaim this. They compare incomes in the richest country in the world with those in Third World countries that still need to develop and are not allowed to. They compare their consumption patterns and living standards to those of a country like Cuba, which has been rigorously blockaded for almost 40 years, a country that is not even allowed to buy an aspirin.

You have probably heard talk that some measures are allegedly going to liberalize the sales of medicines. But to buy medicines — they still have not regulated it and are in no rush to do so — the transactions and the red tape make it almost impossible to buy an aspirin. They have made it look like they are going to liberalize some aspects, but the truth is that until now nothing practical has come of it. Then they tell the blockaded country: Look at socialism, people are suffering, that is what the revolution has led to and they compare it with what consumers have in the empire.

It is as if they tied somebody's hands and feet and threw him into the water and said: Look at that guy, he can't swim! Well, we have been able to swim, even with our hands and feet tied. And we can say: We have things that you do not have, because there is not a single elderly person sleeping under a bridge, covered with newspapers. We do not have a single illiterate person. They do not have many illiterates but they do have mostly functional illiterates. Another type of illiteracy can also be terrible, and that is, political illiteracy.

One often marvels, really, because it is an intelligent people, no doubt, a working people. But how can a system keep its people ignorant of essential values and issues?

Infant mortality in Cuba is lower than in the U.S. capital and survival rates are the same for the city and the countryside, for blacks, mulattos, dark-skinned and white. The United States has a different infant mortality rate for the rich and the poor, for the white and the black. It depends on one's color and wealth. Infant mortality in our country is the same for all, and the very few maternal deaths are the same in the city and the rural areas. It is the same for everybody, irrespective of income, wealth and the rest.

In our country, 85 percent of the population owns their own houses. There is another percentage that lives in houses owned by their work centers. The family doctor lives in a house that is not his or her own, so if he is transferred he leaves it to the doctor taking his or her place. There are also the houses belonging to factories in out of the way places. A very high percentage of the population owns their own houses so they do not pay rent, or even taxes.

In the United States you have to pay a lot more in taxes than what was paid in Cuba as rent under capitalism. We have many things in our poor and blockaded country that they do not have, even material things.

Our athletes win a lot of gold medals and we do not need to buy athletes from other countries. Look at the difficult conditions our peoples have to face if they have an amateur team. Athletes receive great support in our country, including the opportunity to study in sports schools, to obtain a university degree and a modest income. All of a sudden one of these athletes is offered $5 million or $10 million. It is really abusive, immoral that a country should train its athletes for the enjoyment of its people and that a rich foreign country comes along and buys them. Since sport has become increasingly professional and the athletes have become commodities, you cannot imagine how hard it is for a country to keep up the morale and the patriotic spirit of its athletes so that they do not sell out for millions of dollars.

We are proud to have athletes who have been offered contracts of up to $40 million to play for five years and they have refused. All those athletes have is a modest apartment, and they might get to have a modest automobile as an incentive, as a prize for his or her effort. One marvels at people who turn down a $40 million offer in a world so alienated by money.

They usually have athletes from all over the world, but when they manage to bribe a Cuban athlete they proclaim it all through the world as a humiliation for Cuba.

More than 800 participated in the latest competitions. When our athletes went to Puerto Rico for the latest Central American Games, they tried to take away our athletes by offering lots of money. They managed to have tens of them desert; I do not remember the exact number. This time, however, they only managed three and none of them our top athletes. Our boxers, who were there, had won almost every gold medal so they want to buy them. They always want to buy our athletes. This is another form of harassment and plunder.

They are opening schools in Latin America to promote sports, especially for the baseball major leagues. They have calculated that it costs them more to train an athlete in the United States than in Latin America. Well, some go over there, and I know you cannot help being pleased. You are happy, and rightly so, when there is a good pitcher or when a first-class batter hits a home-run over there in the major leagues.

For us, sport is entertainment for almost the whole year round; people want to see their athletes. Some sports competitions last less time; for the volleyball players, for example, the season is shorter. But there is a great effort to take them away.

They use every means they can to try to introduce the ideological virus, to divide, to demoralize. And we need to face all these problems with our openness. But I think we are learning to face everything and also to be more efficient in everything. The day when we again have relatively abundant resources, we will possibly be two or three times more efficient than we were during times of bonanza, and we will make a better use of our resources.

Our excellence is growing in this struggle. Step by step, despite all the evil laws against us, we are growing. It may be five percent, three percent, two percent, 1.5 percent, and if some day a very severe drought, a hurricane or any other phenomenon makes us fall back a point, we will not dismay, we will continue striving. I was telling you that we have 76 percent of what we previously had; someday we will have climbed back to 100 percent.

OUR BATTLE IS NOT ONLY a battle for survival, it is not just surviving for the sake of surviving, no. It is a battle to take part in the struggle for a better world, to participate in that struggle along with the world.

It would be quite an accomplishment for them to defeat the Cuban Revolution, because in every UN forum there is a country present that has been able to resist, a country that has demonstrated how much can be done with so few resources, and its voice is always there. What would they not do to shut off Cuba's voice in any of these forums, in the WTO or in the WHO!

Cuba is always there calculating how much they squander in this or that, the cost of a medicine against AIDS, the $10,000 per year that must be paid for that cocktail that can save the life of an AIDS patient, and asking them where the Africans are going to get the $300 billion they would need every year to give that same treatment to over 30 million AIDS patients in Africa.

There are many questions to ask them and many things to denounce to help build the awareness we need and that the world needs, to find solutions that, I repeat, will not come about because anyone so wishes but because of humanity's need to survive. What is actually under discussion is the survival of a species. It is no longer the survival of a revolution, or an island or a small country. What is being discussed is the survival of the human species.

I think that the idea of the future world is the most important and most noble idea that a revolutionary can harbor. Revolutionaries have always fought for the future. Máximo Gómez and Martí fought for the future. When Martí died at Dos Ríos he knew he was dying for the future. He was not concerned with seeing the results of all that. It would have been extraordinarily useful to have had him longer. It can be said that he died in the prime of youth, when his talent was at its best. They were fighting for the future.

To fight for the future does not mean not to avoid doing every day what must be done for the present. These two ideas must not be confused.

It is possible for our country, in its capacity as a revolutionary state, to devote a great part of its efforts to that struggle for the future, to that struggle against the neoliberal globalization that is crushing us all. It is not the struggle against globalization as an inevitable phenomenon, but the struggle for a more humane and fair globalization.

If they asked the Pope, he would answer: for the globalization of solidarity. If they asked me, I would say what I most deeply believe: the only globalization that can save humanity and preserve the human species is a socialist globalization.

Do I say this out of dogmatism? Do I say it out of ideological fundamentalism? No, not at all! I say it based on a very deep conviction. The world cannot be saved if it persists on the course it is following. In my opinion, there would not be the slightest possibility for the species to survive; neither would there be a possibility for that globalization and that new order that they are establishing to survive — because the masses explode, because the peoples explode, because humanity explodes.

Humanity will not put its neck under the executioner's ax; the preservation instinct, the condition of thinking human beings make this impossible.

Therefore, we think that in the field of ideas a big, difficult battle is being waged, because when everything is global, solutions will also have to be global. I say again, it is a sacred duty to do all that can be done within each person's reach. Now, the great strategic task or the true solutions are global solutions.

The system is not only unsustainable for reasons of survival; it is not only unsustainable because it is unbearable for the masses. The fact is that it is inescapably moving toward inevitable crises, and big changes in history — as we all know — are always the result of big crises. This does not mean that we have to wait for the big crisis to start fighting, to do whatever is possible in every corner of the world. We also have to build awareness about these problems.

There are many schools and many criteria. The only thing I have found all these economists to have in common, including the pundits who advocate neoliberalism and the neoliberal globalization, is their uncertainty. Take careful note of this word: uncertainty. Do not forget that word. There is not a single one of them without uncertainty.

Let me tell you that, without any need for espionage, just by talking with many people in the world who talk with many others, by talking with individuals who have relations, by reading and analyzing every single word that brilliant, eminent analysts write on one side and the other, those in favor of neoliberal globalization and those against it, the only thing one finds is that terrible thing called uncertainty.

I do not remember it right this minute but I am sure many of you do. What was the sign that according to Dante was written at the entrance of hell? Oh! yes: "Abandon all hope!" At the entrance of this world order that they are trying to impose on us you can put up these two signs: "Total uncertainty" and "Abandon all hope."

They are scared. They know that the system is an inseparable sibling of the crises. They have overcome a lot of things, but it is easier to find the cure for cancer or AIDS. We are certain that a cure will be found for these diseases but, for this chaotic, absurd, wild system, or rather, for the consequences of this system, there will be no cure.

The things they make up are incredible. We have seen them when the crises began, from the Mexican to the Russian crisis — which is the next to next to last of the next to next to last of the next to next to last. The crisis began in Mexico and affected some countries of Southeast Asia and then others. Now Japan is in a terrible condition, and that has put Russia in a catastrophic situation, and this is now tremendously threatening, like a big sword of Damocles pending from a fragile thread, to the economies of Brazil, Argentina and the other countries of Latin America and the Third World, including the place where it began, which is Mexico.

The great theoreticians and designers of this world order are afraid of that spreading fire that keeps spreading.

I was saying that there is doubt, uncertainty. The chairman of the International Monetary Fund has great doubts.

They are shaping a world of which they themselves are scared. That guy is intelligent, he cannot be underestimated. Greenspan has the same uncertainty, and the fellow from the World Bank has the same uncertainty; Clinton has the same uncertainty, as does Rubin, the secretary of the treasury; and all the presidents of regional banks have the same uncertainty, they are full of uncertainty. Many of the analyses always end with a phrase: "No one knows what is going to happen."

Of course, they know that something is bound to happen. They were happy a while back. When the first crisis, the Mexican crisis, breaks out they start running all over the place to try to prevent it. They talk about making $50 billion available for Mexico. It is a close neighbor, with almost 100 million people. They are building there a wall 100 times bigger than the Berlin Wall, where more people die each year trying to cross, from thirst, accidents and drowning, than those who died at the Berlin Wall for as long as it lasted. This wall is 3,000 kilometers long... Oh! So that people cannot pass. This is the philosophy of neoliberal globalization: free transit for capital and goods but zero transit for workers, zero transit for human beings.

Yes, let the doors be opened to human beings! Some day the doors of the world will have to be opened. When feudalism is gone, when we cease to be exploited serfs of the modern globe, the roads of the world will have to be opened.

I do not want to scare anybody with this, I am just saying it: Why do they want only capital and goods to cross and not human beings? I am saying it to pose a moral dilemma. If our countries were developed and they had not been colonies for so long and they had not been so exploited, this transit from one place to another would not be necessary. Because, when you come to think of it, any such transit involves an uprooting.

For some time now, the fear of a massive Mexican migration due to a super crisis, encourages those of the North to find solutions. We feel happy if the Mexicans do not suffer a super crisis. But their proximity and all those other elements are pushing in that direction.

Then the crises in Southeast Asia began. Until then — what great hypocrisy — the Asian tigers were *the* model. You could find it in all the books, in all the literature: the Asian tigers, that grow steadily, year after year, 10 years, 15 years, 20 years; it was the end of economic crises; it was possible to grow indefinitely.

But one day the tigers started losing their claws, hair, skin, everything, and all of this overnight, while they were still the model recommended in universities, in economic conferences. They did not tell anyone what was happening there, and they knew it, which is worse. Camdessus, chairman of the International Monetary Fund, tries to justify it now: "Yes, we knew it and we were warning about it."

They knew that the money, the big loans, were distributed among families, that they were distributed among the political clientele, that they were invested in anything, without any concern. Money was pouring into those countries, they invested it in real estate. Hong Kong was full of thousands and thousands of buildings whose value increased. South Korea was full of conglomerates and all sorts of industries in which anyone could invest with all the money they wanted. And the same thing occurred in Thailand, in the Philippines, in Indonesia, and in all of those places.

The International Monetary Fund said: No, we cannot say anything, because if we do we will accelerate the crisis. And they keep silent, until one day it becomes evident that the conditions of a high budget deficit, with high deficits in the current account and overvalued currencies, were created. These were ideal conditions for the speculation wolves, who have billions and billions of dollars and who, like the wolves in the arctic forests, fall upon the reindeer lagging behind, they fall upon any country with the proper conditions. Thus came the catastrophe.

Then came the crisis of Japan, the model of models, which developed by saving more than anybody. Japan received money from no one; the Japanese save over 35 percent of their incomes. Americans nowadays save less than 10 percent. The U.S. specialty and privilege is in investing other people's money. The Japanese invested their own money; they did not want U.S. factories, or U.S. banks, or U.S. insurance companies. The Americans kept demanding that they open up.

The crisis of Southeast Asia begins to affect Japan. They manufacture many articles similar to those of other countries in the region and the United States itself, and they begin to devalue the yen. The Americans said: This is our chance; let's demand from the Japanese that they open up to investment in banks, factories and in everything, to increase consumption. The more confusing things appeared, the less the Japanese increased consumption. There came a moment when the yen was quoted at $147 and Washington ran into a panic, because beyond that, the danger was very serious.

Before that, the crisis in Southeast Asia strikes again. The Indonesian government collapses, there is a social explosion, instability sets in creating a situation that is not very secure at the moment. A new stage begins there. The situation in the other countries of Southeast Asia is increasingly acute; the crisis makes a comeback.

At the same time, 11 nuclear tests in India and Pakistan create, for the first time in the history of the nuclear age, the risk of a regional nuclear war. That same month a deep crisis takes place in Russia. All of this in one month. The truth is that Greenspan, Camdessus and Rubin could barely manage to run from one place to another putting out economic and political fires; but above all, it is the economic fires that threaten to bring about great political cataclysms. All of this takes place in one month.

Then, when the yen plummets to 147 to a dollar, they, who did not want to do anything, prudently undertake intense discussions in Washington. Because it is in Washington where orders are given not only to the U.S. Treasury but also to the World Bank and the International Monetary Fund. They are simply orders. The United States has the power of veto. They hold over 15 percent of the stocks, and with less than 85 percent no agreement can be reached. Therefore, they had to make decisions.

The U.S. Government, advised by all of those brains — because there is no doubt that it has advisers with great experience who have managed great enterprises from the stock exchange, banks, finances, all of them intelligent people — decides to spend some billion dollars buying yens. They rushed to buy yens to increase the yen's value, and raised it to 136 per dollar. They knew that if it was further devalued, it would bring about a catastrophe, because this would inevitably lead to the devaluation of the Chinese yuan, which would add to the Southeast Asian catastrophe, and then, to a greater devaluation of the yen.

They knew that the immediate impact would be felt by Brazil and then by Argentina, Mexico and Latin America. So, they waited to see when the crisis would strike their own stock markets. It is a matter of great importance. Horrified at what was going on in Russia, they said: No, this is too much.

AT THE MOMENT, THEY HAVE not solved any problem, none of those problems. The crisis is increasingly more serious in Russia. Here, in this university, I will say what I have not had the opportunity to express at any other place: the greatest catastrophe in history regarding the construction of a socioeconomic regime is the attempt to build capital-ism in Russia. It is the greatest catastrophe that has ever happened in any socioeconomic experiment.

They criticize socialism. They speak about the failure of socialism and try to build a new type of socioeconomic regime. But if you analyze the history of the countries that have attempted it, whatever their difficulties before, you will find that even the Soviet Union — that immense country with an 80 percent rural population — ended up being the first in outer space. They produced 630 million tons of oil per year, 700 billion cubic meters of natural gas per year, with steel production around 140 million tons, tens of millions of tons of fertilizer, around 200 million tons of grains, despite being destroyed twice by war, and despite all of their mistakes. China advanced, and other countries advanced, but they were blockaded. Whilst conceding the mistakes made in the economic construction of socialism — let alone the political mistakes — it had a hundred times better results than what they have achieved trying to build capitalism in Russia.

Such disastrous results! Such an untenable situation! A rich country, whose GDP is today 45 percent of what it was nine years ago, in spite of the immense aid and all the credits it has been granted. I ask myself: What could Cuba not accomplish with only a small part of Russia's oil? What could Cuba not accomplish with only a small part of Russia's natural gas, its steel-production capacity, its immense lumber forests in Siberia, its factories that manufacture the parts that our tractors, trucks and equipment need today?

There has never been such a failure in history. They received the recipes of capitalism, and what is happening today? The Russian population is decreasing by about one million people a year. Infant mortality in Russia must be around four or five times higher than in Cuba. Life expectancy drops astonishingly. Fifty percent of the Gross Domestic Product is controlled by the Mafia. From $200 billion to $500 billion have fled Russia. Much of it has been invested in residences, in houses, 60,000 houses in Spain and countless houses in southern France, in Austria, in Italy, in Cyprus, everywhere. Only 50 percent of taxes are collected. The national budget of what used to be a great power is now less than the budget of Spain, for example.

Millions of people have not been paid their wages for months. But according to what has been published, the worst part of it is that the strategic missile operators in Central Siberia have not been paid for five months. The situation is so serious that a recently elected governor of the region wrote to the prime minister asking for jurisdiction over those nuclear missiles bases, since he might provide them with clothing and food to and meet their needs.

Has anything similar to this ever occurred in history? Has anything so potentially dangerous ever occurred like keeping unpaid those operating the strategic nuclear missiles? This is it, the rest you can imagine. It is a great risk, an indication of the danger of disintegration.

Can you imagine what the "Yugoslavization" of a country that has more than 20,000 nuclear weapons might mean? These are real dangers. And what have they been doing? They have been applying the recipes of the International Monetary Fund and the neoliberal policies to that country.

Not long ago I met a representative of a rich and powerful Western country, and I said: What are you going to do about this? Are you people crazy, are you so crazy that you will do nothing to avoid a catastrophe in that country? Look what a real danger exists as a result of a crisis, which is the result of the implementation of neoliberal recipes, in an attempt to build capitalism in Russia.

This problem is a source of great concern to all. We want this to be avoided one way or another. The disintegration of that country would be a world catastrophe with unforeseeable consequences.

First, it was a great multinational state they destroyed with those same recipes. Let's have everybody invest mainly in the Caspian Sea oil — there goes U.S. capital — and in Russia's natural gas, anywhere. But they have created a very difficult situation, a very serious situation that is part of the problem.

It must be said that the crisis in Southeast Asia by itself and the almost $100 billion they had to spend in Korea, or promise from different sources, plus the commitments in Indonesia, Thailand, the Philippines, Malaysia, left the International Monetary Fund out of funds, desperately asking the U.S. Congress for an $18 billion contribution that the U.S. Congress does not want to approve.

Now the Russians are desperately asking for funds. What are $10 billion or $15 billion for a bottomless barrel of needs? How can they be urged to bring down their budgets? How long, then, will the millions of workers and nuclear missile operators remain unpaid? What will be left to pay for health care, education, a minimum of utilities, public order? It is a budget that cannot be further reduced a single cent, and to reduce it would invite an outburst. And $15 billion is no money to that country. It is like a drop of water in the desert. One hundred billion dollars are required, perhaps much more. If Korea needed $100 billion according to estimates, how much would Russia need, whose population, although decreasing, is at least three and a half times that of Korea?

The Japanese economy does not take off regardless what measures are taken. The Chinese yuan is being forcibly sustained as the expression of China's will to cooperate in some way to avoid international catastrophe. But not devaluating the yuan is already costing China tens of millions of dollars. How much longer will the Chinese economy be able to stand that? Particularly when it is accompanied by other phenomena like unusual floods resulting from climatic changes and from the deforestation and erosion brought about by the need to produce food. If the Chinese were forced to devalue the yuan, the economy of Southeast Asia would be more seriously affected in the third or fourth comeback of the crisis. The yen would inevitably plunge further and the wave would spread through the rest of the Third World.

Nobody's money is safe in any of those countries — you should know that. If the depositors' money is in the national currency and they sense that a devaluation is coming, it happens like in Moscow: endless queues of people at the bank changing rubles for dollars. But they do not have a lot of dollars there so they have to stop and declare a payments default that is considered a disaster within that scheme.

The other countries with a free exchange, the established model they have imposed on the world, have no way of protecting their reserves. It is absolutely forbidden by the International Monetary Fund and the World Bank to set exchange controls. That is the worst sin described in the theology of neoliberalism. At the slightest risk everybody runs to the banks to take away what little hard currency the country has left.

And what happens with the hard currency that they take away when there is a crisis? They invest it in U.S. bonds, or European bonds. Thus, hundreds of billions have fled and ended up in those places because money seeks security.

Then, due also to historical factors, the only refuge they have left is the U.S. treasury bonds. When the United States took part in World War I, it possessed enormous natural, mineral, oil and agricultural resources. It participated toward the end of that war and did not lose a single factory; it collected a lot of money and ended up with a powerful economy.

Then comes World War II. The United States entered the war at a moment when Roosevelt's policy gained ground against the isolationists. Roosevelt was undoubtedly a great capitalist statesman. At a time of serious recession he began lifting the economy, fought the isolationist trend and embarked on the struggle against fascism. It is a historic merit. But in that war, the already powerful U.S. industry did not lose a single screw, either. They collected all the gold in the world: the gold of Europe, the gold of England, the gold of almost everybody on the whole planet. The war over, its intact industry quickly crossed over to civil production without any competition. The rest of the world was in ruins. It was then that the United Nations emerged, the Security Council with its five countries with a veto power and the Bretton Woods Treaty. That treaty gave the United States an exceptional advantage.

The fact is that in Bretton Woods they had all the gold accumulated and the gold standard was adopted. That institution worked on the basis of the gold standard. For every U.S. dollar that was issued, there had to be a definite amount of gold in the treasury reserves. If you had $35 you had the right to claim an ounce of gold, which was then maintained at $35, the troy ounce, as the bankers call it. Money had a gold backing and its price was stable. If the supply increased, the Americans bought enough to maintain it. Well, that was done to prevent the price of gold from dropping below $35. When there was the threat of a price increase, they began selling gold from their reserve to keep it at $35. Since after the war when that institution was created, until 1971, the U.S. dollar was convertible into gold.

But many things happened during that period. The Vietnam War cost $500 billion without taxes. Wars, which are not popular, are less so if they come with taxes. Pearl Harbor, a major attack that filled the whole population with indignation, was one thing but a war 10,000 miles away, on the other side of the world, begun and carried out in an irresponsible way, was different. It cost $500 billion.

The U.S. gold reserve began to dwindle. When there were approximately $10 billion left, they implemented the great swindle: they suspended the dollar's convertibility into gold, unilaterally, consulting no one. After that the U.S. dollar bill was nothing but a piece of paper, faith its only support, and the fact that there was no other currency. De Gaulle always opposed that, because he realized the advantage this gave the United States: the right to issue money without any gold support.

Then Reagan comes along and carries forward the U.S. military build-up, including the Star War program that was just beginning. The U.S. public debt when Reagan assumed office was $700 billion. Eight years later, at the end of Reagan's term, the U.S. public debt was more than $2 trillion.

How did they solve their budget deficits? Sometimes these were in the order of $150 billion or $200 billion. They sold treasury bonds at a certain interest. Those who bought the bonds kept them in the reserve or in safe banks. The dollar was the only currency, although at a point in time it faced some competition from the Dutch mark, the Japanese yen and a few others. When these had difficulties again it was left as the only reserve currency and treasury bonds as the safest securities.

The countries exported goods and collected dollars. But they did not spend the dollars in U.S. goods or services; they deposited them in their reserves, because every country needs reserves as every central bank does too.

Most of the world reserves of all central banks and of many commercial banks are in U.S. bills, values that did not cost more than the paper and the ink to print them. The result is that the United States is the owner of the world currency. So, if there is the need to buy yens, it buys yens. It prints the money. An important part of that money is not spent; it is put away. If you are given a million dollars in exchange for goods and the right to buy from the person who gave it to you all that he can sell, but you take the million dollars, keep it in your house and do not spend it, then it does not cost the person who gave it to you a single penny.

So the United States enjoys a privileged position today, a very privileged position, which no other country in the world enjoys. In times of panic, the first thing that all those who have money in any currency do, whether they are in Mexico, Brazil, anywhere, fearing a devaluation, is to change it into dollars and deposit it mainly in U.S. banks. It is one of the things they do, according to the interest rates in the banks. If the interest is too low, they might invest it in bonds or other securities.

Now comes the other problem. When stock values in the stock market drops or people perceive they might drop — and this is where the greatest danger lies — all of those whose money is invested in the stock exchange, if they get scared, they quickly sell those stocks and they do not necessarily invest it in other stocks considered less risky. They generally invest in U.S. Treasury bonds. In other words, they put away their money in the form of bonds to try to guarantee its value.

So, under certain circumstances, they do one of two things: they either have stocks or they have national currency. They change the national currency into dollars because they know it is going to be devalued. The central banks spend up to their last penny in hard currency and that money is transferred to the U.S. banks or used to buy stocks in the stock markets of that or another country if there is no fear of investing there.

When stock values start to drop, they do exactly the same thing. They sell them, they collect them and as the stocks are unsafe, they resort to the safest of all the securities historically, until now, the treasury bonds. That is how they are defending themselves and all the maneuvers to prevent a depression.

The real problem will come when the inevitable happens: a global crisis, because there is no longer an isolated phenomenon in a country's economy that does not have an impact on the rest.

The Asian crises are already causing the U.S. exports to decrease because everybody goes to buy the goods in Southeast Asia or in Japan where they can buy a lot cheaper. That is an immediate result, and they fear that that might affect their excellent situation with employment right now. In other words, they too are suffering the consequences.

The fear lies in what might occur in the event of a global financial crisis affecting all of those countries and a situation of panic, because all that edifice I have tried to describe is supported by a pillar known as trust, something a bit more unstable than love. Love might last a long time, even a whole lifetime, but not trust. Trust is ephemeral and depends on many factors. There is an antidote for that thing called trust and that antidote is panic. All you need is panic and the whole edifice collapses. That is why the bosses of the world economy are going to such great lengths to avoid panic.

When there is news that such and such stock market fell so many points in Hong Kong, here or there, the IMF immediately comes out with: "No, no, everything is fine, great, excellent." Clinton immediately begins working the phone: "Everything is great. Our unemployment rate is the lowest we have had in such and such a time, our economy is growing at such and such a rate, inflation is at its lowest, there is no fear, there is security, everything is going excellently."

That is what you call a sedative — librium, the tranquilizer people take when they are nervous — to calm down and avoid panic. Then Rubin, from the treasury, comes out and says: "Everything is absolutely fine, in so many years we have not had such a high level of employment, nor has the economy grown as it is growing, nor is our potential so splendid." The World Bank comes out and repeats the same thing. They have repeated it so much these days that it sounds like a scratched record.

The Federal Reserve says the same thing to calm everybody, because all you need is panic and the same thing that happened in 1929 may happen again. Everybody rushing off to sell their stocks and there is no stopping them. That is the moment of doom.

All that the theoreticians and experts of developed capitalism, the followers of this model and this economic order, have done is try to devise ways so that a depression such as the 1929 does not take place. In this case it would be more serious and global, really global, as global as the world they are designing, and it is all based on something so vulnerable and fragile as trust.

This is without mentioning other factors that are influencing, and will continue to influence, the economy. Billions, hundreds of billions have been invested in many countries of Southeast Asia and elsewhere to produce the same things: refrigerators, TV sets, radios, computer chips. They are creating an enormous production capacity.

Large investments are made in China, and there are 1.2 billion Chinese. It can prove very difficult to surpass that country in manufacturing goods, and they are already producing them and with good quality.

Let us see what happens when the neoliberal theories, with the enthusiastic effort of the WTO, do away with all the customs barriers. There will not even be the possibility of manufacturing jeans to sell in the United States, Canada and other places. The African might very well need jeans but they do not have a penny to buy them with; neither do the Indians, who are 900 million people; nor the people of Bangladesh, who are many millions; nor the hundreds of millions of poor people in Latin America. This is a trick, a consolation. They say, manufacture these garments and the countries are in such a difficult situation that they have no other choice but to find some hope in manufacturing at least shoes or jeans.

Once, chatting with the prime minister of Canada, who was telling me about their billion dollar trade with the United States, and their relations with Latin America and other countries — Mexico, among them — I told him: "Do you export to the United States shoes and all of those things that are produced with cheap labor?" He answered: "No, we export state-of-the-art technology products obtained with intensive capital investment."

Well, they even sell water, electricity, natural gas, oil. I asked him then if the Mexicans could export the same thing to the United States and Canada? The Mexicans, with their assembly plants, export items produced at very low cost with salaries that are one tenth of the salary of a U.S. worker. Even the Americans oppose such an agreement for fear that the factories are taken away to set them up beyond the U.S. borders.

Then I ask if we were destined to export jeans, shoes and items requiring only cheap labor. When I start adding up all the Chinese who can produce these and other things, and all the Indians, and all the Bangladeshis and all the Indonesians, and all the Latin Americans, and all the Haitians and people from all over, I cannot find the customers anywhere. These are nothing but tricks.

They say: "Meanwhile, remove the tariff barriers and let foreign capital pour in." Very well, but foreign capital knows we need it, like thirsty men lost in the desert, and they increasingly demand the lion's share in order to invest, not only in free-trade zones that establish industries, provide jobs.

Of course, in a country with unemployment problems and many needs, it is better to have a person working, even if it is for a modest salary. These countries have no other alternative. It would be more just to receive a transfer of technology and a transfer of capital through soft loans on lenient terms, to be repaid in 20, 25, or 30 years, to set up a private or state-owned national industry. But I will not go into that topic.

Recently, in the Caribbean I met with a group of businessmen who manufacture different types of goods, in small factories, and who are logically seeking to expand their markets. They expressed certain commercial interests. I told them: "When some of those products you are making are manufactured massively in certain countries, what are your possibilities to compete?" They really had to admit that they did not stand a chance.

The fact is that this world order I am talking about affects every country, especially the Third World countries, not Europe, which is quickly uniting in order to have a currency that can compete with the dollar and a market of 400 million customers. It does not hurt us, anyway. From our point of view, to avoid the existence of one single economic power, it is preferable to have two or three.

Today everything depends on one currency, that of the United States. Privilege distributed among three or four is better than privilege in one single hand, because it then gains uncontrollable power. Let that power be distributed, at least in the economic sector. In the military sector it is unthinkable. Let it be distributed among different poles.

The Europeans are quickly uniting beyond borders. They really have human transit over there. In united Europe, there is transit of capital, transit of goods and transit of people; they have no walls. To defend themselves from the colossus, to defend themselves from the con-sequences, to have a place in this globalization, they have to unite even though they spent centuries warring against one another and they speak many different languages.

Our countries are the ones without any security. We put this forward in the World Trade Organization, because we see the straight jacket they want to impose on us. Patent rights for a 50-year term, that is just great! The United States has taken the best talents from all parts of the world and also has the best research centers and all the necessary resources. Now they want to charge patent rights, like the gabelle [tax] in the Middle Ages, for any product coming out of their research centers, no matter how badly needed those products are.

The day must come when intelligence is rewarded. The day must come when works like the *Iliad*, the *Odyssey*, *Don Quixote*, Shakespeare and all the others, become universal property. The day must come when there are other ways to reward talent, to stimulate it, to further it.

Right now, if there are two Central American transnational companies that are jealous of the bananas exported by the small Caribbean islands, subject to drought or hurricanes — two phenomena that are enemies of bananas — and if they are paid a preferential price in Europe, despite the fact that those islands only partake of one percent of the banana trade, the interests of two U.S. companies prevail over the interests of the islands, some of which live exclusively from the banana trade. The WTO rules in favor of the United States.

Now they are cooking up the Multilateral Agreement on Investments in the OECD, a club of the rich, so that others subscribe to it and they can impose on all the countries whatever they agree there. In other words, we already have the IMF, but the WTO is gradually becoming another dangerous instrument of the appalling new order, because there is not enough awareness among our own allegedly developing countries which are the vast majority there.

We need to make the political leaders see the consequences of all of this. Sweep away the custom tariffs, they say. And what are we going to export? Who are we going to compete with? There are no customs revenues and no taxes, and there are no taxes because the investors operate in a free-trade zone or because they demand from the country receiving the investment more and more years of tax exemption, even when they are not in a free-trade zone.

I asked the Grenadians how many years of tax exemption they grant to those who are building hotels there. Hotels, too, are a source of jobs for them. They stimulate other economic activities, give life to the island. It is better than having nothing, since they have no other alternative. Their answer: They have 10 years of tax exemption.

We ourselves have to grant tax exemptions, although not that long. Sometimes, while the investment is recovered. As a rule, it takes five, six or even seven years. We have to do it, because we need that capital, although we dedicate part of the country's resources to build hotels that are the nation's property. Sometimes we let foreign companies manage them for us. They have the expertise and the markets. We then tell them to manage them for a given percentage.

We are told about Sweden and the social conditions there which are now also declining, just like development aid; But if I remember well, business contributes up to 60 percent of their net profits to make possible the social programs, social welfare and social development. We are threatened with being left without taxes and income from custom tariffs. How are we going to meet our needs in education, health care, housing, drinking water, social development, employment? They leave us nothing. That new order simply wants to impose on us the condition of universal wage earners, and it cannot guarantee even that.

If they had been able to conceive something that within their philosophical framework is impossible — that is, a model that would give employment to the six billion inhabitants of the planet, I mean employment for the active labor force of a community that already reaches six billion — you might say: Well they are promising something. They have not conceived it and they cannot conceive it, because their irrational system makes it impossible.

Oftentimes the working hours cannot be reduced, as the French want to do, because then they would compete with the other countries that have not reduced the working hours. And that is absurd for humankind which has created machines that can reduce physical work from 60 hours in the last century to 20 hours per week; sometimes they were more, 70 and 80 hours even.

It may be said today that, with the existing technology, the excess production of all of those things that are not going to have any market might serve to meet the real demands, the real needs of the world population working 20 hours a week. The rest of the time they could use for culture, recreation, studying and a thousand ways that human beings can spend their time. There need not be unemployment.

Cuba is an example. It has more than 60,000 doctors and none of them are unemployed, because they not only work in hospitals and polyclinics; there is a doctor in every ship, every work center, every day-care center, every school, every community. There are almost 30,000 community doctors in the urban areas and the mountains. Of course, we cannot pay them a very high salary, for where are we going to get it? But that person is doing a useful job for society. That person is not a useless, unemployed illiterate, but a professional who gains more and more knowledge daily, who saves lives and promotes health. If there are too many of them, they can be sent to the universities to receive courses like the teachers do, to upgrade themselves during their sabbatical, by studying, and have other doctors substitute for them.

We have 63,000 doctors and around 2,000 medical students still enroll in the university every year. A doctor is a professional who never wants to retire, the older they are the more experienced they consider themselves. We have 21 medical faculties and we are cooperating with some countries in the training of doctors.

And who do we have studying at the universities now? Nurses must graduate from the university. Also health technicians must be university graduates. In other words, we use those capacities to raise our quality standards. Why should there be a surplus of people if they can be trained and used in a rational manner?

Do not let them come around telling us that the market, that wild and crazy beast, is going to organize human society, nor that the law of supply and demand can be above the organizational capacity of human beings or above the million and trillion neurons in the human brain. The market is a chaotic and uncontrollable wild beast.

Let me tell you that I am saying this at a time when the market is fashionable everywhere. They are even talking about a socialist market economy. They will have to describe clearly the meaning of a socialist market economy. Well, if they say that it is a necessary type of distribution, a mechanism for that, we listen — but it cannot be the market that plans and determines humanity's future, the market preserving the environment, the market preserving nature and life.

Who are they going to make believe that story about the market watching over the purity of the air, the good quality of the waters, fruitful seas where the fish necessary for the growing number of inhabitants of this planet can grow, to prevent what occurred when the market filled them with fishing fleets and trawlers that have diminished their ability to produce food, apart from the pollution of that food with mercury and other chemicals harmful to human health that have been dumped into the sea? The Mediterranean alone receives waste from 140,000 European factories.

The time will come when it will not be possible to eat even a sardine without having a jar of antihistamines and antitoxins by one's side, because they are really increasingly poisonous.

And what is that? That is the market. What has destroyed nature? That system has. What has provoked the warming of the atmosphere, the possibility of the polar icecaps melting, the increase of floods on the one hand and of hurricanes on the other, even if dozens of islands and parts of the coastal areas will be under water when the sea level rises? What good will all our docks, ports and current maritime facilities, including recreation centers, do us then? These are real dangers, not fantasy.

They have lately fallen into the habit of referring to people who make this sort of criticism as catastrophists. Since my name is Castro, it is all the same if they call me catastrophist or whatever they like. I know that my rational, mathematical and physical calculations are accurate. Besides, they are the real catastrophists because they are the ones who cause the catastrophes.

In any event, we are warning them not to cause it, and telling them that we are hopeful that the world can survive, that the human species has advanced so much in technological, scientific and intellectual development, as well as in the means to support human intelligence and strength, as to find solutions not even dreamed of before, to produce food and goods for humankind, to preserve nature, which is a decisive issue, and preserve it soon.

Millions of tons of chlorofluorocarbons advancing toward the ozone layer, more and more millions of carbon dioxide, millions, hundreds of million, billions of tons of this gas go to the atmosphere every year.

When they meet to discuss this, the United States is last to accept the slightest reduction or the slightest commitment. They have created the market of the air pollution quotas; I cannot call it otherwise. If a country has a quota of pollution to send up into the atmosphere and saves it, this can then be sold to another so they can pollute, too. Such a humane, very rational, very understanding market! It is really incredible! It is not worthy of a civilized society, of a developed humanity!

It is about these matters — and I know you have been too kind already — that I invite you to think.

ANOTHER TERRIBLE PROBLEM THAT WE are suffering — perhaps the last one I will touch upon — is that of the aggression against our national identities, the ruthless aggression against our cultures, as never before in history, the trend towards a universal monoculture. How can anyone conceive such a world? It is not a world order that combines the wealth and culture of many countries, but a world order that, by definition, destroys culture, a globalization that inevitably destroys culture.

What is one's homeland, if not one's own culture? What is national identity if not a country's own culture? Can there be a greater spiritual wealth than one's own culture, created during eons by humankind? Can our customs be simply swept away, ruthlessly swept away? We have to be aware of that, because the battle of ideas and concepts will be a great battle.

If we are to speak about ideology, let us speak about the ideology of saving the world — not later, but as soon as possible. Let's try to save it and improve it as of now. After we have saved it, we will be able to improve it even more.

I was saying that this battle for survival is not a class struggle, even though classes may be involved in the conflict. This battle for the survival of the Third World countries includes us all: those who have large resources and those who have very little.

I think that both the rich and the poor, if they are sailing on the same ship, would not want the ship to sink. There might be a minimum of collaboration to try to save the ship. We are really sailing in a *Titanic* with a lot of sea beneath and many icebergs in the way. That dramatic story, has now served to invest $300 million in a movie with more than a billion dollars in profits.

The great films are no longer simply films, but a combination of film and commercial operation, and when they have drawn hundreds of millions from the film, they have obtained thousands of millions from the products connected with the picture that are sold, from lion kings, dolls, toys and myriads of objects that absorb families' money. It is all a combination, the merging of commercial and recreation enterprises whose objectives have nothing to do with culture.

A question: Who are the only ones in the world who have $300 million for a film? There is only one answer: the growing, uncontrollable monopolies of the mass media in the hands of the U.S. transnationals.

A few examples will suffice, if you allow me to recall some facts: 50 percent of all the films made and shown in the world today belong to U.S. companies, 75 percent to 80 percent of the TV serials, 70 percent of videos, 50 percent of satellites through which any place can be reached, 60 percent of the world's networks and 75 percent of the internet. All of this is in their hands, and all of this is at the service of neoliberal globalization and the ideas it is putting forward. These are very powerful sources of ideology, information, beliefs, customs that can transform many things.

In the Spanish-speaking Americas, an average of 245 films are premiered per country each year, of which 70 percent are U.S., 10 percent correspond to the local film industry, 14 percent are European and only three percent are Spanish American. Seventy-nine percent of the TV programs imported by the Spanish Americas come from the United States.

Actually, I was amazed when I read not long ago that hamburgers were already in India. The Indians, whose culture is so special, who do not even eat beef, already have McDonald's produced with buffalo meat. Well, you have had it for a long time now. They are here, they are everywhere, but I am talking of India. I can imagine those who are capable of mixing even the meat of a dead oxen killed by accident on a highway with the buffalo meat. Well, the Indians with McDonald's, and chains of McDonald's stores, that is the culture of globalization that is imposed. The Indians have other consumption habits, and they have a lot better and more refined dishes than hamburgers.

The Chinese are consuming McDonald's, the Africans are consuming McDonald's, wherever there is the possibility for that product. The Chinese are consuming Coca-Cola and Pepsi-Cola. The Latin Americans have had the habit for a long time now, but the Chinese did not have it, they drank tea and other things. The Chinese and the Indians are consuming Coca-Cola and Pepsi-Cola. The Europeans are also learning very quickly to consume hot dogs and hamburgers. They gradually acquire the Western customs and habits, they even smoke the cigarettes targeted by critical campaigns in the United States to reduce death by cancer, but which are then advertised and exported to the whole world.

The culture of reading, which was a privilege of our ancestors when over 80 percent of the population was illiterate, is losing ground considerably. Reading habits? No. TV serials? Serials, yes, one after the other, never-ending superficiality of all sorts, escapism.

How much time do children have for studying? The average TV

time of children with electricity in their homes is three hours of their after-school time. The reading habit is gradually disappearing.

Books? What books are available to the Third World? In Finland, for example, where they have a lot of paper and big forests, which they now prefer to exploit as little as possible, they now buy trees from the Russians; they preserve their forests and go to Siberia. The number of books published in Finland between 1991 and 1994 was 246 per 100,000 people, while in India and Madagascar it was barely one per 100,000. The average number of books published in the developed countries is 54 per 100,000 people, while in the countries still to develop it is seven books. That is their possibility of reading, of knowing at least the history of their country.

It is very sad to hear — and it is true — that if a survey is made among Mexican or Latin American children to ask who were Hidalgo and Morelos, or if you ask Central American children who was Morazán, or in Latin America who was Bolívar, they do not know. Yet a great majority of those children know who Mickey Mouse is. That is their cultural legacy to us; they are destroying the most cherished values of our lives, our peoples, our nations, our communities.

Three transnational news agencies circulate 80 percent of the news disseminated in the world by cables. And that is nothing compared to digital television, the increasing number of channels, fiber optics and the possibilities that keep emerging.

Something as sacred as culture is threatened with extinction, because those media are mainly used for commercial and not for educational purposes. Very few Africans have a TV channel, a radio station, and when they do have a TV channel, then all that is shown comes from abroad, from the developed, consumer societies, from the United States in particular.

Are they going to leave us any freedom? They are not even going to leave us the freedom of choosing our food, nor cooking it as our ancestors historically did. All at the service of that unsustainable order.

What will happen when the inevitable depression comes, as it will in a global fashion? Nothing has been devised, nor can anything be devised to prevent it in a world increasingly governed by the law of the market. But this time it will be different! It will not be like in 1929. The stocks are more inflated, a lot more inflated than in 1929, five times, six times inflated, the stocks in the United States. Something which has nothing to do with the creation of new riches, but with what I referred to as trust, the hope that they will continue gaining value: earning money by betting, buying stocks, buying currencies, anything. People invest their money based on that hope.

I already explained in the CARICOM meeting that currently, every day, every 24 hours, speculative operations are carried out with a value of $1.5 trillion. This figure equals 18 times the GDP of the whole world in 15 days. In the calculations I made, it came to around 17 or 18 days. This amount is bet in the world every day. There has never been anything like this.

As I explained, it is money going for money; not money invested in a factory, in an enterprise, in industry or services, but money invested in bonds, currencies, in stocks, anything, even coffee; but not in real coffee, rather coffee quoted in the stock markets, which is quoted at $2 and a buyer thinks that it is going to go up to $2.30, so he buys it to sell it later when it is at $2.30. He has not produced a single coffee bean, he has not grown it; but he invented a game, a lottery with coffee, with sugar and with any other product, and, above all, with stocks.

Before, it was only the rich, the millionaires, the Rockefellers who had stocks in the stock markets. Today, in the United States, tens of millions of people have their savings invested in stocks, and the insurance mutual funds are invested in stocks.

A CRISIS LIKE THAT OF 1929 would be a huge catastrophe. Let us ask Greenspan, Rubin, Camdessus and the director of the World Bank if they think that speculative balloon can be sustained. Exactly the same thing as in 1929. We must tell them: Gentlemen, you have created a World Bank that keeps running around, a monetary fund that has no funds, or not enough, and the crises spread. Are you sure that balloon is not going to deflate?

At the WTO, at the end of their different agendas, I humorously proposed to add a topic: global economic crisis, what can be done? That is what I want to ask those gentlemen, what can be done? Have they invented the philosopher's stone? What have they invented so that these phenomena do not bring about the feared depression?

I personally do not have the slightest doubt. It does not seem like we will have to wait long, bearing in mind some of the things we have listed here and many more. Events are happening very fast. These are times in which events follow one another at great speed.

This is a very new problem. The concepts of globalization are very recent. They have developed with a great force in the last 15 or 20 years, but mainly in the last 10 years. Environmental awareness is also new. Thirty or 35 years ago, very few people spoke about the environment; today everybody talks about it and there is awareness. Events are moving very fast.

I ask myself if this is the last or next to last crisis. We are very interested in, and try to inform ourselves as much as possible about, how events might unfold this year and the next. What will happen in

Russia, Japan and Southeast Asia? If the crisis reaches the other regions how will they solve the problem, plus the pressing political issues, which are very serious? A very serious political problem can be a social explosion in Russia, which is not the same as a social explosion in Yugoslavia or in the Kosovo province; it would be a political catastrophe.

All this means that we are facing the risk of problems that can affect the whole world, because the crisis that is already here is affecting many countries. Sugar producers see the price of sugar at eight cents. Those who produce copper see the price cut in half and the same occurs with nickel, aluminum, rubber. Everybody is seeing the prices of their commodities cut almost in half right now.

The economy of every country is exposed to stock exchange moves and speculation and to losing in a moment of panic all the monetary reserves of a country's central bank, any country. We are not included, because since we were thrown out of all those agencies, we do not have to abide by any IMF recipe or anybody else's. The others have to comply with them, and they are liable to wake up one day without a penny in their reserves.

These are very tough problems: climatic change, the great influence this can have on food prices or people's purchasing power. But this should be no reason for us to do like the IMF, the World Bank, the Federal Reserve Bank and the U.S. Treasury and say: "Be calm, be calm, everything is doing very well. This is a passing phenomenon."

Some of you have young nephews and nieces, or children, or grandchildren five, six or seven years' old. In 50 years they will be a lot younger than what I am now, a lot younger. Fifty years pass very quickly as I certainly know; I sometimes think I am still in school, or it seems only like yesterday. How quickly have 50 years gone by for me! The Cubans who have lived through almost 40 years of revolution and blockade, we know.

Forty years can go too quickly! Sometimes it seems like a second but when those 50 years have passed, the population of this planet will be 10 billion. That will determine the need for more rice, more hamburgers, more wheat, more corn, more milk, more clothes and shoes, more medicines, more housing, more transportation, more drinking water, more recreation, more culture, more spiritual goods that can be produced in infinite quantities, or rather that a rational humanity might produce, not a few thousand transnationals guided by the law of the market.

There is so much spiritual wealth that humanity might create! And humankind does not live on bread alone, as the Bible says. Spiritual goods or riches, spiritual values are missed a lot more when material needs are satisfied, and for those four billion additional population, humanity will have to train doctors, teachers, build hospitals, develop new medicines, which should also prolong life, and defeat cancer, AIDS and other new and old diseases.

The number of those who will have to be fed and aided by a smaller percentage of the people will grow every year. That is why in the United States, England and other places they are beginning to worry and want to raise the retirement age to 65 or more. The lifespan of human beings will be prolonged; it can be prolonged. New medicines and the WHO programs have cut in half the number of children who died 30 or 40 years ago. Productivity must grow. Humanity must be fed!

Does that humanity exist or not? Must it not be fed, educated and given the maximum well-being that does not only lie with material goods? There comes a time when material goods are more than enough. Right now, there are those who have three or four more automobiles than they need. The consumption patterns would also need to be analyzed. All those food chains I talked about, all those media monopolies are wholly devoted to advertising the consumption habits of the developed capitalist societies. It is awful.

How can we imagine every Chinese and every Indian with an automobile at their doorstep! What would be left of the 10 million hectares that the Chinese have today to produce grains, rice, food for 1.5 billion people that they will be in a few decades and at the same time build roads, highways, garages, houses?

Can they continue spreading and imposing on the world a desire for those consumption patterns? Could we not instill a greater desire for culture and spiritual wealth? When humans discover it, oftentimes they prefer that to any other thing. Things for edification not alienation, and television not only for recreation but for education, training, nurturing the human spirit, making the individual better, more generous, not for turning people into wild animals, into killers.

Other statistical data show that in many countries there is an average of five to 10 acts of aggression per hour of television, and that in the period 1996-97 the programs showing violence were 61 percent of the total. Violence and more violence, sex and more sex, which differs from reality, for humankind is not violent by nature, even if the Bible tells us that Cain killed Abel, although television did not exist then!

As for sex, the individual needs to be educated, because as it is instinctively, naturally awakened, there is no need to go around proclaiming it. Isn't that right, young university students? It is exploited and exacerbated for grossly commercial purposes. This also brings about many social phenomena linked to today's world, such as irresponsibility, emotional instability, disappointments, separations, divorce.

Believe me, this is not a priest speaking from his pulpit. I am not and cannot be against the right to divorce, but as leaders of a country, we wish that there were more stability in the family, so the less divorce the better.

It is because stability really helps the children who are the ones most affected and it helps the individual, for instance, to control one's instincts. Nothing is gained by exacerbating them.

Violence and sex are two things much resorted to by these media with a commercial orientation. Everything turns out to be commercial. There is nothing human, nothing that seeks human betterment, but anything that can bring profit even if it destroys humankind, even if it makes social life more complicated.

We must nurture values. There is no alternative; authentic values are those practiced in the greatest freedom.

It is neither a dream nor something impossible that all those fabulous resources that could serve to educate, train and improve humankind, can one day be used for these humane purposes.

I say that time goes by very quickly, not only the time I have used up on this rostrum, but the other — and I say it because I am afraid I might miss the plane — time flies! I said 50 years. You already have an idea that, no matter how many we are, there will be less space. Let us ask ourselves what should be our life patterns, our consumption patterns; what patterns befit us, as an immense, growing humanity.

I think these problems are a source of concern to many people today, one way or another, regardless of social class or religious belief. The great challenge is how to bring together all the talents, all the values and all the ethical systems to achieve those objectives.

I have taken up a few hours of your time, but I did not want to come here to simply say: "Good afternoon. How are you all? We are very happy for the way you have welcomed us!" Of course, all this is true, but I do not have to say what you know so well. I wanted to share some of our ideas, our thoughts. I was not planning to speak too much about Cuba. I was a bit lengthy on that topic to explain some of our experiences. I wanted, rather, to address these issues here, brother to brother, heart to heart, with a frankness equal to the hospitality, the generosity and the affection you have shown our delegation.

You, who have contributed so much to the success of this visit in every respect, you who have been so fraternal, you who have upheld our souls with so much spirit, so much enthusiasm and so much encouragement. Because that trust has not been forged under a clear sky, it has been forged under a deluge of lies, misinformation, slanders; it has been forged under a storm of lightening bolts during these years that we have not even had the opportunity of seeing each other this way, of meeting people to people, in representation, along with other comrades, of the Cuban people.

Let us rejoice for this great progress, let us rejoice that our peoples can come closer, exchange, talk. But your courage is great because your trust has developed under almost impossible conditions. What does this teach us? That one must have confidence in humankind; one must have confidence in the peoples, their talent, their intelligence.

In many parts of the world the representatives of that blockaded [island of] Cuba — slandered through the most sophisticated media — have friends and find so many ordinary men and women who understand their struggle, who understand their cause and express their solidarity with it. Is it not that they, along with us, dream of a better future, of a more just world and of a global, universal society which is truly humane?

What I have described — born from the experience of our fighting, militant people, from the experiences we have lived through, from sleepless eyes that try to see the evolution of events — are my convictions and the convictions of our comrades. We want to leave them here for you, Dominican brothers and sisters, as curators of these ideas. I do not ask you to agree with these ideas, but I do ask you to think about them. We ourselves have to delve deeper and learn a lot more.

4

There is No End of History

Nonaligned Nations Movement Summit, Durban

To endure the global struggle between the superpowers is bad.
To live under total hegemonic domination by one of them is
worse. Let us speak frankly.

It is not possible to resign oneself to a world order whose highest
principals and objectives embody a system that colonized, enslaved
and plundered us for decades. There is no swan-song, no close of
history, no end to the struggle of this movement of nonaligned
countries — the group of peoples that during the Cold War fought,
supported and defended the interests and just causes of Third World
nations in the struggle for national liberation.

We do not have to ask permission or seek excuses from anyone to
exist and to continue the struggle. Even the United States vehemently
sought to be included in this summit as an observer. This way, the
great emperor can see how its modest subjects behave.

The United Nations needs to be reformed and democratized. The
dictatorship of the Security Council needs to end. The General
Assembly needs to recognize its rights and bring together representatives from every country in the world. The Security Council should
be enlarged in proportion to the current number of countries. Its
permanent members should be doubled, even tripled if necessary.

Why the limitation on one representative for Latin America and the
Caribbean, one for Asia and one for Africa? Whose idea was that?

In September 1998, Fidel Castro attended a summit meeting of the
Nonaligned Nations Movement in Durban, South Africa. This speech was
delivered on September 2.

Who accepted it? Why not two or three representatives from each of these regions that together constitute the vast majority of the United Nations? If Western Europe has two members, why do more than four billion people of the Third World not have even one?

The right to veto should disappear. Moreover, it should be impossible and unacceptable to have members of two different categories. If they are not going to rotate, they will only exist to deceive, confuse, divide and diminish the qualifications of new members. Everyone should have the same rights.

The International Monetary Fund should also be transformed and democratized. It needs to cease being an overall politically destabilizing agent and a financial gendarme in the interests of the United States. Nobody should have the power to veto its decisions. This applies to the World Bank as well.

The World Trade Organization, in which we are a majority, cannot be converted into a medium of deceit and division by using it as a tool to impose cruel, global neoliberalism on the world. Nor can it be a party to a binding multilateral accord on investment which is a creation of the Organization for Development and Cooperation in Europe — an exclusive club for the rich in which none of our countries participate but who are, nevertheless, forced to jump onto the bandwagon or be left out with numerous consequences. Freedom of movement should not only apply to capital and commodities but above all to human beings.

No more bloodied walls along the border between the United States and Mexico that costs hundreds of lives each year! End the persecution of immigrants and the accompanying xenophobia! Stop the hypocritical cries of protest when other nations attempt to build nuclear arms while their privileged nuclear capability becomes more and more potent, precise and deadly! This only stimulates interminable proliferation that will never truly lead to total nuclear disarmament.

The arms race has not slowed for one second — not so much in volume as in quality. It serves only to guarantee the privileges of the new order and is a source of profitable and dishonest business. Armaments are increasingly more expensive. Developing nations ruin themselves and kill each other with them. Trafficking in arms is worse than trafficking in drugs.

Neoliberal globalization is rapidly destroying our natural environment, poisoning our air and water, deforesting our lands, eroding our soils into wasteland, squandering our natural resources, changing our climate. How and with what shall 10 billion human beings live? International development aid is decreasing. The average aid budget of 0.7 percent of GDP will never be reached, and has dropped to an average of 0.25 percent. In the richest country on earth — and we all know who that is — it now stands at 0.2 percent.

They think of us as a huge, free-trade zone filled with low-paid workers where no taxes are paid to provide for children, the elderly and sick.

That fact that the population of Africa is left with AIDS, malaria, tuberculosis, leprosy and dozens of old and new diseases is not an issue for the multinationals or the blind eyes of the world markets. Extracting oil, gold, diamonds, platinum, copper, bronze, uranium and other valuable resources is more important.

The unipolar world and its accompanying world order are wiping out sovereignty and independence. Interventions multiply. Terrorism — which kills and wounds innocent people — becomes a pretext for world powers to put into practice their own form of terrorism in dozens of countries in Latin America, Asia and Africa, including Cuba. Launching missiles in all directions without taking into consideration the innocent people who die or the legal ramifications, other than their own all-embracing will.

The world is becoming a Western in the style of old Hollywood movies. Such reprisals have neither moral nor legal justification. This is not the way to fight terrorism. On the contrary, terrorism is encouraged by such brutal actions. Only a universal awareness of the common struggles of the people can eradicate it.

End the economic blockades against other countries! Depriving millions of food, medicine, and other ways of life are terrorist acts of extreme cruelty and true genocide. Such acts must be considered war crimes and should be sanctioned by international tribunals.

End the abuses against the long-suffering Palestinian people and offer them the possibility of peace! Comply with the previously agreed peace accords and return to the Arab peoples the territories taken from them! End the double standard on international questions! End hunger and poverty in the world! End the lack of teachers and schools, of doctors and hospitals! End the interminable pillage of foreign debt that, as more interest is paid and more debt accrues, is blocking our very development.

End unequal exchange such as that used by the conquistadors when they bought gold from the Indians with mirrors and European trinkets!

Pay up on the debt that those who exploited us for so many centuries have accumulated! End the policy of inundating the peoples of the world with the unsustainable life-styles of consumer society! End the destruction of our national identities and our cultures!

Many things must end but, first of all, disunity among us must end. As must the ethnic wars and conflicts among our peoples who are called upon to struggle for their development and right to survive and take their rightful place in tomorrow's world.

And someday, we won't distinguish between ethnic origins; we won't espouse national chauvinism, nor borders, nor rivers, seas, oceans, distances. We will be above that, with all human beings called upon to live in a world inevitably globalized, truly just, filled with solidarity and peace.

We must struggle to achieve that day.

5

Great Crises Always Deliver Great Solutions

South African Parliament, Cape Town

D o not be alarmed. The speech is not as long as it seems, although the translation will take more of our time. I was trying to figure out the impression that I would have upon arrival at this parliament. What could I, and what should I, say that would deserve your interest and your attention, since you have so kindly gathered here to listen to my words.

What I bring here with me, assisted by some data, is therefore just the work of my imagination. Like a love letter addressed to a sweetheart thousands of miles away, even though you don't know how she feels, what she wants to hear, and not even what her face looks like.

For me a speech is just an honest and intimate conversation. That is why I got into the habit of talking to, or establishing a dialogue with, my interlocutors, looking at their faces and trying to persuade them of what I am saying.

If at any time I put aside the paper to add a few things that cross my mind while inspired by some ideas, I hope that those who do not have earphones, the organizers, or the people in charge of seeing to the solemnity and efficiency of this event will understand.

I think about this country and I think about its history. I see in my mind all kinds of developments, events, facts, data, realities that reflect the enormous responsibility and the colossal historical task implicit in creating the new South Africa that you aspire to.

Fidel Castro addressed members of South Africa's parliament in Cape Town on September 4, 1998.

I hope that my presence here will leave, as the sole essential memory, our fervent and sincere wishes to support the enormous efforts that you are making in order to heal the deep wounds that for many centuries have remained open.

This promising country, which was yesterday the target of isolation and universal condemnation, can tomorrow be an example of fraternity and justice. The timely presence, at the precise moment, of a leader of exceptional human and political qualities makes it possible. That man was there, in the dark corners of a jail. He was much more than a political prisoner, sentenced for life; he was a prophet of politics who is today acknowledged even by those who hated and ruthlessly punished him in the past.

Nelson Mandela will not go down in history for the 27 consecutive years that he had lived imprisoned without ever renouncing his ideas. He will go down in history because he was able to draw from his soul all poison accumulated by such an unjust punishment. He will be remembered for his generosity and for his wisdom at the time of an already uncontainable victory, when he knew how to lead so brilliantly his self-sacrificing and heroic people, aware that the new South Africa would never be built on foundations of hatred and revenge.

There are still today two South Africas, which ought not be called the "White" one and the "Black" one; that terminology should forever be dropped if a multiracial and united country is to be created. I would rather put it this way: two South Africas — the rich and the poor — one and the other. One where an average family receives 12 times the income of the other; one where the children who die before their first year of life are 13 per 1,000 and the other where those who die are 57 per 1,000; one in which life expectancy is 73 years, the other in which it is only 56 years; one where 100 percent of the people know how to read and write, another where illiteracy is more than 50 percent; one with almost full employment, another where 45 percent are unemployed; one where 12 percent of the population own almost 90 percent of the land, the other where almost 80 percent of the inhabitants own less than 10 percent of it; one that has accumulated almost all the technical and managerial knowledge, the other doomed to inexperience and ignorance; one that enjoys well-being and freedom, the other having been able to conquer freedom but without well-being.

Such a dreadful legacy cannot be changed overnight. There is absolutely nothing to be gained by disrupting the production system or wasting the considerable material and technical wealth, as well as the productive experience created by the workers' noble hands under a criminal and unjust system that was virtual slavery. Perhaps one of the most difficult tasks of human society is to carry forward social change in an orderly, gradual and peaceful way, so that such wealth could contribute to the optimal benefit of the South African people. In the opinion of this daring guest, whom you have invited here to say a few words, that is the greatest challenge that South Africa is facing today.

I reject demagogy. I would never say a word here to incite discontent, much less to win applause or to please the ears of millions of South Africans who are rightly hurting today because the paradise of equal opportunities for all and the justice that they dreamed of during the long years of struggle have not yet been attained in their country.

There are many nations with similar social and economic problems that are the result of conquest, colonization and an unbearable disparity in the distribution of wealth; but in no place other than here has the struggle for respect for human dignity kindled so much hope. The contradiction between hopes, possibilities and priorities is not only a South African domestic affair, but something that is being debated, and that will still continue to be debated, amongst the honest theoreticians of many countries.

The system of conquest, colonization, slavery, extermination of the indigenous populations and looting of their natural resources in past centuries has had dreadful consequences for the overwhelming majority of the peoples of Asia, Africa and Latin America.

Seventy million Indians were exterminated in the whole of the American hemisphere due to the ruthless exploitation, slave labor, imported diseases or the sharp edge of the conquerors' swords.

Twelve million Africans were violently taken from their villages, from their homes and transported to the new continent, all shackled in chains, to work as slaves on the plantations; and that does not include the many millions who drowned or died during the crossing.

Actually, apartheid was universal, and it lasted for centuries. For our hemisphere, the slaves were the first to revolt, in one way or another, against colonial domination in the very early stages of the 16th century. Major revolts in Jamaica, Barbados and other countries took place in the first decades of the 18th century, long before the revolt of the U.S. slaves. The slaves in Haiti created the first republic in Latin America. Some years later heroic and massive slave revolts also took place in Cuba. The African slaves were the ones who pointed the way to freedom on that continent. In the course of history many crimes have been committed by the Christian and civilized West, as they like to call themselves, and those who created and applied the apartheid system in South Africa, who must carry the full burden of the guilt.

The political miracle of unity, reconciliation and peace under the leadership of Nelson Mandela will perhaps become an unprecedented example in history.

It could be said that there were never so many who wished so much for so few. You, South African citizens and leaders of all parties and of all ethnic origins, are those few for whom all the inhabitants of this planet wish so much and from whom all of us expect so much, from a political and human point of view.

One idea may lead to another: from the new South Africa, the hopes for a new Africa. Economically, South Africa is, from the industrial, agricultural, technological and scientific points of view, the most developed country on the African continent. Its mineral and energy resources are boundless, in many cases exceeding those in all other countries in the world. Today South Africa produces 50 percent of the electricity of this continent, 85 percent of the steel and 97 percent of the coal. It transports 69 percent of all rail cargo; it has 32 percent of all the motor vehicles and 45 percent of the paved roads. The rest of Africa is also immensely rich in natural resources. There is the enormous potential and virgin talent of its children, their extraordinary courage and intelligence, their capacity to assimilate the most complex know-ledge in science and technology. We know this very well because we have been with them; we had the privilege of fighting, together with them, for freedom or for peaceful reconstruction.

Cuba is just a small island next to a very powerful neighbor, but 26,294 professionals and technicians graduated in our education centers and 5,850 students coming from different African countries have been trained there. A total of 80,524 Cuban civilians, among them 24,714 doctors, dentists, nurses and health workers, together with tens of thousands of teachers, engineers and other professionals and skilled workers, have cooperated by rendering international services of different kinds in Africa. In over 30 years, 381,432 soldiers and officers have been on duty or have fought together with African soldiers and officers on this continent for national independence or against foreign aggression. It is a figure that rises to 461,956 in a brief historical period. From the African land in which they worked and fought, voluntarily and selflessly, they returned to Cuba with only the remains of their fallen comrades and the honor of having fulfilled their duty.

That is why we know and value the human qualities of the children of Africa much more than those who for centuries colonized and exploited this continent.

With deep, tearing pain we witness today their fratricidal wars and their economic underdevelopment, their poverty, their famines, their lack of hospitals and schools, the lack of communications. With astonishment we note that Manhattan or Tokyo have more telephones than the whole of Africa together.

The deserts are expanding, the forests disappear, and the soil is subject to erosion. And something awful: old and new diseases — malaria, tuberculosis, leprosy, cholera, Ebola, parasites and treatable infectious diseases — are all decimating its population. Infant mortality shows record-high indexes when compared with those of the rest of the world; also the rate of mothers who die during childbirth; and in some countries, life expectancy is beginning to decrease.

The awful HIV is expanding in geometrical proportions. When I say that whole nations in Africa are at risk of disappearing, it is not an overstatement, and you know it. Each infected person would have to pay $10,000 a year in medication only to survive, while the health budgets can hardly allocate $10 to spend on each person's health. At present prices, $250 billion would have to be invested each year in Africa only to fight AIDS. Owing to this, nine out of every 10 persons dying from AIDS in the world die in Africa.

Can the world contemplate this catastrophe with indifference? Can humanity, with its amazing scientific advances, confront this situation or not? Why go on talking to us about macroeconomic indexes and other eternal lies, prescriptions and more prescriptions of the IMF and the World Trade Organization, about the miraculous virtues of the blind law of the market and the wonders of neoliberal globalization? Why is it that these realities are not taken for what they are? Why not seek other formulas and admit that humankind is able to organize our lives and our destiny in a more rational and humane manner?

An avoidable and deep economic crisis, perhaps the worst in history, is threatening all of us today. In the world, which has become an enormous casino, speculative operations with a value of $1.5 trillion, which bear no relation to any real economy, are carried out every day. Never before has world economic history seen a phenomenon similar to this one.

The shares on the stock exchange markets of the United States have been escalating to the point of absurdity. It was only an historical privilege, associated with a set of factors that made it possible for a wealthy nation to become the world issuer of reserve currency from the reserve banks in every country. Their treasury bonds are the last safe haven for those fearful investors confronting any economic crisis.

When I said that the shares on the stock exchange markets have been escalating to the point of absurdity, I should have said: The prices of the shares on the stock exchange markets of the United States have been escalating to the point of absurdity.

The dollar stopped having gold backing when that country unilaterally suppressed the exchange rates established in Bretton Woods. As in the dreams of alchemists in the middle ages, paper has been turned into gold. Ever since then the value of the reserve world currency has simply become a matter of confidence. Wars like the one in Vietnam, at the cost of $500 billion, paved the way for this enormous deceit. To that should be added the colossal rearmament, which raised the public debt of the United States from $700 billion to $2.5 trillion in only eight years.

So money became a fiction. The values no longer had a real and material basis. Nine trillion dollars were purchased by U.S. investors in recent years through the simple mechanism of the unbridled multiplication of the stock prices in their markets. Thus, we find the colossal growth of transnational corporate investments in the world and in their own country. At the same time as they have had unrestrained growth in domestic consumption, they have been artificially feeding an economy that seemed to grow and grow without inflation and without crisis. Sooner or later the world would have to pay the price.

The most prosperous nations of Southeast Asia have been ruined. Japan, the second most significant world economy, can no longer stop a recession. The yen keeps losing value. The yuan is being sustained with great sacrifice by China, whose high growth will be reduced this year to less than eight percent, a figure dangerously close to the tolerable limit for a country that is conducting a speedy, radical reform and extraordinary rationalization of the labor force in its productive enterprises. The Asian crisis is coming back. The economic catastrophe in Russia is emerging with the greatest economic and social failure in history — trying to build capitalism in that country. All this is despite the enormous financial assistance and the recommendations and recipes supplied by the best minds in the West. Perhaps, at this moment, the greatest political risk lies in the situation created in a state that owns thousands of nuclear warheads, a state in which the operators of the strategic missiles have not been paid their salaries for five months.

The stock exchanges of Latin America have lost over 40 percent of their share value in only a few months; in Russia they have lost 75 percent. This phenomenon tends to spread and become universal. The basic commodities of many countries, such as copper, nickel, aluminum, petroleum and many others, have lately been decreasing in price by 50 percent.

The stock exchange of the United States is already shaking. As you know, they just had what they call a "Black Tuesday." I don't know why they call it "black." Actually it is has been "white Tuesday." No one knows when and how the general panic will be unleashed. Could anyone, at this point, be certain that there will not be a repetition of the 1929 crash? It is just that between then and now there is an enormous difference. In 1929 there were not $1.5 trillion involved in speculative operations and only three percent of the U.S. population had shares in the stock exchange. Today, 50 percent of the population of the United States has its savings and its pension funds invested in shares in those stock exchanges. This is not a fabrication of mine. It is not a fantasy — just read the news. If you wish, add to this the fact that the new world order is destroying, faster than before, the natural environment in which we, the six billion inhabitants of the planet, live at present, and on which 10 billion inhabitants will have to live in another 50 years.

I have discharged my duty. I have just told you what crossed my mind at an altitude of 10,000 meters. Please don't ask me about solutions. I am not a prophet. I only know that great crises have always delivered great solutions.

I trust the minds of peoples and of humankind. I trust the need of humanity to survive. I trust that you, distinguished and patient members of this parliament, will think about this subject. I trust that you will understand that this is not a matter of ideology, race, color, personal income or social class. It is rather, for all of us sailing in the same boat, a matter of life or death. Let us be more generous, more jointly responsible, more humane. Let South Africa become a model of a more just, more humane, future world. If you can achieve it, all of us will be able to.

6

Soweto: Birthplace of Africa's Dignity

Soweto, South Africa

I'm not going to give a speech. I've come to chat with you for a few minutes. A speech would have to be very long, as long as your history, as long as the glorious resistance that these peoples of Africa offered the conquerors, settlers and slave traders. A speech would have to be so long, as long as the list of problems that we have in today's world and it would have to be as long as the list of all those who have fallen in this continent and in other parts of the world for freedom and justice, although we still can't say that true freedom and justice exist in this world. So I'll talk briefly about some things that might help develop our awareness of the idea that freedom and justice in our world may perhaps be closer than ever.

Victory is achieved not only with arms. It is also achieved many times without arms. I don't practice the philosophy of Mahatma Gandhi, but history has shown that many and great battles have been won fundamentally with ideas. That's why I always say that the first thing is the idea; the second, to struggle for ideas; and the third is to triumph with sweat and blood, if necessary, for those ideas.

I thought about this when I arrived here in South Africa and when I visited that modest monument to the memory of those who deserve a monument as high as Mount Everest, which is said to be the highest mountain in the world.

That boy [Hector Petersen] deserves a Himalayan mountain as a

---

As part of his visit to South Africa, on September 5, 1998, Fidel Castro visited Soweto, the township where school students rebelled on June 16, 1976, against the apartheid regime.

monument — that boy and the children who fought and died like him. Who was that boy? How old was he? Why did they kill him? What crime did that boy commit for him to be murdered? What ideas was he defending? More than an idea, little Hector was defending a feeling, that feeling with which we're all born — everyone without exception — a sense of human dignity. That boy was sacrificed for that dignity. And millions of children have been sacrificed for that dignity, just like hundreds of millions — you could say thousands of millions throughout history — of children, old people, men and women, those who suffered, as a result of exploitation, injustice, those who died of hunger, those who died at the hands of other men. Along with humankind's progress in production came the exploitation of some men by others, the enslaving of some men by others, the strongest against the weakest.

That's how history began before writing even existed, when human beings, in relatively more numerous communities, entered into different relations after roaming the jungles in small family groups or in small clans, until this world of today developed.

Other men, a few centuries ago, wanting to get to India by the shortest route and, presuming that the Earth was round, set sail and were lucky not to arrive in China because, if they had, history would have been different. Our hemisphere, according to what geology tells us, was at one time joined to Africa. Apparently, it was a single landmass which, due to a series of natural and physical phenomena, began to split long before there were human beings around. It was not known that there was a continent here.

Then the conquistadors, with 12 horses, disembarked and sowed panic with their superior technology. The harquebus — which was a kind of nuclear weapon at that time because it made a lot of noise — the gunpowder, the crossbows and, fundamentally, the horses were enough for them to take possession of that land in the name of a king. Who gave the king those lands? Why did they arrive putting up a flag in the name of a king who was thousands of miles away, who never even set foot there? I don't remember any king from among them all, over centuries, having ever visited our hemisphere.

But the soldiers arrived with their superior weapons in countries that were very backward technically — not culturally, because there were already cultures that were older than those in Europe. Works of art, architecture… Mexico City, for example, was bigger than any city in Europe, but it was conquered with those weapons and horses.

I've often smiled when thinking about what would have happened if Christopher Columbus hadn't made a mistake and had landed in China instead, which, at that time, according to Marco Polo, had cavalries of hundreds of thousands of soldiers. The 12 Spanish horses would have disappeared in a matter of seconds. But they found there what they called Indians. That's why there are two kinds of Indian — the Indians from India and the Indians that they baptized Indians in the hemisphere that was later called America. Many millions of people lived there, but 70 million died during the conquest and colonization.

Humans discovered that the Earth was round; that it was a round planet, that ships didn't fall into the abyss. Those who fell into the abyss were those who were living there peacefully in that territory when they discovered the Europeans. In other words, with the discovery that we inhabited a round planet, so began one of the cruelest and most unjust historical stages in the history of humanity. If slavery had already disappeared in the Middle Ages, with the discovery [of the Americas], slavery arose anew, around 500 years ago.

That history has a lot to do with us and it has a lot to do with all of you. Since then, scientific knowledge has advanced greatly: mechanics, physics, the exact sciences. Humankind has made extraordinary technological discoveries. We have constructed telescopes that discovered planets and even explored them from a distance. We discovered millions and millions of millions of stars. We discovered the universe and many more things.

Humankind has even launched vehicles into space, to the moon. They didn't conquer it because, on the moon, there was no oxygen or people. Otherwise, they would have taken possession of the moon in the name of the king of Washington. And perhaps the illustrious visitor who preceded me some time ago [U.S. President Bill Clinton], instead of traveling to South Africa, would have traveled to the moon. Humankind explored the planets and discovered that they had no inhabitants. We got to Mars. It was always said that there was intelligent life on Mars. They haven't found it — just rocks and an absence of the essential elements for life.

Other planets have been explored. There are some — I think it's Venus, the one that they called the Goddess of Love — where you would imagine exists a sweet paradise. What they found is that there is a heavy atmosphere with a heat of 400 degrees, which is not really a temperature at which you could make love.

What we know today, which is what's important, is that we have one single, inhabitable planet in our solar system — this one, where there is still an atmosphere, a little oxygen, a little fresh water from time to time, a bit of nature — which has survived the destruction provoked by societies that call themselves civilized.

Yes, maybe there were inhabitants on Mars. Perhaps there was intelligent life there. Maybe they managed to develop a civilization and destroyed that planet, just like some are going to destroy this planet. If we don't stop the destroyers of nature they could end up effectively making this an uninhabitable planet. That's not a fantasy. That's shown by science. It's shown by mathematics, everything.

So, this relatively long tour of the universe brings me to the idea that human beings — you and us, all of us — have to save two things: We have to save the natural environment in which we live and we have to save the human species to which we belong.

I understand that those who have to live in great poverty and who have the problem every day of looking for a job and earning a living don't have the time or even the possibility to meditate very much on these problems of the environment because they are immediately threatened by disease, poverty and hunger.

What a world this is where we need to persuade those who go hungry that to save humankind the natural environment must be saved! So that humankind can live in a world where there is neither injustice nor poverty, where there is no hunger and where children like these don't need to die for dignity, freedom and justice!

Yes, we have to win justice, full justice, full freedom for humankind. But we have to win a world without enemies, a world without some people trampling others underfoot, a world that doesn't have a few people owning everything while the vast majority has absolutely nothing.

We know today that there's one inhabitable planet and that on our planet we are six billion inhabitants. Six billion! And before that boy over there is 17 years younger than the age that I might be and approximately 30 years younger than [Walter] Sisulu's age — some 50 years from now — the Earth will have 10 billion inhabitants. And we'll have to ensure that they can live with dignity and justice, with freedom and bread, with freedom and clothes, with shoes and a roof over their heads, with freedom and schools, with freedom and hospitals, with freedom and medical care, with freedom and recreation, with freedom and culture.

If I'm talking to you about this, it's because I think that the heroic men and women of this famous and legendary township that we're visiting today didn't die just for the well-being of Soweto. They died for the well-being, dignity and freedom of all people in South Africa. They died for the independence, freedom and well-being of all the peoples of Africa, and they died for the dignity, freedom, equality and well-being of all the men and women in the world. That is how I see them and that is why I say that their monument should be as high as the highest mountain. But tall monuments aren't just made of stone. They are made of ideas and they are made of justice.

Many like them have died elsewhere and, one day, they will have that monument of justice, that monument of fraternity, that monument of peace for which we struggle for all the human beings of the Earth.

That's what I see here in Soweto because, for a minute, I think that you, rightly proud of the heroism and courage of this township's children, do not yet realize the full grandeur and the full worth of their sacrifice. I fear that you might not understand the full magnitude of the historic role of Soweto and those children and young people who died on June 16, 1976, whose pictures we have just seen in that humble museum that you have created, so that those who come here can relive, if just for a second, that June 16 — not when Soweto rose up but when the freedom of the oppressed, the dignity of the oppressed rose up.

It happened in Soweto that dignity revolted against all the injustices here and in the rest of the world. Twenty-two years later, nobody forgets them. Rather, everybody remembers them and loves them even more. And this is how, throughout the years, the world will remember that there was a Soweto and there were young people who sacrificed for the dignity of all humankind.

It could be rightly said that this was the birthplace of the liberation of South Africa. But one day, it will be considered the birthplace of dignity for all Africa. And it's not a question of Africa not having struggled. It's not that Africa doesn't have thousands and tens of thousands of heroic deeds, but this remained the most painful place in a system of slavery and injustice that has lasted thousands of years but which, especially in Africa, Latin America and the Third World, lasted hundreds of years.

Apartheid didn't begin in 1948. Apartheid began 500 years ago, when the inhabitants of these lands, like America or a large part of Asia, were conquered and colonized. It began when Africa was conquered and colonized centuries ago. It can never be forgotten that millions and millions of Africans were snatched from their villages and their homes in this continent. There are said to have been 12 million, not counting those who died of disease on the crossing or drowned in those seas. Twelve million Africans were put in chains and sold at auction for a few miserable pesetas to work as slaves for a period that extended for centuries. So, in America, it wasn't just the extermination and enslaving of their natives. They also took over there as slaves many Africans who are now part of our blood, our identity and our peoples.

That's why no one should be surprised by the fact that one day sons and daughters of a people like Cuba, in a beautiful gesture of solidarity, traveled to cooperate and to fight in this continent that contributed so much to our struggles — because the first to rise up against the colonial system in America, long before the British settlers in North America, were the African slaves in the 16th century. Later, in the middle of the 18th century, when there were already millions in Jamaica, Barbados and other countries, they revolted against the colonial system and were savagely repressed. Some were free. They escaped to the mountains and lived in freedom for a long time, because they couldn't accept slavery. None of them accepted it, but not all of them could escape the shackles and the persecution of the dogs hunting them like wild animals in the jungle.

The children and descendants of Africa went through all that suffering for centuries. They rebelled there. Like here, there were many Sowetos in that hemisphere and they sowed the seed and showed the way to our peoples' freedom, the way toward our countries' independence, that even now, unfortunately, has not been fully achieved because of our extremely powerful neighbor who likes to dictate orders, impose conditions and exploit those peoples.

Yesterday in the parliament, I expressed our feelings of solidarity with Africa, the effort that our little country, our little blockaded country was willing to make in order to fulfill a duty to Africa and consistent with our ideas, consistent with our duties, consistent with our consciences.

A lot of people now come to South Africa and to Africa. Don't think that they come because they're interested in Africa's poverty. Don't think that they come because they're interested in the starving people in Africa, the sick people who don't have medicine or the children who don't have schools. We know very well, and you do too, that they come because they're interested in Africa's gold, Africa's diamonds, Africa's nickel, Africa's aluminum, Africa's platinum, Africa's uranium, Africa's manganese, Africa's iron, Africa's chromium, Africa's timber, until not a single tree is left and the continent is a vast desert; and because they're interested in the cheap labor force Africa can provide.

They say that they bring capital, but what is capital? In the past, gold was capital. If you had a green note that said "$10", you could go to the U.S. Treasury and be handed so many grams of gold because, for each bank note, there was a gold reserve. Now, they don't bring gold. No, no. They bring bank notes and take away the gold. Now, they bring bits of paper, a fiction, a lie, a sham.

I'm not going to try to give an economics lesson here. No, I know a few things about economics and, above all, the way our peoples are exploited and cheated. I would just like to say that those who now have hegemony in the world are buying the world's riches with bits of paper. But those are *their* bits of paper that, thanks to the riches accumulated through the plundering of our peoples and the development achieved at the cost of our underdevelopment, constitute a typical mechanism of those economies, an instrument of domination. With them, they take possession of the world's riches. Yes. And what do they pay with? Often with trinkets. Often with things that we could produce here in Africa, with our cotton... Why do we have to buy a suit in New York if all those produced over there are made with raw materials from our countries? All those fine polyester fabrics are made with the oil that comes out of Africa, that comes out of Latin America, that comes out of Asia.

The energy that they consume comes from our raw materials, but the vast majority of Third World countries don't have electricity in many places or telephones or household electrical appliances. All that is produced with our raw materials, extracted from our mines, on the basis of very low wages, in order to export goods to us that they produce with very sophisticated machinery, where, often, by pressing a button, out comes a series of plastic shoes or artificial leather, objects, parts, automobiles, planes. And the finger pressing the button belongs to a guy who went to elementary school and studied high school, who went to college, although you don't need so much knowledge to press a button. Engineers too — those who press buttons are now sometimes engineers! And they also press buttons to launch rockets in whatever direction, with whatever excuse, and they press buttons to start their space voyages.

I wonder: Don't we have any intelligence? Wasn't that boy who died there intelligent? Didn't he have fingers? Didn't he have arms? Didn't he have a heart? Who has to prove that some are more intelligent than others? Before a culture existed in, for example, the United States, the Mayans in Central America already had a developed culture and understood astronomy.

Thousands of years ago, long before they had a civilization in the Middle East and in Mesopotamia, even before Greece and Rome, they already knew how to construct big buildings. They already had a form of writing. They already had libraries. They already had a civilization. And in Egypt, for example, they were already building pyramids, which have existed for thousands of years; to build a pyramid, you need intelligence, you need to know a lot about geometry, architecture and mathematics. That knowledge existed when, in Europe, there was nothing but savage tribes, who came in waves from Central Asia. They weren't more civilized than us, and they didn't know more than us.

Everybody has heard about the Seven Wonders of the World. All those seven wonders existed 2,000 years — maybe I'm wrong, maybe 2,500 years or 3,000 years — before Paris and New York existed.

Who says that civilization and intelligence are the heritage of one group of human beings? I say this in all sincerity. I'm not going to say that one race of humans is more intelligent than another. But I can tell those with racist views who looked at the peoples of Asia and Africa and the Indians of Latin America as inferior people that — due to our close relations with those peoples over many years of this century — we are witnesses to the intelligence, the extraordinary ability and talent of the African peoples, the peoples of Latin America and Asia.

What's more, not just talent but ideas, heroism, such as spending 27 or 30 years in a jail, like Sisulu, and decades in a solitary cell three by two meters, where there wasn't a bathroom or a bed, just the naked floor, abuses, humiliation, isolation from the family, things as terrible as those that Mandela was telling me yesterday — how he never saw one of his daughters after she was 18 months' old until she was already a woman; in that solitary cell, he wasn't even allowed the solace of a daughter. I wonder, why such cruelty?

So, when I had the honor and the privilege of knowing men like these, who never renounced their ideas, I wonder how many heroes have Europe or the United States had? How many among those who despise us could have spent 27 or 30 years in such terrible and painful conditions without renouncing their ideas?

What a monument to the dignity of humankind! What monument to the honor of Africa and to the honor of all the peoples of the Third World! What a monument to the human conscience!

Is it perhaps the case that men who are capable of this would not be capable of creating a better world, a truly human world, a world that is truly capable of equality, a world that is truly worthy of humankind?

I don't want to say anything that might seem to be simple flattery, although I know that you would never see it like that. But out of respect for that shyness any person feels, I'll refrain from saying anything that might sound like simple praise or flattery. I might offend you if I did, and I hold you in too much esteem to use demagogy or falsehood. I just want to express, with all the modesty in the world, my view that our peoples have the capacity to build civilizations as great as those or even greater civilizations at the service of humankind and a thousand times more humane. We can't simply accept some people's right to have everything while others have nothing.

And I ask myself a question, remembering, for example, an outstanding man like Einstein, the famous physicist who created the theory of relativity. It then occurs to me that if Einstein, instead of having been born into an already cultured and supposedly civilized Europe — only a few years before the concentration camps and the Holocaust of millions and millions of human beings, showing how questionable that technological civilization is that lacks a human heart — had been born in Soweto, like Hector Peterson, would Einstein have been Einstein? Perhaps they would have called him Hector. But would he have been able to discover the theory of relativity? Would he have been able to reach sixth grade or junior high school? Would he have managed to graduate from senior high school?

So, how can all that potential talent be developed if in Africa, for example, more than half the population cannot read or write, do not have schools, do not have universities, do not have research centers, do not have the equipment?

How can the population have the equipment? How can they train the doctors and engineers Africa needs? That's how they continue to nurture the hope that they're going to have billions of human beings at their disposal solely as a cheap labor force, but living in poverty, humiliation and neglect. That's what they dream of, I tell you.

I've already told you what they look for when they travel. Right now, there are conflicts in the [Democratic] Republic of the Congo. Why? And why did Lumumba die there? Why was he murdered? Because he wanted to defend the rights of the Congo and because the Congo had a lot of gold, too, and a lot of diamonds, and a lot of platinum and a lot of uranium. It's perhaps one of the regions of the world with the most natural resources. That has been the source of the conflict. And what has the West taken to the Congo over 40 years? More poverty, more backwardness than when Lumumba was alive. Billions and billions of dollars were stolen from there. And where did it end up? In the Western banks. And who stole it? Those who served the interests of the West.

In those 40 years, which are almost the years of the Cuban revolution, our blockaded and poor country, which doesn't even have oil, has trained more than 70,000 medical doctors, out of which — because some of them retire, some of them die — the country now has 63,000. One doctor for every 174 people.

There are many Third World countries that have only one doctor for every 10,000. In Africa, for example, there are countries with one for every 15,000, one for every 20,000. Is that what Western civilization brought us? Is that what they have in store for the peoples of Africa?

Oh! In our country, there was also 30 percent illiteracy when the revolution triumphed, when we freed ourselves from the empire that was the master of all our riches. And we now have between 250,000 and 300,000 elementary and junior high school teachers, and the elementary school teachers are now university graduates. I'm not saying this to boast in any way at all. I'm saying it, simply, to show from experience how different it has been for those who were unable to free themselves from imperial and colonial domination. I've mentioned only two things.

Cuba, a Third World country, also has tens of thousands of scientists. That's why we know what our countries can do and that's why we've had the possibility of sending doctors and teachers to other countries. In a period of approximately 30 years, there have been in Africa more than 80,000 civilian collaborators and 381,000 soldiers and officers who fought alongside African soldiers and officers. The number is so high because, in a country like Angola, we were there for 15 years exercising Sisulu's patience, never to give up, retreat or renounce our duties of solidarity.

We've shared the trenches and we've worked in the hospitals and in the schools with our African brothers and sisters. Who can know their hearts and their talent better than their Cuban brothers? And who can speak more honestly, without a single word of demagogy, about the worthy peoples of Africa, what they can do and what can be done by other peoples with whom we've collaborated in these years?

In Africa alone, there have been over 26,000 Cuban medical doctors, nurses and other health workers. And, if Africa needs more doctors, we've got more doctors because they continue to graduate from our universities — good doctors, because they do not just work in the cities. They also work in the countryside and they go to the mountains. What's more, not just the countryside and mountains of Cuba but any countryside and any mountain anywhere in the world. That's political consciousness! That's internationalist consciousness!

That's how we've tried to educate our people, because you can't think of a better tomorrow, you can't think of a just world on this planet for all human beings, without a profound idea and a profound consciousness of solidarity, fraternity and internationalism. Let's educate humankind in that sentiment. The society that exploits us doesn't instill that sentiment but rather hatred, selfishness and ambition.

When they travel throughout the world, they travel accompanied by a large retinue. They bring their planes full of businessmen because their journeys are to look for business and natural resources, minerals and profits. Not a single businessman came with the Cuban delegation. And, when we've traveled to whatever country in Africa, not a single businessman has come with us. It's enough for us to be able always to feel that we are unselfish friends who do not go around looking for material resources.

We believe in that world we were speaking of and we believe that the people of that world must one day be the masters of the planet. We can't conceive of a world in which a handful of transnational corporations are the absolute masters of the world. That's why I talk about the problems of globalization.

Globalization is inevitable, but not the globalization that they want to impose on us, not that neoliberal globalization. Globalization is a product of science, technology and the development of the productive forces that should be at the service of humankind.

The idea that we defend, above all else, is the right of every human being to develop their talent and their intelligence, their qualities, their best qualities. This is the right of all human beings to freedom, justice, dignity, and respect — the right of all human beings to those things that are indispensable for life.

It's not as if every citizen should have a yacht or a plane. We're not talking about the consumption model of the developed capitalist societies that sow that poison among us every day through television, the radio, the cinema, destroying our cultures — "Drink Coca Cola." And I don't expect to get paid anything at all for the advertising! "Drink Pepsi-Cola," "Eat McDonald's." And you'll now find that even in China and India they drink Coca-Cola and Pepsi-Cola and eat McDonald's.

What we aspire to for humankind is that all are adequately nourished to develop and preserve their health; that all have the possibility of being educated; of acquiring culture; that each has a roof over their head, a secure job. Yes, a secure job. What do they blame for unemployment? The productivity of machinery. Very well, I accept that. I'm happy that machines produce a lot at the touch of a button. Right. But why press the button for 40 or 50 hours a week? Better to press it for 10 hours.

In short, intelligence and scientific and technological advances shouldn't be at the service of a tiny minority of transnational corporations. They should be at the service of humankind. And the machines with computers and automation should not take a human being's place. What we aspire to is that there is work for all people, men and women, in many different kinds of jobs.

Today, there are all those resources for saving nature, for nourishing, educating and providing for the well-being of all people, for getting them to organize rationally, for applying family planning, too. But we need to become aware of that.

What is actually happening? The rich don't multiply. They have one child, two children at most, or none. They keep the population balanced. The poor haven't been able to go to school. They are not aware of these problems. In many Third World countries, they want to have more children as a guarantee for old age. This would not be necessary if culture and well-being were universal. We could all have electricity without polluting the atmosphere, and we could have means of communication. We could even have household electrical appliances, and we could have a roof over our heads. And we could have medicines, medical care; we could all have health, for example, and a longer life. You see what I mean? That is within humankind's reach.

If the machines produce a lot, I repeat, then let human beings work less, let the old people live longer and do what they like, without the need to be pressing buttons. If a small number of us can produce a lot for a lot of people, let's all produce a lot for a lot of people with a minimum of physical effort, since even pressing a button for eight hours every day can be stressful. Let people have more time for sport, for walking, for leisure.

In short, I believe humankind can do it. I believe that world is possible. I believe that we can make it if we understand it, if we win the battle of ideas and of consciousness.

That, fundamentally, is how you won the really difficult battle against apartheid, and there's a lot of apartheid in the world. The symbol has disappeared but thousands of other forms of apartheid remain throughout the world, in different disguises. There's apartheid in a world of rich and poor. There's apartheid in a world where some countries have a [per capita] Gross Domestic Product of $30,000 per year while others don't even have $200 or $300, or maybe $400 or $500. And who are those with tens of thousands of dollars of [per capita] GDP? Those who conquered us when we were free, although we lacked some articles of the so-called civilization. Those who colonized us, exploited us and enslaved us — they are the ones who have the great riches. And who among us has the great poverty? Those who were conquered, colonized and enslaved.

Let's put our heroic will, our extraordinary intelligence to the test in order to win that battle. A battle that — I say again — can find a tremendous weapon in ideas. You can't imagine how much sympathy and support arose in the world when the news of the Soweto uprising against apartheid was known throughout the Earth. Solidarity with the people of South Africa was multiplied by 10, by 100, and it was a decisive factor in that battle, in that victory that, when all is said and done, you won.

That's what I wanted to talk to you about today — although I overextended — and tell you that, in my mind and in my heart, I will always carry the memory of this land, of this people and of those who sacrificed themselves for such a just cause, a humane cause for which it is our duty to fight and for which we will all fight.

7

The Permanent Hurricane of Underdevelopment

Congress of Committees for Defense of the Revolution, Havana

Within 50 years, humanity will be 10 billion people, although [the world] cannot cope with the six billion it has now. Of those six billion, five billion live in the poor, underdeveloped world and only around one billion live in developed countries. It does not mean that all those who live in the developed countries are receiving the benefits of development. No, there are great inequalities in wealth in those developed countries and millions, tens of millions of unemployed, too.

There are also rich people in the underdeveloped countries. They do not have any problems. There is a percentage who live as if they were in Europe. From that point down is where the tragedy begins. That is to say, the rich classes in the underdeveloped countries can have the average consumption level they have in Europe.

Among the underdeveloped nations, there are those with a higher level of development and others with a much lower level.

Hurricanes make for good drama, but there is a permanent hurricane over [Haiti] like the current one, or worse, which is killing every day almost as many people as those killed by the hurricane in a day.

I ask the international community: Do you want to help that country that not long ago experienced an invasion and military intervention? Do you want to save lives? Do you want to show a humanitarian spirit? Let's talk now about a humane spirit and about

---

Fidel Castro addressed the fifth national congress of the Committees to Defend the Revolution (CDR) in Havana, Cuba, September 28, 1998.

the rights of the human being.

We say that we know how 15,000 to 25,000 lives can be saved in Haiti every year. Each year 135 children under five years' old die for every 1,000 live births. Again: 135 children under five for every 1,000 live births!

We have talked with some political leaders who have visited our country about how a health program could save 15,000 of those children and, in a very conservative estimate, a further 10,000 children between five and 15; young people and adults can be saved without large expenses.

In the face of this bitter experience, of the damage that country has sustained — which should remind us of the prolonged tragedy of that people — why isn't help provided there?

Based on the premise that the government and people of Haiti would gladly accept significant and crucial assistance in that field, we propose that if a country like Canada, closely related to Haiti, or a country like France, historically and culturally related to Haiti, or the countries of the European Economic Community, which are moving toward integration, or Japan — if others contributed the medicines, we would contribute the doctors for that program, all the doctors that may be necessary, even if it means sending a complete graduation year or the equivalent.

This country, with over 60,000 medical doctors, can take pride in saying that it has the highest number of doctors per capita in the world. It also has trained doctors anticipating the needs of the Third World, where many of its health professionals have worked. This country has the doctors required by the proposed program.

We met the doctors working in South Africa where it has become evident that language is not a barrier. Our doctors who went to South Africa had to study English and pass a tough exam. There are around 400 there now. Several of them are also working as professors. We know how they are appreciated. Every village is asking for Cuban doctors. They went to villages where English was not spoken. In a really short time, our doctors adapted to that situation. They are learning the villagers' dialect and providing an excellent service. So with a little training in French or the patois spoken in Haiti, and some books as they go along, they can learn the terminology needed for them to communicate with patients. That is not a problem. English is more complicated.

Besides, there is a precedent. Tens and tens of thousands of Haitians, in the first decades of this century, came to Cuba to cut sugarcane and to work practically as slaves; language was not an obstacle for them to cut all the cane that was needed by the U.S.

companies and others who exploited Haitian labor.

It was not necessary to know the language, just as those English-speaking or Spanish-speaking countries did not need to know the language of the African villages to enslave millions and millions of those people and create massive fortunes for the slaveholders.

To heal the sick and to save lives, you do not need prior knowledge of the village language. History has shown this, as well as our recent experience.

The hardest thing to obtain for these programs is the human personnel and we have the human personnel. I am sure there will be enough of volunteers among our young doctors. I am absolutely certain. They are doctors who go to the mountains, who go to the countryside or wherever they are needed. They are in the villages of South Africa.

I am taking advantage of this occasion, when those people are still living the trauma of what has happened [in Haiti], to propose this program to be managed by a UN agency, the World Health Organization.

Haiti does not need troops. It does not need invasions with troops. To begin with, Haiti needs invasions of medical doctors. Haiti also needs an invasion of millions of dollars for its development. That is something we do not have, but the international institutions have plenty. The World Bank has plenty, other financial institutions have plenty and the West has plenty. They have the capacity to show some kindness. Haiti is among the poorest country in the world and certainly the poorest in Latin America. A small area, an eroded soil, deforested mountains, exhausted fishing zones. It has been a victim of military invasions condoned by the United Nations and carried out by U.S. airborne brigades.

That country does not need airborne brigades. It desperately needs medical brigades. We can supply the medical doctors. Let others send teachers and still others send the essential materials for schools, the infrastructure for hospitals and for that country's development. How much longer will it take?

They cannot say that we are going there to indoctrinate the Haitians, because our doctors have not indoctrinated anybody in the villages of South Africa or in the scores and scores of countries where they have worked, beginning with Algeria at a very early stage. The first doctors who set out from Cuba [after the revolution] went to Algeria, right after its independence, when we had no more than 3,000 doctors because the rest had gone to the United States. The revolution opened up the doors of the United States for them, because they wanted to leave our people without any doctors. If it had not been for the revolution, many of those doctors who had been jobless and without any opportunities would not have been given visas to the United States.

So the first internationalist mission of our medical doctors was in Algeria. Around 25,000 doctors and health workers have been in scores of countries throughout the world. And so we make our proposal and submit it for consideration by the countries or groups of countries I have mentioned, aside from our appeal to them to assist the Dominican Republic and the other islands.

The really critical, critical case is that of Haiti. It is a very clear case where, with a relatively modest health program, 15,000 children under five years' old might be saved, thus reducing infant mortality in that age group to 35 for 1,000 live births. We have 9.4, almost four times less. The reduction of that figure to less than 20 requires a more sophisticated medicine, but cutting down mortality to 35 or 30 is relatively easy.

How many mothers could be saved from death in childbirth? And how many people of whatever age who die of infectious diseases, typical of such poor countries as these, or who die of other perfectly preventable or curable diseases? I made a very conservative estimate and I am now offering to cooperate with the international community so that every year no fewer than 25,000 lives can be saved, the vast majority of them children. If that is not done in the world, what will its fate be?

We have the human personnel. It is not an economic cost, it is a human cost. We have the men and women capable of carrying out that program. If they are moved to consider this proposal they may contact us at any time, so that a study can be immediately undertaken into what needs to be done to save that country.

I hope they understand that we do not want any leading role, since this would all be subordinated to the WHO, and that we are not going to indoctrinate anyone at all. It is difficult to indoctrinate a six months' old baby or a one, two, three, four, five, six and seven-year-old in matters related to Marxism-Leninism or theories about communism or political subversion. Our doctors have never done that in the dozens of Third World countries where they have worked and saved countless lives.

WELL, IF YOU WILL GIVE me a little more time, I would like to explain that there is a serious, grave international economic situation. It is there for all to see and they will not be able to blame communism or socialism for that. They will have to blame, from beginning to end, capitalism and its famous market economies as well as the world order that they have imposed.

That is why I have brought some materials, from which I would like to quote a few paragraphs on the economic situation. First, I am going to read two paragraphs to remind you of our speech at the WTO in Geneva:

> The United States also has the peculiar privilege of issuing the currency in which the central bank and the commercial bank deposits worldwide keep most of their hard currency reserves. The transnational companies of the nation whose citizens have the lowest saving rates are purchasing the world's riches with the money saved by people in other countries and the money printed without the gold backing agreed upon in Bretton Woods, and unilaterally ended in 1971.

And I concluded that statement saying:

> Despite so much euphoria no one can be sure of how long the U.S. economic system, ruled by blind laws of the market economy, will be able to prevent a financial meltdown. There are no economic miracles. That is clear now. The absurdly inflated stock values in the stock markets of that economy — unquestionably the strongest in the world — cannot be sustained. In similar situations history is not known to have made exceptions. The problem is that now a big crisis would become global and have unpredictable consequences. Not even the adversaries of the prevailing system could wish that to happen.

I then added: "It would be worthwhile for the WTO to assess these risks and include among the so-called 'new issues' another one: 'Global Economic Crisis: What can be done?'"

This was on May 19. Events have been developing at an increasingly faster pace. Three months and 10 days later, on August 29, 1998, a prestigious English magazine, *The Economist*, a conservative and traditional advocate of the system and of all those theories that are very much in vogue, printed an article entitled "As bad as it gets?" After affirming that, "depending on your definition, a global recession may already have started," it continued:

> The world economy resembles a plane that has lost two of its four engines, with a third now starting to splutter... The Russian ruble is plunging headlong. Latin America may be the next region to hit trouble. Last but not least, Wall Street continues to wobble...
>
> If Wall Street does crash — taking the world economy with it — the blame will doubtless be laid on reckless investment in Asia. But the present fragility of America's stock market also has much to do with

recklessness at home. Despite its recent falls, Wall Street remains expensive by historical standards — as though investors believed that equities were safer now than they have been for years, which they patently are not.

The problem is that those stock markets have exponentially multiplied their value into fabulous sums, exactly the same as what happened in the months before the 1929 crisis. We asked the comrades at the [Cuban] Institute on World Economics to collect all the information and elaborate an analysis. Nothing bears more resemblance to the months prior to the famous 1929 crash, which led to a recession that lasted over 10 years, as what is now happening in the U.S. stock markets. It seems like a carbon copy. The only thing is that then a crisis had very serious repercussions, but this one, in a global world, would be much more serious.

Then come other articles, this one also from the same conservative magazine. This article from September 5 is called: "Heading for meltdown?"

The global economic crisis continues to deepen. The latest horror, Russia's collapse, may be insignificant judged by that economy's puny weight in the world, but it was nonetheless a turning point: the sickness that started in Asia is spreading still, claiming victims far beyond its source.

And then, under the subheading "Luck and judgment":

For the first time since the early 1980s, global slump is a thinkable, even plausible, outcome... Indeed, in some ways, the danger now is greater than it was then.

It is not talking yet about the 1929 crisis. It is talking about another previous crisis that was quite serious but which did not have the same calamitous consequences of the one in 1929.

Much of the world is already deep in recession... the chances are that the worst is not yet over for many big emerging-market economies... not to mention for a handful of rich-country commodity producers, whose export revenues have crashed.

The collapse of basic commodity prices is a phenomenon present today that also preceded other crises such as that in 1929. This means, among many other commodities, coffee, cacao, minerals, aluminum, copper, zinc, and nickel. The last affects us: nickel is at half the price it was a few years ago, barely recouping costs at the plant. Of course, the price of oil, another basic commodity in many countries, has also dropped quite a bit. Oil producers are making desperate maneuvers to try to raise prices.

The article continues: "Mid-week, Wall Street stood some 15 percent lower than at its peak in July. Yet at these prices U.S. equities are still dear." That is the problem, extremely high. "If the market were to fall another 20 percent, say, the shock to U.S. consumers might be enough to bring the country's long expansion to an end. With it would go any hope that the United States could pull the world out of its troubles."

Another article appeared on the same day in the same magazine — "On the edge," it is headed:

The risks of a deep global recession are increasing... The world economy has become far more dangerously poised even during the past month, let alone over the past year. At the annual meeting of the Federal Reserve Bank of Kansas City in Jackson Hole, Wyoming, over the weekend, some central bankers were privately admitting that these are the worst global economic conditions they have seen in their lifetime...

Japan and most of the rest of East Asia is in deep recession. GDP is expected to fall by as much as 15 percent in Indonesia this year, and by six to seven percent in South Korea and Thailand. Russia's government has, in effect, defaulted on its debt; its economic predicament worsens by the day. China may yet respond to the sharp slowdown in its economy by devaluing its exchange rate, and the Hong Kong dollar is under severe pressure. Latin America still teeters on the brink.

Even some developed economies, such as Britain and Canada's, are slowing. And Wall Street has fallen sharply from its peak. Indeed, tumbling share prices have wiped almost $4 trillion off the world's financial wealth over the past two months — the equivalent of Japan's GDP.

That is, in only two months, the world's financial wealth has dropped by almost $4 trillion as a result of a fall in stock values. Such wealth, measured in terms of stock values, has its ups and downs. But that is the trend that has become very much apparent: it has already lost $4 trillion, what we would call in Spanish *billones*, but in English, $4 trillion. In how long? Two months.

When did we raise this prospect? On May 19 [1998]. We had already begun raising it before, but not in an international organization where there were ministers of economy or trade from every member of the WTO. Of course, euphoria reigned at that time. Now, it is not simply what I argued. The most prestigious advocate of the system is saying it.

The Economist continues:

World output grew at an average of four percent in 1996 and 1997, but J.P. Morgan, a U.S. bank, now forecasts growth of a mere 1.5 percent this year and 1.7 percent next... But if the [predictions] turn out correct, this would be the same growth over the two years as in 1981-82, the world economy's worst 'recession' since the 1930s.

Further on, it reads:

Russia's implosion has triggered a new phase in the emerging-market crisis. Its economy accounts for a mere two percent of world output, so its direct impact on world trade and output is tiny. But the indirect effects — through commodity markets, investors' confidence, the cost of capital — are proving far bigger. Coming on top of other financial troubles, Russia's plight could be the straw that breaks the camel's back.

The sickness has spread far and wide: to Eastern Europe, South Africa and Latin America. Venezuela may soon be forced to devalue its currency. Brazil's economy is not in such a bad shape as Russia's, but there are some nasty similarities, not least a big budget deficit (seven percent of GDP). Brazil has suffered a heavy capital outflow in recent weeks...

The prices of industrial commodities are now at their lowest in real terms since the 1930s.

These commodities that are mentioned more than once are the main exports of the Third World countries, although some of them, like certain minerals, are also exported by some developed countries. "This has severely hurt commodity producers, not just in Latin America and Africa, but also in Australia and Canada," the article says. In other words, the conditions are ripe. It continues:

The bubble bursts.

Perhaps the scariest fallout from the latest turmoil in Russia has been the fall in Wall Street and other developed markets. Despite a midweek rally, the Dow Jones Industrial Average [the index that they have for measuring how the New York Stock Exchange is performing] is still down by 17 percent from its peak, wiping out all this year's gains...

But the biggest risk to the U.S. economy is not a slowdown in exports, but a further big fall in its stock market...

It is unlikely to turn into anything like a 1930s-style depression, when America's GDP fell by 30 percent over three years. There are many similarities between now and the late 1920s, such as falling commodity prices and an overvalued stock market.

They then give some arguments, some differences between both periods. It says, for example, in the first place, countries used the gold standard when it was consequently more difficult to ease monetary policy. They invoke a well-known economist:

This restricted their ability to ease monetary policy as economies went into recession after the Wall Street crash of 1929.

Second, governments compounded their tight-money mistake with tight fiscal policies, even in the depth of the depression...

Rather than allowing taxes to fall automatically as income declined, the Americans raised taxes...

Not only do governments have a better understanding of macroeconomics today, but now that public spending takes a much bigger share of GDP, their ability to stabilize demand is greater.

The third difference between today and the 1930s is that there were no global organizations such as the G-7 or the IMF to oversee the world economy. The IMF was set up in 1944 at the instigation of the Americans to head off any future global economic collapse... [and] to provide temporary financial assistance to countries with balance-of-payments problems.

The fact of the matter is that today the whole world has practically rebelled against the International Monetary Fund. They are starting to blame it for all the disasters that are taking place. You can see the number of articles published by the analysts in these specialized magazines, which are practically the last word on matters relating to economics. Other magazines with a different editorial line are even more critical.

I have been reading paragraphs from a magazine that would be the last to say anything against capitalism. It lists some supposed advantages nowadays as compared to 1929. We see defenders of the system coming up with different things in order to avoid the worst. They are terrified that the crisis might spread from Russia to Brazil and from Brazil to the rest of Latin America.

They analyze the conditions in Brazil, with a high budget deficit, a high current account deficit and an overvalued currency, as they put it. We had the opportunity to visit Brazil and talk for many hours with the president of that enormous country about all these issues. It was a very interesting exchange. I will not be committing any indiscretion if I tell you that we have seen Brazil making great efforts to stop the crisis, adopting drastic measures in order to try to prevent an unfavorable economic outcome.

What have they done to avoid a sudden capital outflow, to avoid devaluation of their currency and to keep their reserves? They have considerably increased interest rates. At the moment, it is around 50 percent. So anybody who has money deposited there will reason: "Well, that is better, with interest at 50 percent, instead of taking my money out, I will keep it in the country, making high profits." An interest of 50 percent a year represents a considerable benefit for investors but, at the same time, a high cost for the economy, for operating capital and for national investment.

The president explained to me how, even in agriculture, the interest rate is different: around eight percent or nine percent. They were keeping it lower by protecting it in some way. They were likewise protecting, as far as possible, the export industries because, with such a high interest rate, the aim of which is to protect the country from the actions by speculators, no industry in the world can be competitive.

He explained how, on the other hand, they were maintaining high interest rates for nonessential or, rather, luxury production. They have made additional efforts recently with tough measures to reduce the budget deficit on the eve of elections that will be held in a few days.

Of course, the United States is very worried that the crisis might spread to Brazil. This is an advantage for the Brazilians and the South Americans in general, because the United States considers them to be almost the last defense. All the other defenses have started collapsing and a crisis in Brazil would have grave consequences for all of Latin America.

What happens then in the New York Stock Exchange? Its turn will come. It is to be expected that, strategically, they would try to defend themselves in South America and find some money to support their finances. Of course, the IMF does not have funds.

There remain the problems in Southeast Asia. And nobody knows at this point how the problem of Russia will be solved. Well, I believe that Russia would need $100 billion and the U.S. Congress has opposed this. It is putting up resistance to the handover of some $22 billion. Look, $22 billion in Russia is a drop of water in the ocean!

In all probability, the Americans will take refuge in South America, for their own interests, not for South America. Otherwise, the relapse of the crisis would reach as far as Mexico again and all the Latin American stock markets are already at 50 percent of the values that they had reached before. I do not think that it would have such a catastrophic effect on the region, because they are smaller stock markets, they do not have the tremendous weight of the stock markets in the United States.

The stock values in the United States are enormous. However, their present or, rather, their former value has already dropped by 17 percent of the maximum value. Of course, they say that an additional drop of 15 percent or 20 percent would have dreadful consequences.

Observe that in the U.S. stock markets, stockholders have won $9 trillion in four years. Can you even imagine such a figure? The wealth of the stockholders has grown by that amount! However in 1929, only five percent of the U.S. citizens owned stocks — perhaps less — but never more than five percent. Today, all of the insurance banks and all of the social security funds, all the savings of the middle class and even many of the workers have deposited money in insurance banks, where they accrue enormous sums of money, which, to a great extent, have been invested in these stocks.

All this increases expenditure: the greater the available wealth, due to the rise of stock values, the more they spend. This is what they called a virtuous circle, which is beginning to transform into a vicious circle. And why virtuous? Because by artificially multiplying their wealth and expenses, buying more and more within and outside the United States, investing in everything and everywhere, they stepped up production and services and consequently lowered unemployment and increased the GDP. They have other mechanisms but I shall not go into details.

In substance, since they had more money, they began to spend like madmen. Everyone who owned a car would change it for a new one, and if it were worth $15,000 they would buy one for $20,000; they would also buy yachts, etc., spending money on everything under the sun. With a domestic market of 270 million people, the weight of 50 percent of the stockholders in the stock market has a stronger bearing on the demand for goods and services.

The problem with the balance of payments is not a problem for them — that is paid with treasury bonds. The United States is the only country in the world that can afford to have a $100 billion to $200 billion commercial deficit and yet buy all the raw material it wants. The only country in the world because, among other reasons, there is no longer a gold standard and the bank notes and bonds of that country have become everybody's reserve currency and securities.

When there was a gold standard, any person with dollars could get the gold that the bill was worth. However, during the Vietnam War, the United States lost two-thirds of the gold that it had accumulated after World War II. It was then that it suspended the gold standard, that is, the right of anyone with a dollar to demand the equivalent in gold. But the world moves on, and it had no other alternative but to use that paper as a universal instrument of exchange and reserve currency.

Furthermore, many people deposit their money in U.S. banks. The Japanese are the ones who have deposited the most or acquired treasury bonds, thus preserving a certain interest rate. When shareholders are frightened and panic breaks out, they sell their shares and stop buying gold. They also buy U.S. Treasury bonds that have traditionally maintained their reserve. They have managed to do it, based on the huge benefits derived from the two world wars. They became immensely rich. They only became involved at the end of both wars, did not suffer any material damage, accumulated great wealth and achieved considerable economic development.

At the end of World War II, the United States was the only country that had remained intact; Japan did not exist, the Soviet Union was destroyed; England, France and Germany were also destroyed and all the other countries were penniless. There was only one rich and industrialized country. They had hoarded practically all the gold in the world; the bills they printed circulated universally for their value in gold. They could print bills as long as they had gold. They unilaterally suspended the dollar's conversion into gold. It was a trap; the world had been robbed.

Then the value of gold increased tremendously, immediately. They artificially kept it at a low price. They would buy whenever the price of gold was about to fall. When it was about to go up, they sold gold from their enormous reserves and kept the price at approximately $35 an ounce. Then they suppressed the conversion and a boom in oil prices occurred.

The price of an ounce of gold reached more than $400. They still had approximately $10 billion in gold, and the price of that gold grew tremendously, at least 10 times. The gold standard ceased to exist and there were no more limits. They would print treasury bonds with a certain interest rate for a certain number of years. They preserved the tradition of those bonds that were the safest securities in the market. This is where investors who sell their stocks in times of uncertainty and panic seek refuge. They sell but they do not buy stocks elsewhere, only treasury bonds. Therefore, they have all the money they need to pay for any budget deficit or a deficit in the balance of payments.

Not now! Now, with the progress this has enabled them to make in the economy, they have more or less balanced the budget but not the balance of trade whose deficit grows. They must pay huge amounts of money for their imports, more than what they get for their exports. That is the mechanism.

This way, stockholders have earned $9 trillion and they have spent what they have earned, as they watch their stock values rise. If you have $100,000 and all of a sudden your stocks are worth $200,000, you say: "Oh! Why should I save? I will buy everything I want." So you end up buying a yacht or even a plane. All of this boosted, as I said, the growth of the economy; it boosted employment. Everything was great, an exclusive benefit, an exclusive privilege of theirs. That is why they have bought, well, almost the whole world!

That is why the Europeans want to integrate, in order to survive. They want to have a strong currency so that these tricks cannot be played on them, so that part of the reserve in central banks is made up of euros. It is good for the world that there should be another currency. I wish there were others, two, three more — strong ones — because today the whole world depends on the dollar. It is the main, almost single, reserve currency. They print paper, buy things, and an important part of that paper is put away by other countries in their reserves.

In other words, they have had a very privileged position. Stocks multiplied their value with all the support of an economy growing at a steady rate for a relative long period of time; the unemployment rate was dropping. Inflation, the other enemy they fear like hell, did not increase. On the contrary, the price of products from Japan, Malaysia, South Korea, Thailand and all those countries have dropped after their currencies were devalued. This contributed to keeping inflation down. But Aladdin's lamp begins to lose its magical power.

The great discussion about the U.S. Federal Reserve interest rates — I have already talked about what it meant for Brazil — reflects deep contradictions. If they raise the interest rates, they worsen the situation of all the weakened currencies and the economies of Southeast Asia, Japan, Russia and increase the risks for Brazil, South America and other countries.

What is everybody demanding now? "Hey, please lower the interest rates, lower them." But they are trying to carefully manage the situation, because if they lower the rates too much, everybody begins asking for loans to buy and loans to invest. This can bring about an excess of circulating cash that can immediately turn into inflation.

I told you what the Brazilians do with the interest rate to avoid the capital outflow and keep their reserves. But they cannot maintain a 50 percent rate for too long, despite the exceptions for agriculture and the exporting sectors, because all of the working capital of the other industries and services must pay a 50 percent annual interest rate, and what industry has high enough profits to pay a 50 percent interest rate? In other words, they could bring the economy to a standstill.

For a time, they can hold back the panic and the capital outflow, keep people from exchanging the national currency into dollars, because the exchange of currency there is free. They can exchange it and take it out of the country. But on the other hand, that mechanism is a double-edged sword: it halts the economy and creates an unsustainable situation. They cannot maintain it for long.

In August, Brazil lost billions; I do not remember if it lost $10 or $15 billion of its reserves, just in August and early September. They had been able to accumulate those reserves and they had managed to do so with great hardships and, partly, by privatizing enterprises. There was a telephone company that they privatized which gave them $18 billion. It was an important income, but it was lost in a few days defending the national currency from speculation. They have had to take new, strict measures. The Brazilians are struggling, they are defending their currency, but there is no doubt that they are going to need income from abroad. How much will it be? Well, no one knows exactly.

They offered Mexico — in this case being a close neighbor of the United States was an advantage — up to $50 billion. But when the crisis reached Southeast Asia and then Korea, their favorite international financial institutions had no funds left. So now they are terrified of that spreading fire. I think they will make an effort. It is clear that a good place to entrench themselves is Latin America, to keep the fire from reaching their own hearth.

Unlike the Latin American stock markets, those in the United States have a huge economic weight, because colossal funds are invested in them. I have already told you that in the last four years they had earned $9 trillion, although they must start deducting now.

I have already read the article that affirmed that putting all the stock markets together, the world had lost almost $4 trillion in only two months. That is, not only the United States, part of these losses is theirs, when the value of their stock market shares fell 17 percent from its highest point.

Forgive me for going into details this way, but I am trying to make you understand these mechanisms and how the collapse can take place.

So now they are putting out the fire. I think they have given up trying to put out the fire in Russia. This is very serious because of its implications, including political ones. I think they will try to entrench themselves in Brazil and in South America, trying to prevent a disaster like that in Southeast Asia. The fire will inevitably reach them, and it might happen like in 1982, or worse yet, like in 1929 — or even worse than in 1929 — despite their IMF, their World Bank and all the tricks they have been devising.

They have to analyze well what consequences it would have within the United States for the 50 percent of Americans who have their social security money and their savings in those stocks, if the stocks drop to one half or one third of their value.

That has never happened before. During the great crisis of 1929, the number of people who owned stocks was very small. Its effect, however, was disastrous. What would it be like now when half of that country plus those with the most resources have their wealth invested in the stock market? The fellow who lives under the bridge has no stocks in the stock market. The big transnationals, the big industrial tycoons, the middle class, many professionals, high-income workers, they are the ones who invest. Anyone who has some money, on seeing that values have been rising like foam — and that is where the danger lies — invests there, and encounters these problems which are typical of a capitalist society, typical of a market economy. No one can control that.

There are already a lot of people suggesting the advisability of having the state regulate this in some way, or regulate the operations, the capital that comes on a short-term basis and then leaves. That is against neoliberalism; against everything it has been doing and preaching. Yet, they are beginning to speak with growing energy against allowing the free flow of short-term capital and the absolute freedom that financial capital enjoys today.

The prime minister of Malaysia, who also visited us, has been concerned about this matter for a long time. He has just suppressed the free exchange of currencies and taken a series of measures to defend his country's economy, which has declined due to the devastating blow it received. He told me that the accumulated wealth of 40 years could be lost in two weeks.

All countries are exposed to this. Not a single one can escape. That is why Europe is uniting. No European country alone can escape that enormous power accumulated by the United States. The Europeans are seeking a market of hundreds of millions of people. The United States has a domestic market of no less than 270 million, a very big market. A small country can only have a market of 10 million, no matter how industrialized it may be. They are uniting in Europe, the 15 countries of the Union, amounting to some 300 to 400 million people. They aspire to incorporate more countries in the future to keep safe from the monster; but it could almost be said that the monster is fatally wounded. It is an unsustainable system that is nearing a crisis, as I have explained here.

Besides, they have been too divided in the United States itself. The administration has advisers and acts somewhat more skillfully defending the economic interests of the empire. But others are at war with [the government], with the support of the majority in the Senate and the House, and have not adopted the fast track for the agreements with which the administration wants to tie the Latin American and Caribbean countries to the empire's economic interests.

They are putting up a great resistance against the government's plans for a little increase in the funds of the IMF. But for the IMF $15 billion or $18 billion — I think they had already given $3 billion — is just a drop of water in the desert. It would be difficult to even suppose that they might try to save Russia, instead of entrenching themselves in the last stronghold they have left: South America. But it may so happen that even while they are entrenched, the problems continue to grow and to worsen, because what we are seeing here is a congenital disease of the system.

I HAVE NOT FINISHED, I still have a little more to say. If you are patient enough... Do you want to know how our friend Russia is faring? Are you interested? Very well, I am going to read some paragraphs of articles that have appeared in the capitalist press specialized in economic issues. In this case, they are from the same British magazine [*The Economist*] I already mentioned.

This one is entitled "Russia devalued." Remember that they are the same analysts who time and again applauded everything from perestroika to neoliberalism, privatizations and market economy as the great miracles to improve the [Russian] economy and the life in that country, where with one ruble you could have breakfast, lunch, dinner and you still had some money left — with a ruble!

Afterwards the rate was 6,000 rubles to a dollar. Now, in order to work better with the figures, they took away three zeros, and they established a new ruble equal to $6. Once again it had to be devalued and, instead of six, it is now quoted at approximately 18 per dollar. And this also changes every day. People there have lost their money twice.

When they had the first devaluation, everyone who had some money saved — mark my words — everyone who had money in the bank or anywhere else lost it!

Look how differently it was done in Cuba. When there was a change of currency at the beginning of the revolutionary process, the money in the banks was never touched, and recently, when we took measures to reduce the excess circulating cash, we did not touch the money in the banks either.

The money of all of those who trusted the banks and kept their money there — some who had a little bit, some who had a little more and some who had a whole lot; some, who had accounts in different banks, just in case, based on previous experiences — all the money was respected. Even those who accumulated quite a lot were able to keep their money. Of course, there are many decent, honest people among them. I know very hard-working, honest farmers who, without the agricultural market or anything like it, have accumulated 300,000, 400,000 or 500,000 pesos, because they had very high yields. Ten thousand quintals of potatoes brought 40,000 or 50,000 pesos per year, and they put that money in the bank. There are those who earned their money that way. Others, as you know, earned it either selling at very high prices or one way or another.

But what occurred in Cuba with so much cash circulating after the "special period" set in? We held discussions in the National Assembly, we held discussions everywhere, but we did not touch the money in the banks; there was no change of currency. Those who had that money could use it to buy things from the quota assigned to them, although, right now, unfortunately, in reduced quantities at the historically subsidized prices.

Cuban money can be used to go to a movie and to many recreational activities. Medicines, building materials, electricity, telephone services, rent, sporting events and whatever else the population is entitled to in goods and services are all paid in Cuban pesos. There are important, vital services that do not even need pesos, which are absolutely free. The measures were taken for the people and, naturally, its national currency continued to have the same value in relation to all these things.

At one point in time, those who engaged in exchanging currency were able to get 150 pesos for a dollar. Thanks to the measures taken by the revolution — some of which have brought us the problems we have analyzed — and with a certain recovery of our economy — we still have not climbed back to 1989 level, and some time will pass before we do — the fact is that without all of those resources that Russia has in such abundance, we did not touch the peso and everyone's trust in the banks was preserved. But what is more incredible: the peso was revalued in relation to the dollar, from 150 to 19, 20, 21, 22 or 23, in the exchange bureaus.

So our peso, and all the pesos of those who had money in the bank or elsewhere, was simply revalued. The exchange bureaus bring in a little money, they control, they regulate. If the demand for dollars increases, they raise the price of the dollar. They always guarantee some income, but that was what the speculators who engaged in those dealings, exchanging dollars and pesos, used to earn. And there is a certain amount of income, not much, but it solves some problems and some needs. Do you know what the profits obtained in the exchange bureaus are used for? They are totally handed over to the ministry of domestic trade, for some products or others, or the raw materials to manufacture them, even some goods that are sold in the parallel markets. Well, yes, they are expensive, we know that. This is to meet certain needs and, at the same time, to collect circulating cash in order to maintain the best possible balance between wages and prices, between pesos and dollars. So those exchange bureaus give the country an additional benefit. In this case, the old saying that the bank never loses is confirmed.

But if we let money go into circulation again then we will be back in the same hapless situation. When the peso is devalued so are salaries. If someone earns, let's say, 200 pesos, if they want to buy a dollar some day to spend it in one of those shops, they have the possibility to get that dollar, it costs them 20 pesos. If the exchange rate climbs to 50 or 100 per dollar, they do not have that possibility.

Notice that this country has revalued the peso, the national currency. This has not happened anywhere else, only through the measures implemented and thanks to our socialist system, despite being under a severe blockade and under the conditions of the "special period."

But over there, in Russia, a person who had 6,000 rubles was left with only one dollar. Now, with the new ruble, a person who had 10,000 — there are some over there who make that much in half a minute — or, let us say, 6,000, would have the equivalent of $1,000; when the ruble is quoted at 12, he has the equivalent of $500; when it is quoted at 18, he has the equivalent of $300 and some odd dollars, and when it is quoted at 20 or even more, as it has been the case, what he has left is $300 or less. In a matter of days the worker loses what he has saved from his salary, that is, if they are paying his salary. The nouveaux riches, of course, do not suffer at all; they have their money safe abroad, converted into dollars and invested in large, luxurious mansions.

It is said that the turning point in the global crisis that is so seriously affecting the world economy begins with the recent Russian financial crisis. In Russia, the state was confiscated by all of those gentlemen who had the West's absolute trust, by those who applied all the recipes of the West, by those who privatized everything. And it was "Oh, happy West!"; "how marvelous!"; "that country is really going to develop!"; "what profitable investments we are going to make there!" And they gave them loans for tens of billions of dollars.

But the fall of production in Russia led them to dump into the market all the nickel they had accumulated. We know very well how much that cost us. The Rotterdam docks were full of nickel, and all the copper, all the minerals they could hold, and that has a lot to do with the so-called commodities. That is why the article said that Russia, being a great producer of nickel and of all sorts of raw materials, but unable to use those items in its production, which fell more than 50 percent in relation to what it produced in 1989 and 1990, dumped them all onto the world market.

They said that a bigger economic catastrophe would make them dump everything they have left into the commodities market, reducing these prices even further. This is one of the factors they consider would increase the danger of a big recession. They mentioned two factors in the article: the drop in commodity prices and the overvalued stocks in the U.S. stock markets. That is why they say that although Russia represents only two percent of the world economy, it has a lot of influence. This is without dwelling on other more worrying, serious dangers, just the economic. Well, that catastrophe has come about and now they have no money, the reserves are depleted because everybody rushed to exchange their rubles for dollars, and inevitably they had to suspend the exchange of rubles for dollars. That alone was a sacrilegious violation of all the IMF rules. They had already negotiated a loan of around $22 billion with this institution, but under very strict rules and conditions.

What is this about suspending the free exchange of currency? This is a sacrilege. They suspended their debt payments, another serious sacrilege. How can that be accepted by the IMF or the World Bank or the United States, who is the owner of all that? That business is managed by the United States. It owns 17 percent of shares in the IMF and has a similar participation in the World Bank. It has the power of veto: with 15 percent it can veto any agreement. The United States decides everything that the IMF and the World Bank approve. The Federal Reserve, the U.S. Treasury, the World Bank and the IMF meet to decide what they are going to do. Well, they were scared because of what was happening in Russia, to which they had offered $22 billion. The situation there was really bad; they even spoke about printing money to pay salaries.

The shops began to empty. Before that, everybody had made a run on the banks to change rubles for dollars. The reserve, which was not very high, $14 or $15 billion, was rapidly disappearing. They stopped, they suspended the free exchange. They also stopped the foreign debt payments. There was no hard currency for that, and they could not exhaust what little they had left. Everything that they have done goes against the rules and conditions set by those institutions, which then decided not to hand over the $22 billion.

Now, the gentlemen from the West are so stupid that they are liable not to give them that money. The consequences would be still worse, not only economic consequences but political and security consequences. It would seem as if they had given up on saving that country. You can imagine how worried they are, putting more and more pressure, saying that they will hand over the money only if all those methods are strictly applied.

Over there, more than half of the existing taxes are not collected, and the big enterprises of the multimillionaires that confiscated the state enterprises with the West's support do not pay taxes. They bought the major media, the main radio and television networks.

Just look at the freedom of the press [in Russia] that the West has obtained! The freedom it defends! The people lost the media, which are in the hands of the groups of multimillionaires who also became owners of the big oil and gas enterprises, of all export items. They took over the main industries. They bought the most powerful media. They are the ones in charge, and that is that. They publish what they want published and nothing else. They own the main sectors of industry; they own the media and also the banks.

Just look at how well the banking business was doing, that they established up to 4,000 banks. What did some of these banks do? Many Russians confidently went to deposit their money in those banks and many of those banks declared themselves bankrupt and stole the depositors' money, as simple and unpunished as that. They exchanged the [people's] money for dollars and took it away. In other words, many Russians have been swindled by many of those banks that are in the hands of the Mafia. This is the market economy in its purest form.

There is something called the Mafia, resulting from the reforms that the West so cherishes, defends and glorifies. Now nobody wants to invest because the Mafia has taken over everything. I hope that does not happen to you in the Committees for the Defense of the Revolution, that we do not make the big mistakes that facilitate such things. We are fighting against those who steal in houses or stores. Very well! Over there they robbed the wealth of the socialist state. They invented different mechanisms in order to do it. They even gave out some bonds, which were immediately devalued; then they bought the bonds and they took over the enterprises. It was all very democratic. They gave out some bonds to the workers, but soon those bonds were not worth a single penny. These guys came around, bought them, and that's that; they are the owners of big banks, big enterprises, all of that. They do not pay taxes.

What have they done with the money? The West does not speak of this. Oh, no! They hardly mention it. Every now and then, they feel ashamed and they talk about it in some small paragraph. But the fact is that, since they established that model, from $200 billion to $500 billion have fled Russia. This is something that must be known.

With the free exchange of currency, everyone who could exchange currency did so; feeling unsafe in such situation, they exchanged it, and sent their money to the Scandinavian countries, to Europe. In Spain alone, the wealthy Russians have 60,000 mansions, and they have others in southern France; no one knows how many they have in Austria, in all of Europe in the Scandinavian countries. In Cyprus, a small country, they have a lot of banks and other things. They are experts in confiscating the state's assets, experts in getting money out of the country.

Notice the figure [of Russia's debt]: a minimum of $200 billion and a maximum of $500 billion. Let's say it is $250 billion or $300 billion. Who can withstand that? How can they pay the teachers, the doctors, the scientists, the workers, the army, the missile operators, the pilots? Even those who are orbiting in outer space have been left without a budget, without a budget for the spaceship that has to go fetch them.

The strategic missile operators based in Krasnoyarsk had not been paid for five months. It was so serious that a general who had served in Afghanistan — whose mindset is still unknown, but who clearly wants to run for president after he won the elections in Krasnoyarsk supported by desperate people — negotiated peace in Chechnya. A few days after he took over as governor, he wrote a letter to the former prime minister, asking him to put under his jurisdiction the strategic missiles based in Krasnoyarsk, because he could at least give those people food and clothing.

What kind of order is this, what level of discipline is left, that the governor of Krasnoyarsk writes asking to put under his jurisdiction the strategic missiles of the region: a region turned into a big nuclear power. Meanwhile, the operators there are not paid. It is the last thing a government can do, leave the strategic missile operators unpaid — something terribly dangerous. But this gives you an idea of the situation there.

The army has also not been paid for months, only an elite division of the ministry of the interior, with very high salaries, that the government — in this case we have to say the presidency — has there as a reserve. The first thing done by the new prime minister, formerly the minister of foreign affairs, was to hold a meeting with all the military and order that the army be paid.

But where is the money for that? They said: "Let's print it." So the third big fight with all those international agencies broke out. Print? "No, that is utter madness, absurd, you cannot print, for such and such a reason."

Then they were demanding that they cut the budget. That budget cannot be cut any further. What is it they want, that the strategic missile operators are not paid for a year, that nobody gets paid for a year? How much longer? And the coal miners and the others, how much longer? If they are bringing to a halt the trains on the Siberian railroad, how?

The new government has a very hard task ahead, facing an almost impossible situation.

Some have spoken about rationing; some have spoken about renouncing all those funds, promises that will not solve anything. It has created a frightening situation; there is fear everywhere because no one knows what might happen in that country under such circumstances. But they cannot comply with the conditions demanded by the IMF in order to receive the $22 billion. They cannot, it is impossible.

Everybody who has a ruble left runs to the bank and exchanges it, and takes it away. But as I have told you, the West did not say anything and is not saying anything. You cannot see any of this in these articles, the hundreds of billions that fled that country thanks to those mechanisms that have destroyed the country. The Russian population has declined, the situation is catastrophic, not even money works anymore. There are whole towns living exclusively on bartering. Those who produce coal give others coal for the winter — winter is coming now — in exchange for agricultural produce. What is functioning in Russia today is the barter of goods rather than the use of money.

How can the new government, irrespective of its competence, its earnestness, find a way out of this situation? [The present prime minister] was minister of foreign affairs and once visited Cuba. He is a man whom everyone respects over there. But what is he to do now? Should he accept the IMF's conditions? Who are they going to collect taxes from, how are they going to pay, how are they going to cut the budgets when they are at their lowest level? How? How are they going to pay all those people? Well, should there be a rationing of goods? Of course, that would be the most fair and logical thing to do. That would make them stronger, of course. I am not recommending anything; we stay out of that. I am simply analyzing the situation.

Well, I have told you that the people ran to exchange their rubles for dollars. When the free exchange was stopped, they ran to the shops to buy, without limits, all the goods they could find there, while they lasted. The small shopkeepers must have made a lot of money, because they must have raised the prices. How do you cope with a situation like this? Can they avoid rationing even if they are given the money?

But if they are given the money, they cannot do any rationing or print any bills or any of those things, and they have to pay the debts and they have to cut the budget.

At a very difficult moment, the government has been placed in a very difficult position. That is the predicament right now in Russia and they are between the devil and the deep blue sea. Let us hope that the devil goes by without doing very much harm, but the truth is that they are in a very tight fix.

Did I make all this up? No, allow me, at least, to demonstrate that I did not make it up. The article I mentioned earlier states:

It has not been a good week for Russia. The bundle of measures thrown to the financial wolves on Monday amounts to the end, for the time being at least, of all prospects of further economic reform. [They are still talking about economic reforms, a larger dose of that poison as a remedy.] It may also mark the start of a political degeneration that sees the country slide towards nationalism, autocracy or something nastier. It consigns to the dust bin the last boast of the government's battered reformers, that their policies at least brought currency stability and steady prices...

They have been imposed, it should be remembered, only four weeks after the IMF and other foreign lenders agreed on $23 billion-worth of props for the Russian economy, and only three days after pledges from Mr. Yeltsin that there would be no devaluation and vows from his ministers that all debts would be honored. What went wrong?

The short answer is that much of the lending has gone not to guarantee the deposits of deserving savers, nor even to pay the pensions of impoverished old folks or the wages of unpaid miners.

The danger is that the loss of confidence will continue. If so, the ruble — supposedly freed to float, but in reality to sink — could merely gurgle on downward, the banks could be besieged by depositors large and small and, if no more credit from abroad is forthcoming, the government could be tempted to resort to the printing press to meet their demands. That is the road to hyperinflation, which Russians experienced as recently as 1992 (when, in December, year-on-year inflation reached 2,500 percent), by which time they had seen their savings vaporized. [They have lost their savings twice during this period.] ...

Russians had plenty to complain about: a government so incompetent at collecting taxes that it could provide few services; a payments system so constipated that soldiers, miners, teachers and a host of other workers went without wages; appalling living standards even for those in work; ill-equipped hospitals, overcrowded prisons...

They recommend:

If lending is now to resume, it must only be on the strictest of terms. That should mean explicit conditions about what the money is to be used for — for instance, to guarantee small deposits in commercial banks. It should also mean stern supervision of how it is spent, preferably by appointing foreigners to run the banks in question.

In other words, the intervention of the banks, so that they can be managed by foreigners. Look at this: "Similar control of the tax and customs service will have to be imposed if any support is to be given to the balance of payments." The method used by the United States in the Dominican Republic in the second decade of this century, but to collect taxes: the intervention of customs.

And if the Russians say no? Or, just as likely; say yes but mean no? Then the West should also say no. The West has an interest in promoting democracy and market economics in Russia, though it stands to lose much less than the Russians themselves if these concepts fail to take root. [It says that the Russians would stand to lose more.]

It also has an interest in seeing a country that remains infested with nuclear weapons peaceful and non-belligerent. But it would be wrong to assume that it is in the West's power to bring all this about, certainly not through economic assistance alone. The unfortunate truth is that Russia is condemned by its own history and its own people to a period of acute unhappiness. All happy families resemble one another, Tolstoy might have written, but the Russian family is unhappy in its own way. In the end it will be Russians, not foreigners, who bring its period of misery to a close.

Look at the Western treatment at this moment of super-crisis, they are about to do some crazy deed.

I do believe that the Russians can be saved, I do believe it, I am sure that they can be saved; but I am not saying a single word, nobody has asked for my opinion, neither do we want to assume any responsibility.

Other articles follow, but I will just mention brief phrases from an article in the same magazine: "Russia's nightmare": "Nothing about the measures taken this week to deal with Russia's financial mess gives confidence about the country's future."

Another article: "A detour or a derailment?" "A botched devaluation and a bond default are likely to leave the struggling Russian economy in even worse condition."

The other one is entitled: "Collapse in Russia." Here the things they say about the president of the country are somewhat insulting, and my intention is not to insult anybody, to offend anybody, but to inform and reflect upon these problems a little.

And another one, this time from the *New York Times*, is titled: "Moscow Dashes American Illusions." Subtitle: "Already the question is being asked, 'Who lost Russia?'"

If I could sing I would sing a parody of a song I heard some years ago, which began something like this: "How far behind those times now seem" and change it to "How far behind those dreams now seem." Yes, the dreams of those who had such illusions, of those who recommended these neoliberal recipes, of those who destroyed that state — whatever its limitations or errors might have been — a state that had to be corrected, upgraded, improved, but never destroyed.

Now the West has taken possession of everything, of the Caspian Sea oil; it has introduced itself into all the fragmented former Soviet republics, into Kazakhstan, into Uzbekistan, into Azerbaijan, into all those peripheral countries. It has left the Russian army practically unarmed. They have not been able to supply the armed forces with 20 state-of-the-art aircraft developed by Russian technicians, not even 20 aircraft!

Once Poland joined NATO, it was assumed that after the agreement to withdraw Soviet troops from Eastern Europe there would not be a NATO expansion. But right after that, NATO expanded into Poland, NATO expanded into the Czech Republic, NATO expanded into Hungary, and they are threatening to expand into Lithuania, Estonia and Latvia — even to Ukraine if they can. Although, I think that in these difficult times, since the situation of Ukraine worsens along with Russia's, there may be a better understanding between Ukraine and Russia. But at this rate NATO will soon reach the Kremlin walls.

A totally eastward expansionist policy inspired in bad faith has been applied. What need was there of this? Advancing with the military apparatus where there used to be an army that was strategically on a par with it — only strategically, mind you, because naval superiority and superiority in other branches, in surface units, bases all over the world, would favor whoever was against the Soviet Union during the Cold War. Nuclear strategic parity with the United States had been achieved by the Soviet Union, and now Russia cannot even incorporate 20 aircraft to the country's air force, even though they have all the necessary factories to build them in huge quantities. History will be harsh in passing judgment on those responsible for this catastrophe, the humiliation, the scorn and the dangers that today threaten that people and the world along with them.

What is, then, going to happen in that country? And what if a "Yugoslavization" of Russia, full of nuclear weapons, takes place? It is estimated that they have 20,000 such weapons. Would it not be a tragedy for the world that that country should follow the same road as Yugoslavia, that that country should be dissolved? Can such a thing be conceived? What consequences would it have?

From the economic point of view, nothing scares us. Who is better prepared than Cuba for any global economic crisis? It would affect us, of course. If we have to halt the nickel plants, we halt them; if the price of sugar continues to drop, we will withstand the low prices. We have been withstanding them for a while now; we will see if it is compensated with the low prices of other items.

Our land is in the hands of the people and they will not be idle. What country is better organized and prepared than this? We do not want that crisis, we consider it a tragedy that will bring enormous suffering to the world. In other words, it can be catastrophic.

Those in the United States should be thinking about what will happen within the United States and how the next elections will turn out, not the one coming up in a few days — the next one — if the stock markets collapse and half of the Americans with shares in the stock market lose huge amounts of money.

Reading about the 1929 crisis one can see how the stock brokers committed suicide one after another. Many millionaires committed suicide because they only had $100 million left. And, as I said, only five percent of the U.S. population had stocks then. These were mainly owned by companies.

Well, these things are bound to happen the way things are going. But mind you, an economic crisis in Russia is one thing; its "Yugoslavization" is another. A civil war in that country is something very, very serious. And if I were to advise my enemies, I would tell them: "You had better help Russia. See where you can get the money, maybe by selling those bonds issued by the U.S. Treasury or by printing new bills. Save that country, prevent its disintegration." That is what I would really recommend, and I am not charging them half a penny for the recommendation. I am not doing it to favor U.S. interests; I am doing it for the world.

I would also say to them: "Entrench yourselves also in South America to prevent the crisis from spreading. Help the South Americans because otherwise the fire will soon reach the U.S. economy. Try to understand." And they have to understand it. They cannot be so nearsighted, so arrogant. They cannot continue squeezing others until the very end. They cannot suffocate Russia nor allow the crisis to spread to Brazil.

I will say more: even if they do this, the only thing they will gain is to postpone the crisis for a time. It will come again and it will become even worse. The IMF would have to explode, the whole financial system that has been established, the economic order they have imposed would burst into pieces. They would have to devise something that could save what is possible to save of capitalism; but the present situation is unsustainable. It must change.

They must certainly go quite a bit further if they want to avoid an imminent catastrophe. An increasing number of people are already calling for this. They cannot continue insisting on the rules, the regulations, the outrageous things they are demanding of governments and peoples. They are neither economically nor politically viable, and from the human point of view they are unbearable. The developed capitalist world must inevitably pay a price. It must accept the redistribution of part of the wealth it has accumulated throughout the centuries and some of the technology it has developed. It must cut back the squandering of natural resources, the insulting and irrational luxury. More rationality and less selfishness.

I have only dealt with two or three topics. I have not even mentioned other problems that burden and threaten the world, what for? What we must do now is face the economic catastrophe that awaits us. There will be solutions. Do not ask me what. As I said in the South African Parliament I am not a prophet. I only repeat with the most absolute and deepest conviction: The greatest solutions have always emerged from the greatest crises.

Sooner or later everything will have to change. We are not seeking petty and narrow national interests. We have been withstanding the worst of situations for quite a long time now. We have learned to defend ourselves, to struggle, to achieve many things under extremely difficult circumstances.

We hope the world can be saved. The world has no alternative; it must be saved, and it should save nature, from which the 10 billion people that we will soon be will have to live.

8

The Battle of Ideas

University of Venezuela

I was going to say that today, February 3, 1999, it is exactly 40 years and 10 days since I first visited this university and we met in this same place. Of course, you understand that I am moved — without the melodrama you find in certain soap operas — as it would have been unimaginable then that one day, so many years later, I would return to this place.

Several weeks ago, on January 1, 1999, on the occasion of the 40th anniversary of the triumph of the [Cuban] revolution, I stood on the same balcony in Santiago de Cuba where I had spoken on January 1, 1959. I was reflecting with the audience gathered there that the people of today are not the same people who were there at the time, because of the 11 million Cubans we are today, 7,190,000 were born after that date. I said that they were two different people and yet one and the same eternal people of Cuba.

I also reminded them that the immense majority of those who were 50 years' old then are no longer alive, and that those who were children at that time are over 40 today.

So many changes, so many differences, and how special it was for us to think that the people had started a profound revolution when they were practically illiterate, when 30 percent of adults could not read or write and perhaps an additional 50 percent had not reached fifth grade. We estimated that with a population of almost seven million, possibly a

---

On February 3, 1999, Fidel Castro spoke at the University of Venezuela, Caracas, reminiscing about his visit 40 years earlier in the weeks following the overthrow of the Batista dictatorship in Cuba in January 1959.

little over 150,000 people had gone beyond fifth grade, while today university graduates alone number 600,000, and there are almost 300,000 teachers and professors.

I told my fellow compatriots — in paying tribute to the people who had achieved that first great triumph 40 years before — that in spite of an enormous educational backwardness, they had been able to undertake and defend an extraordinary revolutionary feat. Furthermore, their political culture was probably lower than their educational level.

Those were times of brutal anticommunism, the final years of McCarthyism, when by all possible means our powerful and imperial neighbor had tried to sow in the minds of our noble people all kinds of lies and prejudices. Oftentimes, I would meet a common citizen and ask them a number of questions: whether they believed we should undertake a land reform; whether it would be fair for families to own the homes for which at times they paid big landlords almost half their salaries. Also, if they believed that the people should own all the banks in order to use those resources to finance the development of the country. Whether those big factories — most of them foreign-owned — should belong to, and produce for, the people... things like that. I could ask 10, 15 similar questions and they would agree absolutely: "Yes, that would be great."

In essence, if all those big stores and all those profitable business that now only enrich their privileged owners belonged to the people, were used to enrich the people, would you agree? "Yes, yes," they would answer immediately. So, then I asked them: "Would you agree with socialism?" Answer: "Socialism? No, no, no, not with socialism." Let alone communism... There was so much prejudice that this was an even more frightening word.

Revolutionary legislation was what contributed the most to creating a socialist consciousness in our people. At that time it was those same people — illiterate or semi-illiterate at the beginning — who had to start by teaching many of its children to read and write. The same people who out of love for liberty and a yearning for justice had overthrown the dictatorship and carried out, and heroically defended, the most profound social revolution in this hemisphere.

In 1961, only two years after the triumph of the revolution, with the support of young students working as teachers, about one million people learned how to read and write. They went to the countryside, to the mountains, the remotest places and there they taught people who were up to 80 years' old how to read and write. Later on, there were follow-up courses and the necessary steps were taken in a constant effort to attain what we have today. A revolution can only be born from culture and ideas.

No people become revolutionary by force. Those who sow ideas never have any need to suppress the people. Weapons in the hands of that same people are now used to fight those abroad who try to take away their achievements.

Forgive me for touching on this issue because I did not come here to preach socialism or communism and I do not want to be misinterpreted. Nor did I come here to propose radical legislation or anything of the sort. I was simply reflecting on our experience that showed us the importance of ideas, the importance of believing in humanity, the importance of trusting the people. This is extremely important when humankind is facing such complicated and difficult times.

Naturally, on January 1 this year in Santiago de Cuba it was fitting to acknowledge, in a very special way, that the revolution which had managed to survive 40 years without folding its banners, without surrendering, was mainly the work of the people gathered there, young people and mature men and women. They had received their education under the revolution and were capable of that feat, thus writing pages of noble and well-earned glory for our nation and for our brothers and sisters in the Americas.

We could say that thanks to the efforts of three generations of Cubans, vis-à-vis the mightiest power, the biggest empire in humanity's history, this sort of miracle came true: that a small country would undergo such an ordeal and achieve victory.

Our even greater recognition went to those compatriots who in the past decade had been willing to withstand the double blockade resulting from the collapse of the socialist camp and the demise of the Soviet Union, which left our neighbor as the sole superpower in a unipolar world, unrivalled in the political, economic, military, technological and cultural fields. I do not mean the value of their culture, but rather the tremendous power they exercise to impose their culture on the rest of the world.

However, it was unable to defeat a united people, a people armed with just ideas, a people endowed with a great political consciousness, because that is most important for us. We have resisted everything and are ready to continue resisting for as long as necessary thanks to the seeds planted throughout those decades, thanks to the ideas and the consciousness developed during that time.

It has been our best weapon and it shall remain so, even in nuclear times. Even in times of smart weapons — which sometimes make mistakes and strike 100 or 200 km away from their targets but which have a certain degree of precision — human intelligence will always be greater than any of these sophisticated weapons.

It is a matter of concepts. The defense doctrine of our nation is based on the conclusion that in the end — the end of our invaders — it would be body combat, a man-to-man and a woman-to-invader combat.

We have had to wage, and will have to continue waging, a more difficult battle against that extremely powerful empire: a ceaseless ideological battle. They stepped up this battle after the collapse of the socialist camp when, fully confident in our ideas, we decided to continue forward. More than that, to continue forward alone; and when I say alone I am thinking of state entities, without ever forgetting the immense and invincible support and solidarity of the peoples that we have always had and which makes us feel under a greater obligation to struggle.

We have accomplished honorable internationalist missions. Over 500,000 Cubans have taken part in difficult missions. The children of a people who could not read or write and which developed such a high consciousness that they shed their sweat, and even their blood, for other peoples — for any people in the world.

When the "special period" began we said: "Now, our first internationalist duty is to defend this bulwark." We meant what [José] Martí had described in the last words he wrote the day before his death, when he said that the main objective of his struggle had to go undeclared in order to be accomplished. Martí, who was not only a true believer in [Simón] Bolívar's ideas but also a wholehearted follower, set himself an objective. Martí, in his own words, saw it as his duty as to prevent "the United States from spreading through the Antilles, as Cuba gains its independence, and from overpowering with that additional strength our lands of America. All I have done so far, and all I will do, is for this purpose."

It was his political will and life's aspiration to prevent the fall of that first trench which the northern neighbors had so many times tried to occupy. That trench is still there, and will continue to be there, with a people willing to fight to death to prevent the fall of that trench of the Americas. The people there are capable of defending even the last trench, and whoever defends the last trench and prevents anyone from taking it begins, at that very moment, to attain victory.

Comrades — if you allow me to call you that because that is what we are at this moment — I believe that we are defending a trench here, too. And trenches of ideas — forgive me for quoting Martí again — are worth more than trenches of stones.

We must discuss ideas here, and so I go back to what I was saying. Many things have happened in these 40 years but the most transcendental is that the world has changed. This world of today does not resemble the world of those days.

The revolutionary fever we had come down with from the mountains only a few days before accompanied us when speaking [here 40 years ago] of revolutionary processes in Latin America and focusing on the liberation of the Dominican people from Trujillo's clutches. I believe that issue took most of the time at that meeting — with a tremendous enthusiasm shared by all.

Today, that would not be an issue. Today, there is not one particular people to liberate. Today, there is not one particular people to save. Today, a whole world, all of humankind needs to be liberated and saved. And it is not our task; it is *your* task.

There was not a unipolar world at that time, a single, hegemonistic superpower. Today, the world and all humankind are under the domination of an enormous superpower. Nonetheless, we are convinced that we will win the battle without panglossian optimism — I believe that is a word writers sometimes use.

These are objective reasons, and I am sure humankind will provide all the indispensable subjective ones. For this, neither nuclear weapons nor big wars are necessary, but ideas. I say this on behalf of that small country we mentioned before, which has struggled staunchly and unhesitatingly for 40 years.

You were calling me — to my embarrassment — the name by which I am known, I mean "Fidel." I have no other title, actually. I understand that protocol demands the use of "His Excellency the President" and so on and so forth. When I heard you chanting: "Fidel! Fidel! What is it with Fidel that the Americans cannot put him down?" I had an idea. So I turned to my neighbor on the right and said: "Well, actually, what they should be asking is: What is it with the Americans that they cannot put him down?" And, that instead of saying "him" they could say: "What is with the Americans that cannot put Cuba down?" That would be more accurate. I realize words are used to symbolize ideas. I never take credit, nor can I take credit, for that myself.

Yes, we all hope to live long, all of us! In the ideas that we believe and in the conviction that those following in our steps will carry them forward. However, your task — it should be said — will be more difficult than ours.

I WAS SAYING THAT WE are living in a very different world. This is the first thing we need to understand. Furthermore, the world is globalized, really globalized. It is a world dominated by the ideology, the standards and the principles of neoliberal globalization.

In our view, globalization is nobody's whim; it is not even anybody's invention. Globalization is a law of history. It is a consequence of the development of the productive forces — excuse me, please, for using this phrase which might still scare some due to its authorship — it is a consequence of scientific and technologic development, so much so that even the author of this phrase, Karl Marx, who had great confidence in human talent, was possibly unable to imagine it.

Certain other things remind me of some of the basic ideas of that thinker among great thinkers. It comes to mind that even what he conceived as an ideal for human society could never come true — and this is increasingly clear — if it was not in a globalized world. Not for a second did he think that in the tiny island of Cuba — just to give you an example — a socialist society, or the building of socialism would be attempted, least of all so near to such a powerful capitalist neighbor.

Yes, we have tried. Furthermore, we made it and we have defended it. And we have also known 40 years of blockade, threats, aggression and suffering.

Today, since we are the only ones, all the propaganda, all the mass media ruling the world are used by the United States in the ideological and political warfare against our revolutionary process in the same way as it uses its immense power in all fields, including its economic power, and its international political influence in the economic warfare against Cuba.

We say, "blockade," but blockade does not mean much. I wish it were an economic blockade! What our country has been enduring for a long time is true economic warfare. Do you want evidence? You can go anywhere in the world, any factory owned by a U.S. company, to buy a cap or a kerchief to export to Cuba. Even if produced by nationals of the country in question with raw materials originated in the same country, the U.S. government thousands of miles away bans the sale of such a cap or kerchief. Is that a blockade or economic warfare?

Do you want an additional example? If by any chance one of you wins the lottery — do you have lottery here? — Or finds some treasure and decides to build a small factory in Cuba, you can be sure of receiving very soon a visit from a senior U.S. diplomat, perhaps even the ambassador himself. He will try to persuade you, put pressure or threaten reprisals so that you do not invest your little treasure in a small factory in Cuba. Is it a blockade or economic warfare?

Neither does it allow the sale of medicine to Cuba, even if that medicine is indispensable to save a life, and we have had many examples of such cases.

We have withstood that warfare, and like in all battles — whether military, political or ideological — there are casualties. There are those who may be confused, some are softened or weakened by a combination of economic difficulties, material hardships, the parading of luxury in consumer societies and the nicely sweetened but rotten ideas about the fabulous advantages of their economic system, based on the mean notion that humans are animals moved only by a carrot or when beaten with a whip. We might say that their whole ideological strategy is based on this.

There are casualties, but also, like in all battles, other people gain experience, fighters become veterans, enhance their qualities and help preserve and increase the morale and strength needed to continue fighting.

We are winning the battle of ideas. The battlefield is not limited to our small island, although the small island has to fight. Today, the world is the battlefield — everywhere, in all continents, in all institutions, in every forum. This is the good side of the globalized struggle. We must defend the small island while fighting throughout the huge world they dominate or try to dominate. In many fields they have almost total domination, but not in all fields, nor in the same way, nor in absolutely every country.

They have discovered very intelligent weapons but we, the revolutionaries, have discovered an even more powerful weapon: humans think and feel. We have learned this around the world, in the countless internationalist missions we have discharged in one place or another. Suffice it to mention a single figure: 26,000 Cuban doctors have taken part in these missions.

The country that was left with only 3,000 out of the 6,000 doctors it had at the triumph of the revolution, many of them were unemployed and always wanting to migrate to obtain better salaries. The revolution has been able to multiply the 3,000 who stayed by training more and more doctors from those who began studying first or second grade in the schools immediately established throughout the country after the revolution. These people have such a spirit of sacrifice and solidarity that 26,000 of them have accomplished internationalist missions just as hundreds of thousands of Cubans have worked as professionals, teachers, construction workers and combatants. Yes, combatants, and we take pride in saying this because fighting against the fascist and racist soldiers of apartheid and contributing to the victory of African peoples will forever be a reason to feel proud.

In this ignored effort — highly ignored — we have learned a lot from the peoples. We have come to know those peoples and their extraordinary qualities. We have learned, not only through abstract notions but also in ordinary everyday life, that all people may not be equal in their features but all are equal in their talents, feelings and other virtues. This proves that, in terms of moral, social, intellectual and human abilities, all human beings are genetically equal. Many have made the big mistake of taking themselves for a superior race.

I WAS SAYING THAT LIFE has taught us many things, and this is what nurtures our faith in the people, our faith in humanity. We did not read this in a little book, we have lived through it; we have had the privilege of living through it.

There is no need here for an extensive explanation of what

neoliberalism is all about. How can I summarize it? Well, I would say this: Neoliberal globalization wants to turn all countries, especially all our countries, into private property.

What will be left for us of their enormous resources? Because they have accumulated an immense wealth not only looting and exploiting the world but also working the miracle alchemists longed for in the Middle Ages: turning paper into gold. At the same time, they have turned gold into paper and with it they buy everything, everything but souls, or rather, everything but the overwhelming majority of souls. They buy natural resources, factories, whole communication systems, services, and so on. They are buying even land around the world, assuming that if it is cheaper than in their own countries it is a good investment for the future.

I wonder: What is it they are going to leave us after turning us practically into second-class citizens — pariahs would be a more precise term — in our own countries? They want to turn the world into a huge free-trade zone. It might be more clearly understood this way because what is a free-trade zone? It is a place with special characteristics where taxes are not paid; where raw materials, spare parts and components are brought in and assembled or various goods produced, especially in labor-intensive sectors. At times, they pay not more than five percent of the salary they must pay in their own countries and the only thing they leave us with are these meager salaries.

Sadder still: I have seen how they have made many of our countries compete with one another by favoring those who offer more advantages and tax exemptions to investors. They have made many Third World countries compete with one another for investments and free-trade zones.

There are countries enduring such poverty and unemployment that they have had to establish dozens of free-trade zones as an option within the established world order. It is this or not having free-trade zone factories and jobs with certain salaries, even if these amount to only seven percent, six percent, five percent or less of the salaries the owners of those factories would have to pay in the countries they come from.

We stated this at the World Trade Organization, in Geneva, several months ago. They want to turn us into a huge free-trade zone; then with their money and technology they will start buying everything. It remains to be seen how many airlines will remain national property, how many shipping lines, how many services will remain the property of the people or the nations.

That is the future we are offered by neoliberal globalization. But you should not think that this is offered to the workers only. It is also being offered to the national businessmen and to the small- and medium-size owners. They will have to compete with the transnational companies' technology, with their sophisticated equipment, and their worldwide distribution networks; then they will have to look for markets without the substantial trade credits their powerful competitors can use to sell their products.

We in Cuba can have a great factory, let's say a fridge factory. Let us assume that other Third World countries manufacture fridges of acceptable quality and even at a lower cost. Their powerful competitors constantly renew their designs, invest huge sums of money to lend prestige to their trademarks, manufacture in many free-trade zones paying low wages or tax-free. They also have abundant capital or financial mechanisms for credits that can be repaid in one, two or three years. They flood the market with electrical appliances produced in a world riddled with anarchy and chaos in the distribution of investment capital, under the generalized motto of export-based growth and development, as the IMF advises.

What space is left for national industries? How can they export and to whom? Where are the potential consumers among the billions of poor, hungry and unemployed living in a large part of the globe? Shall we have to wait until all of them can buy a fridge, a TV set, a telephone, an airconditioner, a car, a PC, a house, a garage, fuel and electricity or until they get an unemployment subsidy, market shares and a safe pension? Is that the path leading to development, as they tell us millions of times over by all possible means? What will happen to the domestic market if the accelerated reduction of customs barriers — an important source of budget revenues in many Third World countries — is imposed on them?

Neoliberal theoreticians have been unable to solve, for instance, the serious problem of unemployment in most of the rich countries, let alone the developing countries, and they shall never find a solution under such a ridiculous conception. It is a huge contradiction in the system that the more they invest and resort to technology, the more people are left jobless. Labor productivity and the most sophisticated equipment born out of human talent multiply material wealth as well as poverty and layoffs. So what good are they to humankind? Perhaps to help reduce working hours, have more time for resting, leisure, sports, cultural and scientific upgrading? That is impossible because the sacred law of the market and competition patterns — increasingly more imaginary than real — in a world of transnationals and mega-merges would not allow it. Anyway, who is competing and against whom? Monopoly and merger-oriented giants against giants. There is not a corner in the world for the other alleged players in this competition. For wealthy countries, state-of-the-art industries; for Third World workers, manufacturing jeans, T-shirts, garments, shoes; planting flowers, exotic fruits and other products increasingly demanded in industrialized societies because they cannot be grown there. We know that in the United States, for instance, they even grow marijuana in greenhouses or in courtyards, and that the value of the marijuana produced in that country is higher than all their corn production, although they are the biggest corn producers in the world. In the long run, their laboratories are, or will wind up being the biggest narcotics producers in the globe, for the time being, under the label of sedatives, anti-depressants and other products that young people have learned to combine in various ways.

In the happy, developed world, tough agricultural tasks like picking tomatoes — for which a perfect machine has not yet been invented, a robot capable of picking them according to ripeness, size and other characteristics — cleaning the streets and other unpleasant jobs that nobody wants to do in consumer societies, how do they solve this? Oh! That is what Third World immigrants are for! They themselves do not do that type of work.

For those of us made into foreigners in our own countries, what they leave is the manufacture of blue jeans and things like that. Under their "wonderful" economic laws, they make us produce blue jeans as if the world population already was 40 billion and every person had enough money to buy a pair of jeans. No, no, I am not criticizing the garment — I am criticizing the jobs they leave for us that have absolutely nothing to do with high technology. So, our universities will become redundant and be left to train low-cost technical staff for the developed world.

You may have read in the press these days that the United States, in view of the needs of their computer, electronic and other industries has decided to grant visas to 200,000 highly-skilled workers from the Third World. You had better be careful because they are looking for trained people. This time it is not to pick tomatoes. [Americans] are not very literate, and many people can see this when they confuse Brazil with Bolivia or Bolivia with Brazil, or when surveys show that they do not even know many things about the United States itself. They do not even know if a Latin American country they have heard of is in Africa or Europe — this is not an overstatement. They do not have all the geniuses or highly skilled workers for their state-of-the-art industries, so they come to our world and recruit a few who are then lost to our countries forever.

Where are the best scientists of our countries, in which laboratories? Which of our countries has laboratories for all the scientists it could train? How much can we pay that scientist and how much can they pay?

Where are they? I know many outstanding Latin Americans who are there. Who trained them? Oh! Venezuela, Guatemala, Brazil, Argentina or another Latin American country; but they had no opportunities [to work] in their homeland. Industrialized countries have the monopoly of laboratories and the money. They recruit them and take them away from poor nations — not only scientists, athletes, too. They would like to buy our baseball players the way slaves were sold on one of those platforms...

They are treacherous. Since there is always a soul to be tempted — so the Bible says, referring to the first human beings who were supposed to be better, right? Because supposedly they were not so wicked nor were they familiar with consumer societies. In those days there was no dollar. All of a sudden, even an athlete who is not absolutely first rate, gets paid a couple of million, or four, five or six million. Since Major League batters seem to be so bad, they have some success [over there]. I mean no offense to U.S. professional athletes; they are hard-working, highly motivated people. They are also a commodity bought and sold in the market, although at a high price; but there must be shortcomings in their training because they smuggle in some Cuban pitchers — who, would rank first, second or third — or a shortstop, or a third base. These [Cubans] get there and the pitcher strikes out their best batters and the shortstop does not let a ball get past him.

We would be rich if we auctioned Cuban baseball players. They no longer want to pay U.S. baseball players because they are too expensive. They have organized academies in our countries to train players at a very low cost and pay them lower salaries, but still salaries of millions of dollars a year. Together with this, all the TV advertising, plus cars from here to there and beautiful women from all ethnic groups linked to automobile advertising and the rest of the commercial advertising you see in some tabloids, can tempt more than one of our compatriots.

In Cuba we do not waste any newsprint or other resources in such frivolous advertising. The very few times I have watched U.S. television, I can hardly stand it because every three minutes it stops for a commercial, maybe a person working out on an exercise bike which is the most boring thing in the world... I am not saying it is wrong, I say it is boring. Any program, even soap operas are interrupted in their sweetest moments of love...

In Cuba we buy some soap operas from abroad because we have not been able to cover our needs and some made in Latin American countries are so popular with the Cuban audience that they even cause people to stop working. At times, we also get good films from Latin America, but practically everything circulating in the world is all Yankee-made, canned culture.

Actually, what little paper we have in our country is used for textbooks and for our few newspapers with few pages. We cannot use resources to print those glossy magazines with so many pictures, read by beggars in any street of our capitals, advertising fancy cars with their beautiful escorts or even a yacht and other things, right? That's how they poison people with propaganda, so that beggars are also cruelly influenced and made to dream of a heaven — unattainable for them —

offered by capitalism.

In our country we operate differently. Still, they have an influence with the image of a society that is not only alienating, and economically unequal and unfair, but also socially and environmentally unsustainable. I usually say, by way of example, that if consumerism means that in Bangladesh, India, Indonesia, Pakistan or China there may be a car in every household... I apologize to those present who have one. I mean no criticism, but a warning against a model not applicable in a world that has yet to develop. You will surely understand me, because Caracas cannot accommodate many more cars. You know they are going to have to build avenues three or four stories high. I can imagine that if they were to do the same in China, then the 100 million hectares of arable land would have to be transformed into highways, gas stations and parking-lots, leaving practically no space to grow a single grain of rice.

The consumption pattern they are imposing on the world is sheer madness, chaotic and absurd. It is not that I think the world should become a monastery. However, I do believe that the planet has no other choice but to define what consumption standards or patterns are both sustainable and obtainable, and educate humankind in these.

Every day, fewer people are reading books. And why should human beings be deprived, for example, of the pleasure of reading a book, or of many other cultural and recreational satisfactions, not only for the sake of acquiring material wealth but also spiritual richness? I am not thinking about men and women working, as in the times of [Frederick] Engels, for 14 or 15 hours a day. I am thinking of men and women working four hours a day. If technology so allows it, then why work eight hours? It is only logical that, as productivity increases, less physical and mental effort will be required; that there will be less unemployment and the people will have more spare time.

Let us call a free human being someone who does not need to work all week, Saturdays, Sundays or double shifts included, to make ends meet, dashing at all hours in large cities, rushing to the subway or to take a bus... How are they going to convince us that this is a free human being?

If computers and automatic machines can work wonders in terms of the generation of material goods and services, then why cannot humans benefit from the science created with their intelligence for the well-being of humanity?

Why must anyone endure hunger, unemployment, early death from curable diseases, ignorance, the lack of culture and all sorts of human and social afflictions for exclusively commercial reasons and profits? Why, for the sole interest of an over-privileged and powerful elite operating under frenzied economic laws and institutions which are not, were not and will not be eternal?

Such is the case of the well-known market laws. The market has become today an object of idolatry, a sacred word pronounced at all hours. Why should this be so when it is possible to generate all the wealth required for meeting reasonable human needs compatible with the preservation of nature and life on our planet? We must ponder and reach our own conclusions. Obviously, it is reasonable for people to have food, health, a roof, clothing and education. Also adequate, rational, sustainable and secure transportation; culture, recreation, a broad variety of options and many more things that could be within the reach of human beings and not, of course, a private jet or a yacht for each of the 9.5 billion who will live on the planet within 50 years.

They have impaired the human mind.

Thank goodness that these things did not happen back in the days of the Garden of Eden or Noah's arc in the Old Testament. I can imagine that life was a bit more peaceful then, even if they did have a flood. We are also the victims of floods, all too frequently. Observe what happened recently in Central America. No one knows for sure if as a result of all the climatic constraints we might end up buying tickets or standing in line to board an arc.

They have instilled all this in people's minds. They have alienated millions and hundreds of millions of people and made them suffer even more, as those people are unable to meet their basic needs because they do not even have a doctor to see or a school to attend.

I mentioned the anarchic, irrational and chaotic formula imposed by neoliberalism: the investment of hundreds of billions without rhyme or reason; having tens of millions of workers manufacturing the same things: television sets, computer parts, and clips or chips, whatever they are called... an endless number of gadgets, including a large numbers of cars. Everyone is doing the same thing.

They have doubled the capacity for manufacturing cars. Who will buy these cars? Buyers can be found in Africa, Latin America and in many other parts of the world. The only problem is that they don't have a dime to buy either cars or gas, or to pay for the highways or repair shops, which would ultimately ruin Third World countries even more by squandering the resources needed for social development and further destroying the environment.

By creating unsustainable consumerism in industrialized countries and sowing impossible dreams throughout the rest of the world, the developed capitalist system has caused great injury to humankind. It has poisoned the atmosphere and depleted its enormous nonrenewable natural resources, which humankind will need in the future. Please, do not believe that I am thinking of an idealistic, impossible, absurd world; I am merely trying to imagine what a real world and a happier person could be like. Without mentioning commodities, it suffices to mention a concept: inequality has made more than 80 percent of the people on the planet unhappy. [New] concepts and ideas are required that will make possible a viable world, a sustainable world and a better world.

I find amusing the writings of many theoreticians of neoliberalism and neoliberal globalization. Actually, I have little time to go to the cinema or to watch videos, however good they may be. I rather amuse myself reading the articles these gentlemen write. I can see their analysts, their wisest and most perceptive commentators, immersed in many a great contradiction, in confusion and even despair. They want to square the circle. It must be awful for them.

I recall that once they showed me a squared figure with two lines on the top like this, one in the middle and another one downwards. The object of the game was to draw over the lines with a pencil without lifting it once. I don't know how much time I lost attempting to do this instead of doing my homework or studying math, languages or other subjects. In my childhood we used to invent games ourselves in which we lost a lot of time.

But [these articles] amuse me and I truly enjoy them; I am also thankful for what they teach me. And do you know whose articles and analyses humor me the most? Oh, the most conservative ones who do not even want to hear about the state; they want no mention of it, whatsoever. Those who want a Central Bank on the moon so that no human being will dare to lower or raise interest rates. It's unbelievable!

They are the ones who make me happiest because they say certain things, so that I ask myself: "Am I mistaken? Couldn't this article have been written by a left-wing extremist, a radical?" But what is this? After reading the latest book by [George] Soros I reasoned: "Well, this man is a theoretician. He is also an academic and, furthermore, he has I don't know how many billion dollars as a result of speculative operations. This man must know all about this, all the mechanisms and the tricks." However, he entitled his book: *Capitalism's Global Crisis*, which is quite something. There he states with absolute seriousness and apparently with such conviction that I said to myself: "Goodness, it seems that I am not the only madman in this world!" Actually, many have expressed similar concerns. I pay more attention to them than to the adversaries of the current world economic order.

The leftists want to prove that the system will inevitably collapse. This is only logical since it is their duty and, after all, they are right. However, the others do not want this to happen and become despondent, writing many things when faced with a crisis. They are baffled. They have lost faith in their own doctrines.

Then, those of us who decided to resist in solitude... I do not mean geographical solitude but almost complete ideological solitude. In the aftermath of these disasters there is a skepticism, which is then heightened by the expert and powerful propaganda machinery of the empire and its allies. All of this caused many people to feel pessimistic and confused since they lacked the necessary elements for analyzing circumstances from a historical perspective; consequently, they lose hope.

Those first days were truly bitter, and earlier, as we watched how many people, here and there, became turncoats — and I am not criticizing anyone but the coats... Then, again, things change so quickly! Those illusions are now long gone — as we say in Cuba: lasting less than a candy bar in a schoolyard.

They took their neoliberal and market recipes to the former Soviet Union, causing destruction, truly incredible destruction, dismembering nations. They brought about the economic and political dismantling of the federal republics reducing life expectancy in some cases by 14 and 15 years, multiplying infant mortality by three to four times and generating social and economic problems which not even a resurrected Dante would dare to imagine.

It is truly pathetic. We try to be as well-informed as possible about everything that happens everywhere; we have no other choice but to be more or less well informed, otherwise we would be disoriented. We have quite a clear notion of the disasters that the market god, its laws and principles have caused along with the recipes that the International Monetary Fund and other neocolonizing and recolonizing institutions have practically imposed on every country. Even wealthy countries like the Europeans have found it necessary to unite and establish a currency so that experts like Soros do not try to bring down even the pound sterling, a currency that reigned not so long ago as a medium of exchange and was the sword and the symbol of a dominating empire that was the master of the world's reserve currency. All these privileges are now in the hands of the United States while the British had to suffer the humiliation of watching the fall of their pound sterling.

Such was the case of the Spanish peseta, the French franc and the Italian lira; they staked their bets on the immense power of their billions because these speculators are gamblers who play with marked cards. They have all the information, the most prominent economists, Nobel Prize laureates, such as the case of the famous company that was one of the most prestigious in the United States, called the Long Term Capital Management. With a total fund of almost $4.5 billion, the company raised $120 billion for speculative operations.

Those from Long Term, as it is commonly known, made a mistake and lost. It was a disaster and it was necessary to rescue that company, violating all international, ethical, moral and financial norms that the

United States had imposed on the world. The head of the Federal Reserve declared in the Senate that if that fund was not bailed out, there would inevitably be an economic catastrophe, both in the United States and in the rest of the world.

Another question: What kind of economy prevails today where a handful of multi-millionaires can cause an economic catastrophe in the United States and in the world? I do not mean the big ones, not Bill Gates and others like him since Bill Gates' fortune is about 15 times the initial capital with which Long Term mobilized enormous sums from investors, obtaining loans from over 50 banks. But oh! The international economy would have collapsed had it not been bailed out. This was stated by one of the most competent and intelligent persons in the United Sates, the chairman of the Federal Reserve.

That distinguished gentleman knows more than a thing or two. The problem is that he does not say everything he knows because part of the method consists of a total lack of transparency and strong doses of sedatives in case of panic, accompanied by sweet and encouraging words: "Everything is all right, the economy is running smoothly." This is the accepted and invariable technique. However, the chairman of the Federal Reserve had to admit before the U.S. Senate that a catastrophe would have occurred if the Fed had not done what it did.

These are the bases of neoliberal globalization. Don't worry; you may subtract one or 20 more from their fragile structure. What they have created is unsustainable! However, they have caused anguish for many people throughout the world. They have ruined nations with the International Monetary Fund's formulas and continue to impoverish countries. They cannot avoid the ruin of these countries, yet they do not cease to do foolish things, and in the stock markets they have inflated the prices of shares and continue to do so ad infinitum.

In the U.S. stock markets, more than one third of families' savings and 50 percent of pension funds have been invested in shares. One can imagine the impact of a catastrophe similar to that of 1929, when only five percent of the population had their savings invested in the stock market. Today, they would feel terrified and run in haste. That was what they did in August after the crisis in Russia, whose share of the world's gross product is only two percent. That crisis made the Dow Jones, the key index of the New York Stock Market, fall in one day by more than 500 points; 512 to be exact, causing an enormous commotion.

The truth is that the leaders of this dominating system spend most of their time running around the world, from banks to financial institutions. And when they saw what occurred in Russia, a track and field Olympics ensued. They met with the Council on Foreign Relations in New York. Clinton delivered a speech, stating that recession and not inflation was the real danger. In a matter of days, in practically a few hours, they made a 180 degree shift, and instead of increasing interest rates they actually lowered them. On October 5 and 6, all the directors of central banks met in Washington. Speeches were delivered, an indeterminate number of criticisms were raised about the IMF and measures were adopted supposedly to reduce the danger. A few days later, the U.S. government met with the G-7, which decided to contribute $90 billion to stop the crisis from extending to Brazil and from there to the rest of South America. They were trying to impede the flames from reaching the over-inflated stock markets of the United States. A small pin, the smallest of holes and the balloon would deflate. These are the risks threatening neoliberal globalization.

That was what they did. Then some of us, myself included, concluded: "They have resources, they have the possibility to maneuver and postpone the great crisis for a time." They could postpone it, but not ultimately avoid it. I reflected on the matter and said: "Apparently they have succeeded thanks to all the measures adopted or imposed: lowering interest rates; $90 billion to support the Fund which had no funds; the steps taken by Japan to confront the bank crisis; Brazil's announcement of harsh economic measures and the timely statement that the U.S. economy had grown more than expected in the third quarter."

It seemed that things would hold on. However, only a few days ago, we were again surprised by the news from Brazil on the current economic situation. This truly hurts us very much for reasons connected to this very issue, that is, the effort that our peoples must make to join forces and wage the hard struggle that awaits us. Actually, a destructive crisis in Brazil would have an extremely negative impact on Latin America.

At present, despite everything they did, Brazilians are faced with a complicated economic situation, regardless of the fact that the United States and the international financial institutions used up a large part of their recipes and ammunition. Now, after the first months since the great scare, they are demanding new conditions and seem more indifferent to the fate of Brazil.

As for Russia, they intend to keep it on the brink of an abyss. This is not a small country. It is the largest territory in the world with a population of 146 million and thousands of nuclear weapons where a social explosion, an internal conflict or any other event can cause terrible damage.

Yet, these gentlemen who manage the world economy are so insane and reckless that, after ruining a country with their recipes, it does not even occur to them to use some of their own printed paper, because that is precisely what the treasury bonds are, a refuge for terrified speculators. When faced with any risk, speculators would buy U.S. Treasury bonds. It does not occur to them to use some of the $90 billion designed for the IMF to prevent an economic or political catastrophe in Russia. What occurs to them is to impose a bunch of impossible conditions. They demand that budgets, which are already below the indispensable limit, be cut. They also demand free conversion and immediate payment of high debts; a host of requirements that would deplete the remaining reserves of any country. They refuse to think; they have not learned their lesson. They intend to maintain that country in a precarious situation, at the edge of the sword, with humanitarian assistance, imposing conditions and generating truly serious dangers.

However, the Russian issue has not been solved — a country they impoverished, thanks to their advisers and formulas. Nor have they solved the Brazilian issue, a problem they were so very much interested in solving, since it could affect them very closely. Therefore, it seemed to me that this was the last stronghold of the U.S. stock markets.

It was a close call. Some of the measures I've mentioned stabilized the situation a bit. Once again the sale and purchase of shares was unleashed and once again they are off on a race to outer space, preparing the conditions for an even greater crisis, and relatively soon. No one knows what the consequences for the U.S. economy and its society will be.

It is impossible to imagine what would occur in the event of another 1929. They believe they have done away with the risk of a crisis like that and actually they have solved nothing. They have not even been able to prevent the Brazilian crisis, which may consequently affect the whole integration process in Latin America and the interests of all our countries.

However, there is an explanation for everything, and after waiting and watching how they think, what they say, what they do, one can actually guess what is in their minds. The important thing with those people is not so much to believe what they are saying but to try to penetrate their brains — with the least possible trauma as we would not want to harm them — to know what they are actually thinking, to know what they have not said and why they have not said it.

For us this is a matter of profound interest, a source of reflection, encouragement and reaffirmation of our convictions. Because we lived through days of uncertainty and bitterness that I previously described, and witnessed the loss of faith of many progressive men and women. Now, we can see that the truth is gaining ground and that many people are now beginning to think more profoundly. And those who claimed the end of history and the final victory of their anachronistic and selfish concepts are now in decline and undoubtedly demoralized.

THESE PAST EIGHT YEARS — SINCE 1991, in other words, from the collapse of the Soviet Union to the present — have been hard years for us in every sense, especially in terms of ideas and concepts. Now we see that the high and mighty, those who thought they had created a system or an empire that would last 1,000 years are beginning to realize that the bases of that system, of that empire, are falling apart.

What is the legacy of this global capitalism or this neoliberal capitalist globalization? Not only the capitalism that we know from its very origins, that capitalism from which this one was born, which was progressive yesterday but reactionary and unsustainable today. A process many of you, historians, and those who are not, like the students of economics, must know. A history of 250 to 300 years, whose primary theoretician, John Adams, published his book in 1776, the same year as the Declaration of Independence of the United States. He was a great talent, undoubtedly, a great intellect. I do not think he was a sinner, a culprit or a bandit. He studied the economic system that emerged in Europe while it was in full bloom. He examined and outlined the theoretical bases of capitalism — the capitalism of his day, because John Adams could have never imagined this one.

In those days of small workshops and factories, Adams felt that the individual interest was the prime stimulus of economic activity, and that private and competitive quest constituted the basic source of public welfare. It was not necessary to appeal to an individual's humanity but one's love of oneself.

Personal property and management were all that was compatible with the world of small-scale industry that John Adams knew. He did not even live to see the enormous factories and the impressive masses of workers at the end of the 19th century. He could much less imagine the gigantic corporations and modern transnational companies with millions of shares, managed by professional executives who have nothing to do with the ownership of these entities and whose main function it is to occasionally report to the shareholders. (Those executives decide, however, which dividends are paid, how much and where to invest.) These forms of property, management and enjoyment of the wealth produced have nothing to do with the world [Adams] lived in.

Nevertheless, the system continued to develop and gained considerable momentum during the English Industrial Revolution. The working class emerged and so did Karl Marx, who in my view, with all due respect to those who may be of a different view, was the greatest economic and political thinker of all times. No one learned more about the laws and principles of the capitalist system than Marx. Right now, more than a few members of the capitalist elite, anguished by the current crisis, are reading Marx, seeking a possible diagnosis and remedy for today's evils. Socialism, as the antithesis of capitalism, surfaced with Marx.

The struggle between the ideas symbolized by both men of thought,

[Marx and Adams], has persisted for many years. Capitalism continued to develop under the principles of its most prominent theoretician until approximately World War I.

Before the war, a certain level of globalization existed. There was a gold standard for the international monetary system. In 1929, there was the great crisis followed by the great recession that lasted over 10 years. Then, another important thinker emerged, John Maynard Keynes. He is one of the four pillars of economic thought who had an enormous political impact on the last three centuries and bore the indelible seal of each of his predecessors. Keynes was a man of advanced ideas for his time, different from Karl Marx although quite respectful of Marx, coinciding with him in certain concepts. He elaborated the formulas that extricated the United States from the great depression.

Of course, he did not do it alone. A group of scholars was under his influence. At that time, there were practically no economists, nor were they taken very seriously. I don't know if this was for better or for worse, it all depends... However, highly trained groups [of economists] began to emerge. They had plenty of statistical information and conducted extensive studies during the Roosevelt administration in a country that was both exhausted and anguished by endless years of recession; many of them became prominent cabinet members. Keynes's theories helped pull capitalism out of the worst crisis it had ever known.

There was a temporary suspension of the gold standard that was later reestablished by Roosevelt in 1934, if I remember correctly. It was maintained until 1971 when Mr. Nixon came along and the great empire embezzled us all.

Perhaps you are rightly wondering why I am talking about this. I have mentioned these three characters — although I still have not referred to the fourth person. It is very important to know the history of the system that currently rules the world; its anatomy, principles, evolution and experiences — in order to understand that this creature, which came into being almost three centuries ago, is reaching its final stage. It is almost time to perform an autopsy on it before it finally dies, lest that many of us die with it, or if this takes too long, that all of us would die as well.

I mentioned the gold standard because it had a lot to do with the problems that we are now confronting. Toward the end of World War II, an attempt was made to establish an institution that would regulate and step up world trade. The economic situation was in a shambles as a consequence of the long, destructive and bloody war. Therefore, the well-known Bretton Woods Agreement was established by a number of countries, including the most influential and the wealthiest.

The United States was already the richest nation accumulating 80 percent of the world's gold. A fixed exchange currency was established based on gold, combining gold with the U.S. bank note, which then became the international reserve currency. This gave the United States a special privilege and enormous power, which it has continued to use in its own best interest. It gave that country the power to manipulate the world economy, set rules, and prevail in the International Monetary Fund where 85 percent of the votes are required to make any decision. So with its 17.5 percent, the United States may obstruct any decision of that institution. Thus, it controls and is practically the owner of the IMF. It has the last say and has been able to impose worldwide the economic order that we suffer today.

However, Nixon cheated before that. Initially the United States had $30 billion in gold whose price was maintained through a strict control of the market at $35, the so-called troy ounce. Soon, it began to incur in tax-free expenditures, tax-free wars. The United States spent more than $500 billion on the Vietnam adventure. By then, they were running out of gold. They only had $10 billion left and, at that pace, they were going to lose it all. In a speech delivered on August 17, 1971, Nixon openly declared that he had suspended the U.S. dollar's conversion into gold.

As I already explained, they were able to maintain a fixed price for gold thanks to a strict control of the market, the aforementioned $35 an ounce. If there were an excess gold supply in the market they would buy; after all, it did not cost them anything. They would hand over those bank notes and receive gold in exchange, thus avoiding a drop in prices. If an excessive gold demand threatened to raise its price, they would do the opposite. They would sell gold from their abundant reserves, in order to lower its price. Many countries backed their currency with gold reserves or with U.S. bank notes. At least, there was a relatively stable monetary system for trade.

From the moment that Nixon, defrauding the whole world and everyone who owned one of those bills, announced that the value of U.S. dollar bills would no longer be received in physical gold he suspended the most sacred commitment undertaken through an international treaty. He did this unilaterally, by presidential decree or through some other legal procedure. It was not even a congressional decision, and the world had hundreds of billions of dollars in the central banks' reserves.

They kept the gold. Later, prices rose. The value of the remaining gold, worth $10 billion, rose to more than the $30 billion they initially had in physical gold. They also kept all privileges of the system, the value of their treasury bonds and their bank notes that continued to be the compulsory reserve currency in the countries' central banks. In order to get those dollars the countries had to export all their goods, while the United States only had to pay the printing costs. Consequently, U.S. economic power became even greater, and in exchange, it began to destabilize the world. How? The other currencies suffered fluctuations. Their values changed from day to day. Money speculation was unleashed; speculative sales and purchases of currencies amounting today to colossal sums, based on the constant fluctuation of their values. A new phenomenon had emerged, which is now out of control.

Currency speculation, which only 14 years ago involved $150 billion a year, now amounts to more than $1 trillion a day. I would like to point out, so that we may understand each other in this Babel Tower of figures and numbers, which often give rise to confusion as well as translation mistakes and misunderstandings, that I am not referring to the term *billón* in Spanish. There is much confusion between the meaning of *billion* in English and *billón* in Spanish. The former equals one thousand million and the latter one million million. This is what they call a "trillion" in the United States. A new term has just begun to circulate, the *millardo* that also represents one thousand million. In order to avoid any confusion, I said that the currency speculative operations reached a figure of more than a million million dollars a day, that is, one trillion.

It has grown by 2,000 times in 14 years as a result of the measures adopted by the United States in 1971 that caused the fluctuation of all the currencies, either within certain limits or freely. Consequently, we now have this new capitalism, something that would have never occurred to John Adams, not even in his worst nightmares, when he wrote his book, *The Wealth of Nations*.

Other new and equally uncontrollable phenomena have emerged: the hedge funds. In fact, there are hundreds or thousands of these. Think of what might be happening, and what the repercussions might be, after the chairman of the U.S. Federal Reserve declared that one of them might have caused an economic cataclysm in the United States and the rest of the world. He is well informed. He should know in detail what is really happening.

One can guess, judging by certain articles published in a number of conservative magazines, because they know. At times, they need to print something that will support their arguments. However, they try to be extremely discreet. But there are no longer so many foolish people in the world and it is not hard to discern what they did not want to say. A phrase published in a very famous British magazine criticizing the measures adopted by Greenspan in connection with the well-known hedge fund said more or less that perhaps Greenspan had additional information. I cannot exactly recall the phrase used, which was subtler.

However, it is possible to discern from this magazine, which is careful about what it prints and is a highly specialized journal, that it knew more than it was saying. And although it did not agree with the decision of the chairman of the Reserve, it knew perfectly well what he meant when he ascertained that "it is necessary to save this Fund." Undoubtedly, both the magazine and Greenspan knew why the latter felt that there could be a chain of bankruptcies of the most important banks in strategic centers.

The fourth personality who has definitely influenced the latest stage of capitalist economic development thinking is Milton Friedman. He is the father of the strict supply-side economics applied by many countries throughout the world and which the IMF advocates so strongly: the last recourse against the inflationary phenomenon that surged with extraordinary strength after Keynes.

At present, we can find a number of countries immersed in a depression, others in inflation, with recipes and measures that destabilize governments. The world has already realized that the International Monetary Fund will economically ruin and politically destabilize the countries it assists or tries to assist. Now more than ever we can rightly say that the assistance of the International Monetary Fund is like the devil's kiss.

Allow me to point out some facts which respond to the question I asked: "What is the legacy of capitalism and neoliberal globalization?" After 300 years of capitalism, the world now has 800 million hungry people. Now, at this very moment, there are one billion illiterates, four billion poor, 250 million children who work regularly and 130 million people who have no access to education. There are 100 million homeless and 11 million children under five years of age dying every year of malnutrition, poverty and preventable or curable diseases.

There is a growing gap between the poor and the rich, within countries and between countries; a callous and almost irreversible destruction of nature; an accelerated squandering and depletion of important non-renewable resources; pollution of the air and underground waters, rivers and oceans; climatic changes with unpredictable but already perceptible consequences. During the past century, more than one billion hectares of virgin forests were devastated and a similar area has become either desert or wasteland.

Thirty years ago hardly anyone discussed these issues; now it is crucial for our species. I don't want to give any more figures. All this is very easy to demonstrate and its disastrous results are self-evident.

In face of all this, perhaps many are wondering, "What is to be done?" Well, the Europeans have invented their own recipe. They are uniting. They have already approved and are in the process of implementing a single currency. The good wishes of the United States, according to their spokespersons, have not been lacking — good wishes which are as great as they are hypocritical, because everyone knows that what they really want is for the euro to fail. They say, "What a wonderful thing, the euro is very good, it is an excellent idea." This is the case of a rich, developed

Europe with an annual GDP per capita of $20,000 in some countries and of $25,000 to $30,000 in others. Compare these countries to others in our world with $500, $600 or $1,000.

And what shall we do? This is a question that we must all ask ourselves within this context, at a time when they are trying to swallow our countries. You can rest assure that this is what they would like to do. We should not expect another miracle like that when the prophet was delivered from the gut of a whale, because if that whale swallows us, we'll be thoroughly digested at full speed.

Yes, this is our hemisphere and I am here speaking from no other place than Venezuela, Bolívar's glorious homeland, where he dreamed, where he conceived the unity of our nations and worked for its attainment at a time when it took three months to travel from Caracas to Lima on horseback, when there were no cellular phones, no planes, no highways, no computers, nor anything of the sort. And yet, he foresaw the danger that those few, recently independent colonies, far up North, could pose. He was prophetic when he said, "The United States seems destined by Providence to plague the Americas with misery in the name of liberty." He launched the idea of our peoples' unity and struggled for it until his death. If it was a dream then, today it is a vital necessity.

How can solutions be worked out? They are difficult, very difficult. As I said, the Europeans have set a goal and are immersed in a tough competition with our neighbor of the North; this is obvious, a strong and growing competition. The United States does not want anyone to interfere with its interests in what it considers to be its hemisphere. It wants everything absolutely for itself. On the other hand, China in the Far East, is a huge nation and Japan is a powerful, industrial country.

I believe that globalization is an irreversible process and that the problem is not globalization *per se*, but rather the type of globalization. This is why it seems to me that for this difficult and tough undertaking, for which the peoples do not have much time, the Latin Americans are the ones who should hurry the most and struggle for unity, through agreements and regional integration, not only within Latin America but also between Latin America and the Caribbean. There we have our English-speaking sister nations of the Caribbean, the CARICOM members, who after barely a few years of independence have acted with impressive dignity.

I say this based on their behavior towards Cuba. When everybody in Latin America, except for Mexico, severed all ties with our country in response to U.S. pressures, the Caribbean nations, together with Torrijos, were the first to break through. They have struggled to break Cuba's isolation until the present time when Cuba maintains relations with the immense majority of Latin American and Caribbean countries. We know them and we appreciate them. They cannot be left to their own fate; they cannot be left in the hands of the WTO and its agreements. They cannot be left at the mercy of the U.S. banana transnational enterprises, which try to take away the small preferences that they so badly need. You cannot mend the world by leveling everything to the ground; that is the way the Yankees do it, by razing everything.

Several of these countries live from their plantations and produce only one percent of the banana market, two percent at the most, which is meaningless. The U.S. Government, to protect a U.S. transnational that owns three plantations in Central America, filed an appeal with the WTO and won. Now the Caribbean nations are very worried because similar procedures may be applied to take these preferences away, and because measures are being adopted to liquidate the Lome Convention, by virtue of which they enjoy some considerations as former colonies and countries in dire need of resources for development. It is unfair to take these considerations away from them.

It is not fair to treat all nations equally, as there are marked differences in their levels of development that cannot be ignored. It is not right to use the same recipe for all. It is not right to impose a single formula. Formulas for controlling and developing economic relations are of no use if they will only benefit the wealthy and the powerful. Both the IMF and the WTO want everything *tabula rasa*.

The OECD, the exclusive club of the wealthy, was rather secretly preparing a supranational Multilateral Agreement on Investments to establish the laws that would govern foreign investment — something like a worldwide Helms-Burton Act. They had almost everything ready when a nongovernmental organization got hold of a copy of the draft. The copy was disseminated through the internet creating a scandal in France, which rejected such a draft agreement; apparently they had not paid much attention to what was brewing at the OECD. Later, I think the Australians did the same; consequently, the draft, which had been worked out so secretly, was abandoned.

This is how many important and decisive international treaties are produced. Then, they put the draft on the table so that those who want to sign it may do so and those who do not, well, everyone knows what happens to those who do not want to sign. Not a single word was discussed with the countries that were to apply such standards. This is how they treat us. This is how they handle the most vital interests of our peoples.

They will continue. We must be very alert with these institutions. We must say that they were laying a big trap for us. So far, we have managed to sidestep it, but they will continue with their scheming to make our living conditions even worse. It was not only a matter of competing with everyone in the whole world and making desperate concessions in every field. The Multilateral Agreement on Investments was intended to facilitate their investments in the conditions they deem fit, respecting the environment if they wish, or poisoning the rivers in every country if they feel like it, destroying nature without anyone being able to demand anything from them. But Third World countries are a majority in the WTO and, if we can stop them from deceiving and dividing us, we can fight for our interests. Cuba could not be excluded from the WTO because it has been a member since its foundation.

But they do not want China in — at least they are putting up great resistance. China is making a great effort to enter the WTO because a 1,000 percent tariff can be applied to countries not belonging to this institution and their exports can be completely blocked. The richest countries are setting the rules and requirements that best suit them.

What is it that suits them? What is it they are after? They want to see the day when there will be no tariffs, when their investments will not be charged by the tax authorities in any country. They obtain years of tax exemption as a concession from underdeveloped countries thirsty for investments, where they get the lion's share and the right to do as they please in our countries with no restrictions whatsoever. They also impose the free circulation of capital and goods throughout the world. Of course, the exception is that commodity called Third World people — the modern slaves, the cheap labor power so abundant on our planet — who flood the free-trade zones in their own land or sweep streets, harvest vegetables and do the hardest and worst paid jobs when legally or illegally admitted into the former metropolis.

This is the type of global capitalism they want to impose. Our countries, full of free-trade zones, would have no other income but the meager salaries of those fortunate enough to get a job, while a bunch of billionaires accumulates untold fortunes.

The fact that a U.S. citizen, no matter how great his talent and expertise in technology and business matters, owns a $64 billion fortune, which is the annual income of more than 150 million human beings in the poorest countries, is something awesomely unequal and unfair. That this capital has been accumulated over a few years, because the stock value of the large U.S. enterprises double every three or four years through stock exchange transactions inflating the value of assets *ad infinitum*, shows a reality that cannot be considered rational, sustainable or endurable. Someone is paying for all that: the world and the astronomical figures of the poor, hungry, ill, illiterate and exploited people populating the Earth.

What year 2000 are we going to celebrate, and what kind of a new century will we live in? The world will reach that 21st century with people wrapped in papers living under New York bridges, while others amass enormous fortunes. There are many tycoons in that country but the number of those living under bridges, at the entrance of buildings or in slums is incomparably higher. In the United States, millions live in critical poverty, something in which the fanatical advocates of the economic order imposed upon humanity cannot take pride.

A few days ago I was talking with a U.S. delegation visiting Cuba, actually well-informed, friendly and outstanding religious people and scientists, and they told me that they were engaged in building a pediatric hospital in the Bronx. I asked them: "Is not there a pediatric hospital in the Bronx?" And they answered: "No." "And how many children are there in the Bronx?" I asked. And they said: "Four hundred thousand children." So there are 400,000 children in a city such as New York, many of them of Puerto Rican descent, of Hispanic descent in general, and Black, who do not have a pediatric hospital.

They also said that there are 11 million U.S. children who do not have medical insurance. They are mostly Black, mixed, Native American or the children of Hispanic immigrants. Do not think discrimination in that society is based only on skin color — no, it is not. Whether they have blond or dark hair, they are at times treated with contempt simply because they are Latin American.

There was a time when I visited that country, when I sat in cafeterias or stayed in those motels at the side of the road, and more than once I felt their contempt; they almost felt furious to have a Hispanic around. It impressed me as a society full of hatred.

Most of the 11 million children without medical insurance belong to those minorities living in the United States. They have the highest infant mortality rate. I asked them what was the infant mortality rate in the Bronx and they said they thought it was about 20 or 21 per 1,000 live births. There are worse places — in Washington itself it is quite high — and in areas where Hispanic immigrants mostly live it is 30 or more. It is not the same everywhere.

Their infant mortality is higher than that of Cuba. The blockaded country, the country targeted by their war and from which they stole 3,000 doctors, today has an infant mortality of 7.1 per every 1,000 live births. Our rates are better and they are very similar throughout the country. It is six in some provinces, not precisely in the capital; it may be eight in others, but it is within two or three percentage points of difference with the national average, because medical care reaches all social sectors and regions.

Even after the beginning of the "special period," in these eight terrible years, in 1998 we were able to reduce infant mortality to 7.1 from 10. It was an almost 30 percent reduction, even when we had entered a very difficult stage after the demise of the socialist camp, especially the Soviet

Union, with which we had most of our trade. Also the U.S. economic war against Cuba grew more severe. In 1993, for example, despite all our efforts, the per capita daily calorie intake had declined to 1,863 from 3,000 and to approximately 46g of animal or plant protein from 75g. Among other essentials, a very inexpensive, subsidized liter of milk was guaranteed to children under seven years of age.

We have managed to help the most vulnerable groups. If there is a severe drought or any other natural disaster we try to find resources wherever we can to protect everyone, especially the children and the elderly.

The establishment of new, very important scientific centers has been one of the advances of the revolution during the "special period." Our country produces 90 percent of its medications, even though some raw materials must be imported from very distant places. We have shortages of medications, that is true, but everything possible has been done to always have the most essential ones in stock, to have a central reserve, in case some may be missing one day, and we are trying to have more reserves.

These actions had to be taken because we must anticipate in order to have the capacity to protect those in greatest need. Of course, it is also possible to receive medications sent by relatives abroad; we facilitate this as much as possible; we do not charge anything at all, no tariff is paid for that, but we do all we can for the state to offer these resources to our entire population.

Despite the said decline in food consumption, we have been able to reduce infant mortality by 30 percent. We have also maintained and even raised life expectancy. On the other hand, not a single school was closed; not a single teacher lost their job; on the contrary, teacher-training colleges and institutions are open for all those who wish to enroll.

I must clarify that we have not been able to do the same in all professions. In medicine, we have already had to set certain limits, looking for higher qualifications, for a higher standard for those entering the profession. We have graduated many doctors in our struggle against our neighbor and we let them migrate if they wanted to. In that battle we established 21 medical colleges.

Right now we are offering 1,000 scholarships to Central American students to be trained as doctors in our country and an additional 500 each year for 10 years; we are establishing a Latin American medical school. With the cuts we have made in expenses, even in defense expenditure despite the dangers we face, we will be able to locate the medical school in the former facilities of an excellent school for civil and military navy captains and technicians, whose school has been moved to another facility. The medical school will be ready in March [1999] and the first Central

American students will arrive for a six months' premedical catch-up course to refresh their knowledge and prevent later dropouts. In September more than 1,000 Central American students will be studying their first year of medicine in Cuba. I don't know if it is necessary to add that their studies will be absolutely free of charge.

Perhaps I should say — and do not take it as an advertisement for Cuba but as an example of what can be done with very little — that we offered 2,000 doctors to the Central American countries hit by Hurricane Mitch. We have said that, if a developed country or some developed countries — and some have already responded — supply the medications, our medical personnel are ready to work in Central America saving every year — I repeat, every year! — as many lives as were lost in the hurricane, supposing there were about 30,000 casualties, as reported. Twenty-five thousand of those lives to be saved would be children.

According to estimates, medications required to save a child often cost only a few cents. What cannot be bought at any price is a trained physician ready to work in the mountains, in the remotest places, in swampy areas, full of insects, snakes, mosquitoes and some diseases that do not exist in our country. And none of them hesitate. The immense majority of our doctors have volunteered for that task. They are ready for this and 400 of them are now working in Central America; 250 doctors are already working in Haiti, a country that received the same offer after Hurricane George hit it.

The percentage of lives that can be saved in Haiti is higher because infant mortality there is 130 or 132. It means that by reducing it to 35 — and in our country we know very well how to do it — 100 children a year for every 1,000 live births would be saved. That is why the potential is greater. Its population is 7.5 million, and the birth rate is very high, thus, doctors there could save more lives. In Central America the average [infant mortality] rate in the countries hit by the hurricane is about 50 or 60, almost half of the lives that can be potentially saved.

I warn you that these are conservative estimates. On the other hand, we do not want our doctors working in the cities because we do not want any local physician to be affected in any way by the presence of the Cuban doctors. Cuban doctors offer their services in the places where there are no doctors and where other doctors would not go. On the contrary, we want to have the best relations with local doctors, we want to cooperate with them, whether they are in private practice or not. If they are interested in a case, it is all right with us.

We have said that cooperation with local doctors is necessary, as is cooperation with other sectors. Our doctors are not going there to preach political ideas; they are going to accomplish a humanitarian mission. That is their task. There should also be cooperation with priests and pastors, since many of these have been carrying out their work in isolated places. Some of our first doctors to arrive lived in parish facilities.

We are very pleased with this cooperation. They are working in delicate situations, where there are indigenous people who speak their own language, people with great dignity, and peasants who live in small villages. That facilitates the doctors' work because in Cuba peasants live far from each other in the mountains, so they must walk long distances to visit the patients regularly, while in a village they can visit more than once a day.

A program is being implemented there that says much about what can be done with a minimum of material resources. What is most important and those gentlemen, the managers of the financial institutions I have mentioned do not know it, is that there is a capital worth much more than all their millions: the human capital.

Perhaps, one day I will meet one of those assistants to Bill Gates, who is a computing champion, so that I can ask: "Can you tell me how many Americans have served abroad since the Peace Corps was created?" This is to determine if there have been more [volunteers] than the number of Cubans who have [served abroad], due to the generous and cooperative spirit of that slandered and ignored island and people, against which a war is being waged — a war never waged against the apartheid fascists. I am speaking about an economic war. I know many decent, altruistic Americans and it is meritorious that so many altruistic people live in a place whose system sows only selfishness and the venom of individualism. I respect these Americans. I have met some of those who have served with the Peace Corps; but I am sure that since their creation they have not been able to mobilize the number Cuba has mobilized.

Once, when Nicaragua requested 1,000 teachers we invited volunteers and 30,000 offered. Later, when the bandits organized and supplied by the United States who waged that dirty war against the Sandinistas murdered some of our teachers — who were not in the cities, but in the most isolated places in the countryside, sharing the peasants' living conditions — 100,000 volunteered to go. This is what I mean! And I must add that most of them were women, because women are the majority in that profession.

That is why I am discussing ideas; that is why I am discussing consciousness. That is why I believe what I am saying, that is why I believe in humankind. Because when so many of our fellow countrymen and women went or were ready to go to those places, consciousness and the idea of solidarity and internationalism proved to be a mass phenomenon.

I will complete my idea. I already said that they took half our doctors and more than half of the professors from the only medical school in Cuba. We accepted the challenge — there is nothing like a challenge —

and today Cuba has 64,000 doctors, one for every 176 people, twice the number of doctors per capita in the most industrialized of all the countries in the First World. And what I did not say is that since the beginning of the "special period" we have incorporated 25,000 new doctors into health institutions and communities throughout the country in towns, country, plains and mountains. This is really human capital!

It is much easier to conquer a person than to buy them. Fortunately, it is much easier, because with its so-called easing of the blockade — intended to deceive the world — what the U.S. administration is actually saying is that every American should buy a Cuban. I say: "So, let us raise the price then, because there are 27 Americans for every Cuban." After all it has done against our country, after intensifying its economic war under the pressure of the extreme right, this administration had the ultimate idea: to buy us one by one. Not ministers, administrative cadre or political leaders but common citizens, by granting permission to every American — always with the administration's prior consent, of course — to send remittances to Cubans, even if they are not related.

Very well, now we know we are worth something since there are people willing to pay for us, a very rich government trying to buy us out. There are four billion poor in the world and they are not willing to pay a dime for any of them. Our quotation in the market has been climbing.

I am telling you this because we are extending our medical care program to Suriname, which requested over 60 doctors. Even authorities from an autonomous province in Canada requested our doctors. They say: "We can't find doctors wanting to serve in the Arctic Circle. They don't want to come." We immediately told them: "Yes, but you discuss it with your government. It is up to you." Of course, conditions would be different, not because we would profit from it but because it is only logical for things to be different in case of an industrialized country. The doctors' services would be reasonably although modestly remunerated, since what moves us are not economic interests, but sincere wishes for international cooperation in the field of health, in which we have abundant human resources.

If the Canadian official can overcome all the obstacles to take the doctors there, we will have Cuban doctors from the Amazonian jungle to the Arctic Circle. But we are focused on the Third World. We pay our doctors their modest salaries in our country. It is good, we are all happy about that and our doctors are very happy with this arrangement; their morale is very high and they come from a great internationalist tradition.

We have received requests for cooperation from other places. Thus, the idea emerged of helping Haiti and later Central America. Now we see it is extending through Latin America and the Caribbean. We have no money, but we have human capital.

You should not think I am boasting when I say that they would have to bring together all the doctors in the United States — however many they are — to try to find 2,000 volunteers ready to go to the swamps, mountains and inhospitable places where our doctors go. It would be worthwhile to see what would happen, even though I know there are also altruistic doctors over there, that's for sure. But to find 2,000 willing to leave the standard of living a consumer society offers and go to a swamp in the Mosquito Coast, a place that not even the Spanish conquerors could stand — and that is really saying something — that, perhaps, they may be unable to do. But Cuban doctors are there: that is human capital. If we take one out of every three doctors, we could offer the rest of Latin America the program we have offered Haiti and Central America, in places where similar conditions exist, where children and adults die for lack of medical care, in places no one else goes to. We have made the offer and it seems it will be accepted; and our country will be in a position to respond. Such is the kind of human capital that can be created!

How many lives can be saved? We have suggested the idea of having the countries in our region unite to save a million lives every year, including the lives of hundreds of thousands children. The cost of saving a million lives can be accurately estimated and saving the lives of children is the least costly, because older people need more laboratory tests and radiography, more medications and all that, while children survive almost by themselves after the first year of life. At times a vaccine worth a few cents saves a life. Polio is a case in point.

We believe that a million lives can be saved every year with a small part of the money wasted in extravagant expenditure and there are doctors ready for the task. There may be more than enough medications in Europe, but they will not save a million lives without the 15,000 to 20,000 doctors required to undertake a program such as this.

I AM TELLING YOU ABOUT this so you know what Cuba is today, why Cuba is like that and what the prevailing standards are in Cuba, a country so miserably slandered in matters of human rights. A country where in 40 years of revolution there has never been a missing person, where there has never been a tortured person, where there are no death squads and no political assassinations — nothing like that has ever happened. A country where there are no elderly people abandoned, no children living in the streets, without schools or teachers, no people left to their own lot.

We know very well what has happened in some of the places where our neighbors from the North have been, such as those who organized the 1954 ousting of the government in one of the most important countries in the Central American region. They brought in their advisers with their handbooks on torture, repression and death. For many years there were no prisoners, this category did not exist, only dead and missing persons. A hundred thousand missing persons in just one country! And 50,000 killed. We could add what happened in many other countries with torture, murders, missing persons, repeated U.S. military interventions under any pretext or no pretext at all.

They do not remember that, they do not speak about that; they have lost their memory. In the light of the terrible experience undergone by the peoples of our America, we challenge them. We will demonstrate with actual facts, with reality, who has a humane sense of life, who has true humanitarian feelings and who is capable of doing something for humankind that is not lies, slogans, misinformation, hypocrisy, deception and everything they have been doing in our region throughout this century.

I know you do not need me to clarify all this for you but since I broached the subject I feel it is my duty to say so. One frequently meets misinformed persons who believe at least some of the tons of lies and slanders that have been cast against our country in an attempt to batter us, to weaken us, to isolate us, to divide us. They have not been able to divide us and they won't be able to!

I have said all these things to you in the greatest intimacy. I could not come now and speak to you as I did in 1959 about organizing an expedition to solve a problem in a neighboring country. We know very well that today no country can solve its problems by itself. That is a reality in this globalized world. We can say here: "Either we are all saved or we all sink."

Martí said: "Humanity is my homeland." This is one of the most extraordinary things he said. That is how we have to think: Humanity is our homeland!

I remember a case in Cuban history of a Spanish officer who during the Ten Years' War — the first war for the independence of Cuba — when the Spanish government executed eight innocent medical students accused of desecrating the tomb of a rightist Spanish extremist, broke his sword in an eternal gesture of indignation and protest and exclaimed: "Humanity comes before one's homeland." Of course, some parts of humankind are closer to home. When we think of humankind, the first thing that comes to our mind is our Latin American and Caribbean brothers and sisters, whom we never forget. Then, comes the rest of that humanity on our planet. We will have to learn that concept, those principles contained in Martí's words — not only learn them, but feel them and practice them.

It is the Latin American countries' duty to unite without losing a single minute; the Africans are trying to do it. In Southeast Asia they have ASEAN and are looking for other forms of economic integration. Europe is doing it at a swift pace. That is, there will be subregional and regional alliances in various parts of the world.

Bolívar dreamed of an extended regional federation from Mexico to Argentina. As you well know, the gentlemen from the North sabotaged the Amphictyonic Congress. They opposed Bolívar's idea of sending an expedition commanded by Sucre to liberate the island of Cuba and remove all risks of threat or counterattack by the fearful and tenacious Spanish metropolis; so we were not forgotten in Venezuelan history. Now that we are free from the domination of a much stronger power, our most sacred duty is to defend our freedom for the very interests and security of our brothers and sisters in this hemisphere.

Obviously, we must work out various forms of cooperation and integration, step by step, but with swift steps if we want to survive as a regional entity with the same culture, the same language and so many things in common. Europe does not have a common language — I don't know how an Italian understands an Austrian or a Finn, how a German speaks with a Belgian or a Portuguese — but they have been able to create the European Union and they are quickly advancing toward a greater economic integration. Why can't we consider this type of formulae? Why don't we encourage all the unitary and integrationist trends in every country sharing our language, our culture, our beliefs and the mixed blood running through the immense majority of us? And, where there is no mixed blood in our veins, there should be mixed blood in our souls.

Who were those who fought in the Ayacucho battle? Men from the lowlands and from Caracas; Venezuelans from the West and the East, Colombians, Peruvians and Ecuadorians who were together; that is how they could do what they did. The unforgettable cooperation of Argentines and Chileans was also present. Our greatest sin is that we lost this, after almost 200 years.

Eleven years from now we will celebrate the 200th anniversary of the proclamation of the Venezuelan independence and later, that of other countries. Almost 200 years! What have we done in those 200 years, divided, fragmented, Balkanized, submitted as we have been? It is easier to control the seven dwarfs than to control a boxer, even if he is a lightweight. They have wanted to keep us as divided, neighboring dwarfs so they can control us.

I was discussing the need for unity not only in South America but in Central America and the Caribbean as well, and this is the moment to say this, given what is happening in Venezuela. They have tried to divide us. The great power in the North wants NAFTA and nothing more; a Free-Trade Agreement and fast track — I believe fast track means quick, right? A quick step? Yes, I also recommend a fast track for us, a fast track to unite. The Latin American answer to the fast track from the North should be a fast track from the Center and the South.

Brazil should have our support and encouragement. We know very well that the United States does not like the existence of MERCOSUR, for it is an important embryo of an alliance that may grow. Some neighboring countries are not too far away from MERCOSUR. We see it as a sub-regional alliance, as a step toward a regional alliance, first of South America and then another step, as quickly as possible, to embrace the Caribbean and Central America.

We are considering the need to advance in the contacts, the concept, the arrangements and the practical steps that may be taken in that direction before we can afford to consider the creation of a common currency. We believe that in that field the most we can do right now is to elaborate ideas and concepts. Meanwhile, we need to avoid, at all cost, the political and economic suicide of replacing our national currencies with the U.S. currency, despite the difficulties and fluctuations imposed by the present economic order. That would be tantamount to the annexation of Latin America to the United States. We would not be considered independent nations any more and we would be renouncing every possibility of taking part in the restructuring of the future world. Under the present circumstances it is absolutely indispensable to unite, to come together and to expand our forces.

The meeting of the Caribbean Basin states will be held in the Dominican Republic on April. Later, almost immediately, there will be a meeting with the European Union in Rio de Janeiro. We have some common interests with the Europeans. Living under the slavery of only one currency, as we are now, is a tragedy, and we are happy that with the euro, a rival to the Olympic champion, to the gold medal winner, has come into being.

The strengthening of the United Nations is another necessity that cannot be deferred. The United Nations must be democratized. The General Assembly, where all the member countries are represented, should be granted the highest authority, as well as the functions and role befitting it. The Security Council's dictatorship must end together with the dictatorship the United States exercises within that body.

If the veto power cannot be eliminated because those who have the last word about such a reform are precisely those with the power to veto it, we strongly demand at least that the privilege be shared. The number of permanent members must be suitably increased from the five they are now in compliance with the growth of UN membership and the great changes that have taken place in 50 years. The Third World, where a great number of countries emerged as independent states after World War II, should have the possibility to share equal prerogatives in that important UN body. We have defended the idea of having two representatives for

Latin America and the Caribbean basin, two for Africa and two for the underdeveloped regions in Asia, as a minimum. If two are not enough, the figure could be increased to three, in one or more of the above-mentioned regions. We constitute the immense majority at the UN General Assembly and cannot continue being ignored.

We would not oppose the admission of other industrialized countries, but we give absolute priority to the presence of permanent representatives of Latin America and the Caribbean and the other above-mentioned regions in the Security Council, with the same prerogatives as its other permanent members. If it is not so, we will have three categories of members: permanent members with veto power, permanent members without veto power and non-permanent members. And there is still more of this madness. Aiming at dividing and thus preserving the privileges of their present status, at the same time as reducing the prerogatives of the potential new permanent members, the United States has come up with the idea of rotating that position among two or more countries from the various regions; that is, to reduce this vital reform to zero, to nothing, to simple salt and water.

There is another way to regulate the worrying veto prerogative with an increase in the number of members needed to apply it; that is, the General Assembly may be given the possibility of taking part in the main decisions. Wouldn't this be more democratic and fair?

A battle must be waged there. All Third World countries should unite. We say that to Africans when we meet with them, also to Asians, to the Caribbeans, to everyone in every international agency: the United Nations, the Nonaligned Nations Movement, the Lome meetings, the Group of 77, everywhere. We are a large number of countries sharing common interests, wishing to advance and develop; we are the overwhelming majority in almost all international institutions, and you may rest assured that we are advancing in building an awareness about the fate imposed on us. We must work, persuade, fight and persevere. We must never be discouraged.

Those in the North are constantly scheming to divide us. I am going to give you four examples concerning Latin America.

They do not like MERCOSUR, which has already achieved some measure of economic success, even though it is but an embryo of the great regional integration we hope for but which they do not want at all. What is it they propose? Well, many things. First, they organize those hemispheric meetings leaving out Cuba, a reaction to the first Ibero-American Summit in Guadalajara.

They propose the idea of having only one Latin American permanent member in the Security Council, to have several important members of our region confronting each other. They immediately add the advisability of rotating the position among Brazil, Argentina and Mexico, of course with no veto power. Then, they create the special category of strategic ally for Argentina. That plants distrust and restlessness among important fraternal neighbors that should closely unite and cooperate, particularly now when MERCOSUR is advancing.

They made the Machiavellian decision of releasing the sale of sophisticated arms to countries in the region, which may unleash a costly, destructive and fissiparous arms race among them. Why arms when there is neither a Cold War nor the ghost of the Soviet Union or any other foreign threat to security but that coming from the United States itself? Can these arms contribute to the unity, cooperation, integration, progress and peace among us? What do we need to open up our eyes and finally understand the geo-strategic purposes of this policy?

They have not been able to isolate our small country everywhere. We already take part in the Ibero-American Summits. We are members of the Association of Caribbean States. We belong to the Latin American Economic System and have been included in the Latin American Integration Association. We maintain excellent relations with the Caribbean Community (CARICOM). We will be present in the important Summit of the European Union, Latin America and the Caribbean to be held in Rio de Janeiro. We have been admitted as observers among the countries in the Lome Convention. We are active members of the Group of 77 and hold an outstanding place as founding members of the Nonaligned Nations Movement. We belong to the WTO and are very present at the United Nations, which is a great forum and an institution that, once democratized, may become a basic pillar for a fair and humane globalization.

What are we doing there? Talking, explaining, submitting problems that we know touch a large part of humankind very intimately because we are free to do it. There are fraternal countries in Africa, Asia, Latin America and other places that would like to submit many things with much energy but do not have the same possibilities as Cuba. Being excluded from all international financial institutions, blockaded and subjected to economic warfare, invulnerable to any retaliation of that type, strengthened by 40 years of long, hard struggle that gives us an absolute liberty to do anything, Cuba can speak up. Others may be in crucial need of a credit from the World Bank or from the Inter-American Bank or from another regional bank, or of some negotiation with the International Monetary Fund, or of an export credit, which is one of the many mechanisms used by the United States to limit their possibilities of action. That is why quite often Cuba has taken upon itself such a task.

In spite of everything, there are people in our impoverished world who are so courageous that, for example, at the United Nations, the

Cuban motion against the blockade received the support of 157 votes against two. We had spent seven years on this exercise. The first time there were some 55 votes in favor and four or five against and all the rest, abstentions or absences. Who could want to be at odds with the Yankees? Because voting there is by show of hands.

But people lose fear and fear was gradually lost; dignity may grow and it does. The following year, there were more than 60, then more than 70, then over 100. Now, after we have the support of almost 160 countries and only two are against, it can hardly grow anymore. In the end, there will be no country supporting this inhuman, cruel and unlimited action except the United States, unless a day comes when the United States votes for us and supports the Cuban motion!

We are making progress, gaining ground. People know, intuitively or instinctively, that we are very often slandered. The majority of people have a great instinct! Besides, people know them, how they are everywhere doing all sorts of things, abusing people and sowing selfishness and hatred. People know them. Contempt is difficult to hide and the Third World countries suffer under such arrogance and contempt.

The various U.S. administrations with their blockade, their constant harassment and their exclusions have given us the possibility of fighting them face to face and of being even joyful to be excluded in exchange for the freedom to speak without compromise in any forum of the world where there are so many just causes to defend.

For the reasons I have already explained we may have some sympathies with other countries. To those who are the mainstay of reaction and injustice in our times, we can speak the truth and always the truth, with and without relations, with and without a blockade. They should entertain no illusions that, if some day they lift the blockade, Cuba will stop speaking as frankly and honestly as it has done for 40 years! It is a historic duty.

I BEGAN TELLING YOU THAT [Venezuela] is a country I love dearly. This is when I began to tell you about my love for history, for universal history, for the history of revolutions and wars, for the history of Cuba, the history of Latin America, and especially for that of Venezuela. That is why I identify so much with Bolívar's life and ideas.

Fate would have it that Venezuela should be the country to fight the most for the independence of this hemisphere. It began here, and you had a legendary precursor like Miranda, who even led a French army in campaign, waging famous battles, which during the French Revolution prevented an invasion of French territory. He had also fought in the United States for that country's independence. I have a wide collection of books about Miranda's great life, although I have not been able to read them all. The Venezuelans, therefore, had Miranda, the forefather of Latin America's independence, and later Bolívar, the Liberator, who was always for me the greatest among the greatest men in history.

[Responding to the audience:] Please, put me in the forty-thousandth place. One of Martí's phrases is deeply engraved in my mind: "All the glory in the world can fit into a kernel of corn." Many great people in history were concerned about glory and that is no reason to criticize them. Perhaps it was the concept of their time, a sense of history, the future, the importance of events in their lives that they took for glory. This is natural and understandable. Bolívar liked to speak about glory; he spoke very strongly about glory. He cannot be criticized; a great aura of glory will forever be attached to his name.

Martí's concept, which I entirely share, associates glory with personal vanity and self-exaltation. The role of the individual in important historical events has been very much debated. What I especially like about Martí's phrase is the idea of an individual's insignificance as compared to the enormous significance and transcendence of humanity and the immeasurable reach of universe, the reality that we are really like a small speck of dust floating in space. However, that reality does not diminish human greatness a single bit. On the contrary, it is enhanced when, as in Bolívar's case, he carried in his mind a whole universe of just ideas and noble sentiments. That is why I admire Bolívar so much. That is why I consider his work so immense. He does not belong to the stock of men who conquered territories and nations, or founded empires that gave fame to others; he created nations, freed territories and tore down empires. He was also a brilliant soldier, a distinguished thinker and prophet.

Today, we are trying to do what he wanted to do and what still remains to be done. We are trying to unite our peoples so that tomorrow human beings will be able to know and live in a united, fraternal, just and free world. That is what he wanted to do with the white, black, native and mixed peoples of our America.

I seem to perceive at this moment an exceptional situation in the history of Venezuela. I have witnessed two unique moments: first, that moment in January 1959, and 40 years later, I have seen the extraordinary volatility of the people on February 2, 1999. I have seen a people reborn. A people such as I saw in Plaza del Silencio [Silence Square] where I was a bit more silent than I have been here... Those were unquestionably revolutionary masses.

It was once again very impressive to see the people in such extraordinary high spirits although under different circumstances. Back then hopes had been left behind. I do not want to explain why; I leave that to the historians. This time hope lies ahead. I see in these hopes a true rebirth of Venezuela, or at least an exceptionally great opportunity for Venezuela. I see it coming not only in the interest of Venezuelans; I also see it in the interest of Latin Americans. I see it as something in the interest of other peoples in the world as it advances — because there is no other choice — toward a universal globalization.

There is no way of escaping it, and there is no alternative. So I am not trying to flatter you with my words. I rather remind you of your duty, the duty of the nation, of the people, of all those who were born after that visit [in 1959], of the youngest, of the more mature, who really have a great responsibility ahead of you. Opportunities have often been lost, but you would not be forgiven if you lose this one.

The person speaking to you here has had the privilege and the opportunity of accumulating some political experience, of having lived through a revolutionary process in a country where, as I have already said, people did not even want to hear about socialism. And when I say people, I mean the vast majority. That same majority supported the revolution, supported the leaders, and supported the Rebel Army — but there were ghosts that they were afraid of. Like Pavlov did with his famous dogs, the United States created conditioned reflexes in many of us, including who knows how many millions of Latin Americans.

We have had to fight a lot against scarcity and poverty. We have had to learn to do a lot with very little. We had good and bad moments, the former especially when we were able to establish trade agreements with the socialist bloc and the Soviet Union and demanded fairer prices for our export products. We resorted to diplomacy and the eloquence that revolutionaries in a country that had to overcome so many obstacles must have.

Actually, the Soviets felt great sympathy for Cuba and great admiration for our revolution. It was very surprising for them to see that after so many years a tiny country, right next to the United States, would rebel against that mighty superpower. They had never contemplated such a possibility and they would have never advised it to anyone. Luckily we never asked anybody for advice, although we had already read almost a whole library of the works of Marx, Engels, Lenin and other theoreticians. We were convinced Marxists and socialists.

With that fever and that blind passion that characterizes young people, and sometimes old people too, I absorbed the basic principles that I learned from those books and they helped me understand the society in which I lived. Until then it was for me an intricate puzzle for which I could not find any convincing explanation. I must say that the famous *Communist Manifesto*, which Marx and Engels took so long to write — you can tell that its main author worked conscientiously — impressed me tremendously. For the first time in my life I realized a few truths.

Before that, I was a sort of a utopian communist, drawing my own conclusions while studying the first political economy course they taught us in law school from an enormous book with some 900 mimeographed pages. It was a political economy inspired by the ideas of capitalism but which mentioned and analyzed very briefly the different schools of thought. Later, in the second course, I paid much more attention to the subject and after meditating on it all, I ended up a utopian communist. I call it that because my doctrine had no scientific or historical basis whatsoever but was based on the good intentions of a student recently graduated from a Jesuit school. I am very grateful because [the Spanish Jesuits] taught me some things that have helped me in life — although very distant from any of the ideas I uphold today — above all, to have strength, a certain sense of honor and definite ethical principles.

I left that school an athlete, an explorer and a mountain climber. I entered the University of Havana ignorant about politics, without a revolutionary private tutor, who would have been so useful to me at that stage of my life.

That is how I came to have my own ideas, which I maintain with growing loyalty and fervor. Maybe it is because I now have a little more experience and knowledge, and maybe also because I have had the opportunity of meditating about new problems that did not exist during Marx's time.

For example, the word *environment* was probably never pronounced by anyone during Karl Marx's lifetime, except Malthus, who said that the population grew in geometric progression and that there would not be enough food for so many people. He, thus, became a sort of forerunner of today's ecologists, although he maintained ideas concerning the economy and salaries we cannot but disagree with.

SO I AM WEARING THE same jacket I wore when I came to this university 40 years ago, the same one I wore when I attacked the Moncada garrison [in July 1953], when we disembarked from the *Granma* [in December 1956]. I would venture to say, despite the many pages of adventure that anyone can find in my revolutionary life, that I always tried to be wise and sensible, although perhaps I have been more wise than sensible.

In our conception and development of the Cuban Revolution, we acted as Martí said when, on the eve of his death in combat, he addressed the great anti-imperialist goal of his struggle: "I have had to work quietly and somewhat indirectly, because to achieve certain objectives, they must be kept under cover; to proclaim them for what they are would raise such difficulties that the objectives could not be attained."

I was discreet, but not as much as I should have been because I would explain Marx's ideas about class society to everyone I met. So, they began to take me for a communist in the people's movement whose slogan in its fight against corruption was "Dignity against Money." I had joined that movement as soon as I arrived at the university. Toward the end of my university studies, I was no longer a utopian communist but rather an atypical communist who was acting independently. I based myself on a realistic analysis of our country's situation.

Those were the times of McCarthyism and Cuba's Marxist party, the People's Socialist Party, was almost completely isolated. However, within the movement I had joined, which had now become the Cuban People's Party, in my opinion, a large mass had a class instinct but lacked a class consciousness: peasants, workers, professionals, middle-class people — good, honest, potentially revolutionary people. Its founder and leader [Eduardo Chibás], a man of great charisma, had dramatically taken his own life a few months before the 1952 coup d'état. The younger ranks of that party later became an important part of our movement.

I was a member of that political organization which, as usually happened, was already falling into the hands of rich people, and I knew by heart what was going to happen after the then inevitable electoral triumph. But I had come up with some ideas on my own — just imagine the things a utopian can think up! — about what had to be done in Cuba and how to do it, despite the United States. Those masses had to be led along a revolutionary path. Maybe that was the merit of the tactic we pursued. Of course, we were reading the books of Marx, Engels and Lenin.

When we attacked the Moncada garrison we left one of Lenin's books behind, and the first thing the propaganda machine of Batista's regime said during the trial was that it was a conspiracy of corrupt members of the recently overthrown government, bankrolled with their money, and communist, too. No one knows how both categories could be reconciled!

In the trial, I assumed my own defense. It was not that I thought myself a good lawyer but I thought that I was the person who could best defend myself at that moment. I put on a gown and took my place with the lawyers. It was a political and not a penal trial. I did not intend to be acquitted but to disseminate ideas. I began to cross-examine all those killers who had murdered dozens upon dozens of our comrades and were there as witnesses; I turned the trial against them. So the next day they took me out of there, they put me away and declared me ill.

That was the last thing they did although they really wanted to do away with me once and for all; but I knew very well why they checked themselves. I knew the psychology of all of those people. It was due to the mood and the situation with the people, the rejection and huge indignation caused by all the murders they had committed. I also had a bit of luck. But the fact is that at the beginning, while they were questioning me, this book of Lenin appears. Someone takes it out and says: "You people had a book by Lenin."

We were explaining who we were: followers of Martí, that was the truth, that we had nothing to do with that corrupt government that they had ousted from power, that our objectives were such and such. However, we did not say a word about Marxism-Leninism, neither did we have to. We said what we had to say, but since the subject of the book came up at the trial, I felt really irritated and said: "Yes, that book by Lenin is ours, we read Lenin's books and other socialist books, and whoever does not read them is ignorant." That is what I told the judges and the rest of the people there. That was insufferable. We were not going to say: "Listen, that little book was planted there by somebody..."

Our program had been presented when I defended myself at the trial. Therefore, if they did not know what we thought it was because they did not want to know. Perhaps they tried to ignore that speech, which became known as *History Will Absolve Me*, with which I defended myself all alone. As I explained, I was expelled, they declared me ill, they tried all the others and sent me to a hospital to try me in a small ward. They did not exactly hospitalize me, but put me in an isolated prison cell. In the hospital, they turned a small ward into a courtroom with the judges and a few other people crammed into it, most of them from the military. They tried me there, and I had the pleasure of saying there all that I thought, everything, quite defiantly.

I wonder why they were not able to deduce our political thought, for it was all there in the open. You might say it contained the foundation of a socialist program, although we were convinced the time was not ripe, that the right time and stages would come. That was when we spoke about the land reform among many other things of a social and economic nature. We said that all the profits obtained by all those gentlemen with so much money — that is, the surplus value but without using such terminology — should be used for the development of the country, and I hinted that it was the government's responsibility to look after the development of the country and that surplus money.

I even spoke about the golden calf. I recalled the Bible once again and singled out "those who worshipped the golden calf," in a clear reference to those who expected everything from capitalism. That was enough for them to deduce our way of thinking.

Later, I have contemplated that it is likely that many of those who could be affected by a true revolution did not believe us at all, because in the 57 years of Yankee neocolonialism, many a progressive or revolutionary program had been proclaimed. The ruling classes never believed our program to be possible or permissible by the United States. They did not pay much attention to it. They heeded it and even found it amusing. At the end of the day, all those programs were abandoned and people would become corrupt. So they probably said: "Yes, the illusions of these romantic young men are very pretty, very nice, but why worry about that?"

They did not like Batista. They admired the frontal attack against his abusive and corrupt regime, and they possibly underestimated the thoughts contained in that declaration, which were the basis of what we later did and of what we think today. The difference is that many years of experience have further enriched our knowledge and perceptions about all those problems. So, as I have said, that is the way I have thought since then.

We have undergone the tough experience of a long revolutionary period, especially during the last 10 years, confronting extremely powerful forces under very difficult circumstances. Well, I will tell you the truth: we achieved what seemed impossible. I would venture to say that near miracles were performed. Of course, the laws were passed exactly as they had been promised, always with angry and arrogant U.S. opposition. It had had great influence in our country, so it made itself felt and the process became increasingly radicalized with each blow and each aggression we suffered.

Thus began the long struggle we have waged until today. The forces in our country polarized. Fortunately, the vast majority was in favor of the revolution and a minority, around 10 percent or less, was against it. So there has always been a great consensus and a great support for that process up to now. One knows what to worry about, because we made a great effort to overcome the prejudices that existed, to convey ideas, to build a consciousness, and it was not an easy work.

I remember the first time I spoke about racial discrimination. I had to go on television about three times. I was surprised at how deeply rooted — more than we had supposed — had become the prejudices brought to us by our northern neighbors: that certain clubs were for white people only and the rest could not go there, as well as certain beaches. Almost all the beaches, especially in the capital, were exclusively for whites. There were even segregated parks and promenades, where according to the color of your skin you had to walk in one direction or another. What we did was to open all the beaches for all of the people and from the very first days we prohibited discrimination in all places of recreation, parks and promenades. That humiliating injustice was incompatible with the revolution.

One day I spoke and I explained these things. There was such a reaction, such rumors and so many lies! They said we were going to force white men into marrying black women and white women into marrying black men. Well, just like that other preposterous invention that we were going to deprive families of the parental custody of their children. I once again had to go on television on the subject of discrimination to reply to all those rumors and machinations and explain the matter. That phenomenon, which was nothing but an imposed racist culture, a humiliating, cruel prejudice was very hard to eradicate.

In other words, during those years, we devoted a great deal of our time to two things: defending ourselves from invasions, threats of foreign aggression, dirty war, assassination attempts, sabotages, etc. and building consciousness. There was a moment when there were armed mercenary bands in every province of our country, promoted and supplied by the United States. But we confronted them immediately, giving them no time. They had not the slightest chance to prosper because our own experience in irregular warfare was very recent and we were practically one of the few revolutionary countries that totally defeated these bands despite the logistical support they received from abroad. We had to devote a lot of our time to that.

ONE PROBLEM I SEE, ONE source of concern I have is that many expectations have been raised in Venezuela by the extraordinary results of the elections, and this is logical. What do I mean? I mean the natural, logical tendency of the people to dream, to wish that a great number of accumulated problems be solved in a matter of months. As an honest friend of yours, in my own opinion, I think there are problems here that will not be solved in months, or years.

That is why I read the data. We are daily analyzing similar data in our country: the price of nickel or sugar; the yield of a hectare of sugarcane; if there is a drought, if there is not; how much income we are getting; how much we owe; what must be purchased urgently; the prices of powdered milk, cereals, indispensable medicines, inputs for production and all the other things and what is to be done.

At a given point in time our sugar production was boosted, almost doubled. There were good prices, we purchased machinery and began to build the infrastructure. Investments in industry and agriculture increased, limited only by Soviet technological resources, which were more advanced in some fields and less advanced in others. They generally consumed too much fuel.

But we bought all the steel we needed that was not covered by our national production. Half a million cubic meters of timber arrived in Cuba from Siberia every year, purchased with sugar, nickel and other products that, thanks to the sliding prices — the agreement we had reached before the oil prices surge — increased their prices as the price of oil increased. And do you know how much we got to consume? Thirteen million tons a year. Not only due to all the transportation services, the mechanization of agriculture and port facilities, the construction of tens of thousands of kilometers of highway, hundreds of big and small dams, mainly for agriculture, houses, dairy farms, all equipped with milking machines, thousands of schools and other social facilities, but also because of the power consumption in industries and homes. The electrification of the country benefited 95 percent of the population. There were resources but we were not able to manage them with maximum efficiency.

Now we do, we have learned. In times of abundance, you do not learn much, but in times of scarcity, real scarcity, you learn quite a lot. But we did all those things that allowed us to achieve these results in the economic, social and other spheres I have talked about.

Our country also holds first place in education, in teachers per capita. Recently, UNESCO issued a very rewarding report. A survey was conducted among 54,000 children in the third and fourth grade of elementary school about their knowledge of mathematics and language, in 14 Latin American countries, among the most advanced. An average was obtained: some were above the average and others were below, but Cuba ranked first by a wide margin, almost twice the average of the rest of Latin America. In all the parameters, such as students' age per grade, retention rate, non-repeating students and other factors which measure the quality of elementary school, we hold, without exception, the place of honor, placing our country, all by itself, in category one.

There are a large number of new teachers and every passing year they accumulate more knowledge and experience, just like there are many doctors who gather more and more knowledge every year. The same thing happens with professionals in general and several fields in particular. The percentage of the gross income that we invest in science is incomparably higher than that of the most advanced countries in Latin America, with tens of thousands of scientific workers, many of them with postgraduate degrees and constantly improving their knowledge. We have done a lot of things and invested mainly in human capital.

What do I fear? It is this: You people lived through periods of abundance — okay, long ago. In 1972 the price of oil was $1.90 a barrel. For example, at the triumph of the revolution, Cuba could buy the four million tons of fuel it consumed with a few hundred thousand tons of sugar, at the normal world sugar price existing then. When the price of fuel suddenly rose we were saved by the already mentioned sliding price [agreement with the Soviet Union]. But when the crisis came — after the Soviet Union was lost and our basic market with it, as well as all our agreed prices — we had to cut by half the 13 million tons of oil which was our consumption by that time. A large part of what we were exporting we had to invest in fuel, and we learned to save.

I have already talked about baseball players. I would add that in every small village there were baseball players and they would use tractors and wagons to transport the players and fans to the games. There were even some tractor drivers who used their tractors to go visit their sweethearts. We had gone from 5,000 tractors to 80,000.

The people owned everything. We had changed the system, but we had not learned much about management and control. We also made some idealistic mistakes. But we had a lot more things to distribute than what we have today. Some said that Cuba had "socialized poverty." We answered: "Yes, it is better to socialize poverty than to distribute the scarce wealth there is among a small minority that takes everything and leaves nothing for the rest of the people."

Now more than ever, we are forced to distribute what we have as equitably as possible. However, there are now some privileges in our country. The reasons were inevitable for us: family remittances, tourism, opening to foreign investment in certain branches of the economy, something which has made our work in the political and ideological field more difficult, because the power of money is great; it must not be underestimated.

We have had to struggle hard against all that. On the other hand, we had reached the conclusion that living in a glass case might be very pure; but those who live that way, in totally aseptic conditions, when they [leave that glass case] they may be finished off by a mosquito, an insect, a bacteria, or any of the bacteria, parasites and viruses that the Spaniards brought over with them, which killed a great many native people in this hemisphere. They lacked immunity. We said, "We will learn to work under difficult conditions because, at the end of the day, virtue flourishes in the fight against vice." Thus, we have had to face many problems under the present circumstances.

[In Venezuela] you had a period of huge incomes when the price of oil rose from $1.90 a barrel in 1972 to $10.41 in 1974; to $13.03 in 1978; to $29.75 in 1979; until reaching the fabulous price of $39.69 in 1980. In the following years, from 1981 to 1985, the average price per barrel was $30.10, resulting in a true stream of income in convertible currency. I know the story of what happened later, because I have a lot of friends who are professionals, and every time I saw them I would ask about the situation, what was their salary then and what was their real income 10 years later. I witnessed how that income dwindled year after year until today.

These are times of abundance for neither Venezuela, nor for the world. I am fulfilling an honest duty, a friend's duty, a brother's duty, by suggesting to you, who are a powerful, intellectual vanguard, to meditate profoundly about these topics. We want to express to you our concern that this logical, natural and human hope, stemming from a sort of political miracle that has taken place in Venezuela might, in the short term, turn into disappointment and a weakening of such an extraordinary process.

I ask myself: "What economic feats or miracles may be expected immediately with the prices of Venezuelan export commodities so low and oil at $9 a barrel? What with the lowest price in the last 25 years, a dollar which has a lot less purchasing power now, with a larger population, an enormous accumulation of social problems, an international economic crisis and a neoliberally globalized world?"

I cannot and should not say a word as to what we would do under such circumstances. I cannot. I am here as a guest, not as an adviser, an opinion giver or anything like that. I am simply meditating. Allow me to say that there are some important countries, whose situation is worse than yours, which I hope can overcome their difficulties. Your situation is difficult, but not catastrophic. That would be our perception if we were in your place. I will tell you more with the same frankness. You cannot do what we did in 1959. You will have to be more patient than we were, and I am referring to that sector of the people who wants radical economic and social changes in the country.

If the Cuban Revolution had triumphed in a moment such as this, it would not have been able to sustain itself, I mean that same Cuban Revolution which has done all it has done. It emerged — and not because it was so calculated, but by a rare historical coincidence — 14 years after World War II, in a bipolar world. We did not know a single Soviet citizen, nor did we ever receive a single bullet from the Soviets to carry out our struggle and our revolution. Neither did we let ourselves to be guided by any type of political advice after the triumph, nor did anybody ever attempt it, because we were very reluctant to accept that. We, Latin Americans in particular, do not like to be told what to do.

At that moment, of course, there was another powerful pole and so we anchored ourselves to that pole, which had come out of a great social revolution. It helped us to face the monster that cut off its oil and other vital supplies and reduced its imports of Cuban sugar bringing them down to zero as soon as we enforced a land reform law. Therefore, from one minute to the next, we were deprived of a market that had taken more than a century to build.

The Soviets, on the other hand, sold us oil. At world price, yes; to be paid in sugar, yes; at the world price of sugar, yes, but we exported our sugar to the Soviet Union and we received oil, raw materials, food and many other things. It gave us time to build a consciousness; it gave us time to sow ideas; it gave us time to create a new political culture. It gave us time! Enough time to build the strength that enabled us later to resist the most incredibly hard times.

All the internationalism that we have practiced, which has already been mentioned, also made us stronger.

I do not think any country has endured more difficult circumstances. I am not at all boastful if I tell you, objectively, that no country in the world could have resisted. There might be some. If I think of the Vietnamese, I think the Vietnamese are capable of any kind of resistance. I think the Chinese were equally capable of performing any kind of feat.

There are people with peculiar characteristics and conditions, deeply rooted, unique cultures, inherited from age-old ancestors, which give them an enormous capacity for resistance. In the case of Cuba, it was a culture largely inherited from a world that became our enemy. We were completely surrounded by hostile regimes, hostile campaigns, a blockade and all sorts of economic pressures, which made our revolutionary tasks extremely difficult. We spent six years in war against the bandits employed by our powerful neighbor to implement its dirty war tactics. Also, many years fighting terrorists, assassination attempts... This is evidence of the inefficiency and failure of those who so often tried to accelerate the natural and inevitable process of life toward its end.

Now we can say the same thing a lieutenant said who took me prisoner in a forest near Santiago de Cuba in the early hours of dawn, several days after the attack against the Moncada army garrison. We had made a mistake — there is always a mistake. We were tired of sleeping on the ground, on roots and stones, so we fell asleep in a makeshift hut covered with palm fronds. Then, we woke up with rifles pointed against our chests. It was a lieutenant, a black man, with a group of obviously bloodthirsty soldiers who did not know who we were. We had not been identified. At first, they did not recognize us. They asked our names. I gave a false name. Prudence, huh? Shrewdness? Perhaps it was intuition or maybe instinct. I can assure you that I was not afraid because there are moments in life when you consider yourself as good as dead, and then it is rather your honor, your pride, your dignity that reacts.

If I had given them my name, that would have been it: tah, tah, tah! They would have done away with that small group immediately. A few minutes later they found some weapons nearby. Some comrades who were not in a physical condition to continue the struggle had left these behind. Some of them were wounded and we had all agreed they should return to the city to turn themselves in to the judicial authorities. Only three of us stayed, only three armed comrades! And we were captured the way I have just explained.

But that lieutenant... what an incredible thing! I have never publicly told this story in detail. This lieutenant was trying to calm down the soldiers but he could hardly restrain them. When they found the other comrades' weapons while searching the surroundings, they were infuriated. They had us tied up with their loaded rifles pointing at us. But the lieutenant moved around calming them down and repeating in a low voice: "You cannot kill ideas, you cannot kill ideas." What made this man say that?

He was a middle-aged man. He had taken some university courses and he had that notion in his head, and he felt the urge to express it in a low voice, as if talking to himself: "You cannot kill ideas." Well, when I look at this man and I see his attitude, in a critical moment when he was hardly able to keep those angry soldiers from firing, I get up and speak to him alone: "Lieutenant, I am so and so, first in command of the action. Seeing your chivalrous attitude, I cannot deceive you. I want you to know whom you have taken prisoner." And the man says, "Do not tell anyone! Do not tell anyone!" I applaud that man because he saved my life three times in a few hours.

A few minutes later they were taking us with them and the soldiers were still very irritated. They heard some shots not far from there, got ready for combat and said to us, "Drop down to the ground." I remained standing and I said, "I will not drop to the ground!" I thought it was some kind of trick to eliminate us, so I said, "No." I also told the lieutenant who kept insisting that we protect ourselves, "I am not dropping to the ground; if they want to shoot let them shoot." Then he says — listen to what he says: "You boys are very brave." What an incredible reaction!

I do not mean that he saved my life at that moment, but he made that gesture. After we reached a road, he put us in a truck and there was a major there who was very bloodthirsty. He had murdered many of our comrades and wanted the prisoners handed over to him. The lieutenant refused, saying we were his prisoners and he would not hand us over. He had me sitting in the front seat of the truck. The major wanted him to take us to the Moncada [barracks] but he did not hand us over to the major. So there he saved our lives for the second time. He did not take us to the Moncada barracks. He took us to the precinct, in the middle of the city, saving my life for the third time. You see he was an officer of that army we were fighting against. After the revolution, we promoted him to captain and he became aide to the first president of the country after the triumph.

As that lieutenant said, ideas cannot be killed. Our ideas did not die; no one could kill them. And the ideas we sowed and developed during those 30 odd years until 1991, when the "special period" began, were what gave us the strength to resist. Without those years we had had to educate, sow ideas, build awareness, instill feelings of solidarity and a generous internationalist spirit, our people would not have had the strength to resist.

I am speaking of things that are somewhat related to matters of political strategy. Very complicated things because they can be interpreted in different ways. I have said that not even a revolution like ours, which triumphed with the support of over 90 percent of the population, with unanimous, enthusiastic support, great national unity, a tremendous political force, would have been able to resist. We would not have been able to preserve the revolution under the current circumstances of the globalized world.

I do not advise anyone to stop fighting, one way or another. There are many ways, among them the action of the masses, whose role and growing strength are always decisive.

Right now, we ourselves are involved in a great combat of ideas, disseminating our ideas everywhere; that is our job. It would not occur to us today to tell anyone: "Make a revolution like ours." Under the circumstances that we think we understand quite well, we would not be able to suggest: "Do what we did." Maybe if we were in those times we would say: "Do what we did." But in those times the world was different and the experience was different. Now we are more knowledgeable, more aware of the problems and, of course, respect and concern for others should come first and foremost.

At the time of the revolutionary movements in Central America, when the situation had become very difficult because the unipolar world already existed and not even the Nicaraguan revolution could stay in power, when peace negotiations were initiated, we were visited quite often because of the long friendship existing with Cuba, and we were asked our views. We would tell them: "Do not ask our views about that. If we were in your place, we would know what to do, or we might be able to think what we should do. But you cannot give opinions to others when they are the ones who will have to apply opinions or criteria on matters as vital as fighting until death or negotiating. Only the revolutionaries of each country themselves can take that decision. We will support whatever decision you make."

It was a unique experience, which I am relating in public for the first time. Everyone has their own options but no one has the right to convey to others their own philosophy on facing life or death. That is why I say that giving opinions is a very delicate matter.

This does not hold true for criteria, viewpoints and opinions about global issues that affect the planet, recommending tactics and strategies of struggle. As citizens of the world and part of the human race, we have the right to clearly express our thoughts to those who want to hear, be they revolutionaries or not.

We learned a long time ago how our relations with the progressive and revolutionary forces must be. Here, I limit myself to conveying ideas, reflections, and concepts in keeping with our common condition as Latin American patriots because, I repeat, I see a new hour in Venezuela, an immovable and inseparable pillar of the history of our America. One has the right to trust one's own experience or viewpoint. Not because one is infallible or because one has not made mistakes, but because one has had the opportunity to take a 40-year-long course in the academy of the revolution.

That is why I have told you that you do not have a catastrophic situation, but you do have a difficult economic situation that entails risks for the opportunity that is looming.

There have been very impressive coincidences. This situation in Venezuela has taken place at a critical moment in the integration of Latin America; a special moment in which those further to the south, in their endeavor for unity, need help from those in northern South America. In other words, they need your help. This has come at a moment in which the Caribbean countries need you. It has come at a moment when you can be the link, the bridge, the hinge whatever you want to call it, or a steel bridge between the Caribbean, Central America and South America.

Nobody like you is in such a position to struggle for unity and integration, something so important and of so much priority at this difficult moment. It concerns the survival not only of Venezuela but of all the countries sharing our culture, our language and our race.

Today more than ever we must be followers of Bolívar. Now more than ever we must raise the banner with the concept that humanity is our homeland, aware that we can only be saved if humanity is saved. We can only be free — and we are very far from being free — if and when humanity is free. If and when we achieve a really just world, which is possible and probable, although from much observing, meditating and reading, I have reached the conclusion that humanity has very little time left to achieve this.

This is not only my opinion but the opinion of many other people I know. We recently held a congress with 1,000 economists, 600 of them from different foreign countries, many eminent people, and we discussed the papers presented. Fifty-five papers were discussed and debated concerning these problems of the neoliberal globalization, the international economic crisis, things that are happening. I should have added that, unfortunately, I am not very hopeful that the prices of your commodities will increase in the next two or three years.

Our nickel has also declined by half its price. You see, not so long ago it was $8,000 a ton, and now it is $4,000. Two days ago, sugar was six and a half cents, a price that does not even cover production costs; the cost of fuel, spare parts, labor force, productive inputs and so on. That is a social and not only an economic problem. Hundreds of thousands of workers live by the sugar mills and are very much attached to them with deeply rooted traditions of sugar production, traditions that have been transmitted from generation to generation. And we are not going to close their factories although, right now, we are facing losses in sugar production.

We have some resources. Tourism, developed mainly with our own resources, has gained momentum in these years and we have made several decisions that have proved effective. I am not going to explain how we have managed to achieve what I have already explained. But I should say that we did it avoiding shock policies, the famous therapies that have been so insensitively applied elsewhere.

We consulted with all the people about the austerity measures we applied. They were discussed with all the trade unions, the workers and the peasants. We discussed what to do with the price of a given item, what price to increase and why, what price not to increase and why. That was also discussed with all the students in hundreds of thousands of assemblies. Then the measures were submitted to the National Assembly and later they were taken back to the grassroots again. Every decision was previously discussed because nothing is implemented unless there is a consensus and that is something that cannot be achieved by force.

The wise men in the North believe or pretend to believe that the Cuban Revolution is sustained by force. They have not been clever enough to realize that in our country, a country educated in high revolutionary and humane concepts, that would be absolutely impossible. This is only achieved through consensus and nothing else; no one in the world can do this without the people's massive support and cooperation. But consensus has its own rules. We learned to create it, to maintain it and to defend it. A united people ready to fight and win can be tremendously strong. Once there was a small disturbance that was not essentially political. It was a moment when the United States was encouraging through every means illegal exits to its territory. Cubans received automatic residence rights, something the United States does not grant to citizens of any other country in the world. This was encouragement for anyone to make a raft stronger than the Kon-Tiki or to use a motorboat to travel to that rich country assisted by the Gulf Stream. Many people have sporting vessels. Others stole boats and were welcomed as heroes, with all honors.

In an incident where a passenger boat was stolen in the port of Havana to create a migratory disorder there was some turmoil; some began to throw stones against some store windows. What did we do then? We have never used soldiers or policemen against civilians. We have never had a fire engine using powerful water jets against people, as one can see in those images from Europe itself almost every day, nor people wearing masks as if ready for a trip to outer space. No, it is consensus that maintains and gives the revolution its force.

That day I remember I was just getting to my office about midday when I heard the news. I called my escorts, who were carrying weapons, and told them: "We are heading for the disturbances. You are forbidden to use your weapons!" I really preferred to have someone shoot at me than using weapons in this type of situation. That is why I gave them categorical instructions and they dutifully went there with me.

How long did the disturbances last? Minutes, seconds perhaps. Most of the people were perched on their balconies. They were somewhat shocked, surprised. Some lumpen elements were throwing stones. And, suddenly, I think even those who were throwing stones started to applaud. Then the whole crowd moved and it was really impressive to see how the people react when they become aware of something that might harm the revolution!

Well, I intended to get to the Havana City Museum where the city historian was. How was [Eusebio] Leal? He was said to be under siege in the museum. But some blocks away, near the sea wall a whole crowd was walking with us and there were no signs of violence. I had said: "Not one unit should be moved, not one weapon, not one soldier." If you trust the people and if you have the trust of that people, you do not have to use weapons ever. We have never used them in our country.

So what you need is unity, political culture and the conscious and militant support of the people. We built that through a long process. You, Venezuelans, will not be able to create it in a few days, nor in a few months.

If instead of being an old friend, someone to whom you have given the great honor of receiving with affection and trust, if instead of being an old and modest friend — I say it candidly, since I am totally convinced of it — if it were one of the Venezuelan forefathers who was here; I dare say more, if it were that great and talented man who dreamed of the unity of Latin America who was here, talking to you right now, he would say: "Save this process! Save this opportunity!"

I think you can be happy, and you will be happy, with many of the things you can do. Many already are within reach and depend on subjective factors and on very little resources. Yes, you can find resources, and you can find them in many things to meet priorities, fundamental, essential requirements. But you cannot dream that the Venezuelan society will now have the resources it once had, under very different circumstances. The world is in crisis, prices for raw materials are very low, and the enemy would try to make use of that.

Rest assured that our neighbors to the North are not at all happy with the process that is taking place in Venezuela, nor do they want it to succeed.

I am not here to sow discord, quite the opposite. I would recommend wisdom and caution, all the necessary caution, and no more than necessary. But you have to be skilled politicians. You will even need to be skilled diplomats. You should avoid frightening many people. Based on my own experience of many years, not on my own intelligence, I suggest that you subtract as few people as possible.

A TRANSFORMATION, A CHANGE, A revolution in the sense that word has today — when you look farther than the piece of land where you were born, when you think of the world, when you think of humankind — requires the participation of the people. Better add than subtract. Look how that lieutenant who commanded the platoon that took me prisoner was added to our cause, not subtracted from it. I took that man the way he was, and I have met some like him throughout my life. I would say I have met many like him.

It is true that the social environment, the social situation is the main factor in forging the human conscience. After all, I was the son of a landowner who had quite extensive land in a country the size of Cuba, though perhaps not considered so extensive in Venezuela. My father had about 1,000 hectares of land of his own and 10,000 hectares of leased land that he exploited. He was born in Spain and as a young and poor peasant was enrolled to fight against the Cubans.

Recently, in an important U.S. magazine someone trying to offend the Spaniards annoyed because the Spaniards have increased their investments in Latin America, published a very harsh article against Spain. One could see from that article that they were really angry. They want everything for themselves. They do not want a Spanish peseta invested in these lands, let alone in Cuba. Among other things, the article said that in spite of his attacks against imperialism Fidel Castro admires the reconquest. The article construed things as if there was a Spanish reconquest. It was entitled "In Search of the New El Dorado"; and at one point in its furious attack it mentioned that the Cuban ruler, the son of a Spanish soldier who fought on the wrong side during the war of independence, does not criticize the reconquest.

I think about my father, who perhaps was 16 or 17 when he was drafted over there and sent to Cuba as things were done in those days, and stationed in a Spanish fortified line. Could my father be accused of fighting on the wrong side? No. In any case, he fought on the right side — he fought with the Spaniards. What do they want? That he should be an expert on Marxism, internationalism and a host of other things when he could barely read and write? I consider that they drafted him and he fought on the right side. The Yankee magazine is wrong. If he had fought on the Cuban side he would have been on the wrong side, because that was not his country. He knew nothing about it. He could not even understand what the Cubans were fighting for. He was a conscript. He was brought here as they brought hundreds of thousands of other people. When the war ended, he was repatriated to Spain and he came back to Cuba a little later to work as a farmhand.

Later, he became a landowner. I was born and I lived on a large estate; it did not do me any harm. I had my first friends there, the poor children of the place, the children of waged workers and modest peasants, all victims of the capitalist system. Later I went to schools that were more for the elite, but I came out unscathed, luckily. I really mean luckily. I had the fortune of being the son, and not the grandson, of a landowner. If had I been the grandson of a landowner I would have probably been born and brought up in a city among rich children, in a very high-class neighborhood, and I would have never developed my utopian or Marxist, communist ideas nor anything similar.

No one is born a revolutionary, nor a poet or a warrior. It is the circumstances that make an individual or give them the opportunity of being one thing or the other.

If Columbus had been born a century before, no one would have heard of him. Spain was still under Arab occupation. If he had not been wrong and there had really been a path directly to China by sea without an unforeseen continent in between, he would have lasted 15 minutes on the coast of China. Remember that the Spaniards conquered Cuba with just 12 horses and in those days the Mongols already had cavalries with hundreds of thousands of soldiers. See how things come to be!

I will not say anything about Bolívar, because he was born where he should have been born, the right day and in the way he should — that's it! I leave aside the scenario of what would have happened if he had been born 100 years before or 100 years later, because that was impossible.

[Responding to the audience:] Che? Che [Guevara] has been present here every second, in my words, speaking from here.

Now I will really finish. Some businessmen are waiting for me. How will I change my discourse? Well, I will tell them the same thing, honesty above all else. I believe that in this country there is a place for every honest person, for every sensitive person, for every person who can listen to the message of the homeland and of the times. I would say, the message of humanity is the one you should convey to your fellow countrymen and women.

9

National Sovereignty and the War in Yugoslavia

International Congress on Culture and Development, Havana

A mong the subjects discussed [at this congress] some caught my particular attention. I find they are among the subjects related to culture and politics that I mostly appreciate. For example, the need for states to promote a correct policy of environmental education; the importance of history to convey values and defend national identities; the need to reject colonialist or hegemonic models; the advisability of avoiding damage to national identity from tourism; the necessity to meditate on the current world, to build a public awareness and to transmit ideas which I consider of basic importance; and the urgent need to foster a true revolution of human ethics through education and the implementation of the right cultural policies.

Finally, there is an item 12 with which I agree, although I don't know if absolutely everybody does. It reads: "The capitalist economy cannot guarantee the prospective development of humanity because it does not take into account the cultural and human losses that result from its own expansion." I would go a little further and say that not only does it not guarantee the prospective development of humanity but that, as a system, it puts at risk humanity's very existence.

As a fundamental part of the integration policy that is up for debate you have raised the need for culture to be given a priority over the other objectives of that integration.

Speech at the International Congress on Culture and Development, held in Havana, June 11, 1999.

We feel that, united we would be worth the sum of many and very rich cultures. In this sense, when we think about "Our Americas," as [José] Martí called it, it is the Americas down from the Rio Bravo [Rio Grande] — although it should have been from the Canadian border because that portion also belonged to our Americas until an insatiable expansionist neighbor seized the whole territory of the west of what is today the United States. It is that integration which I have in mind, including the Caribbean nations also.

The Caribbean nations are still not present in these Ibero-American Summit conferences. Fortunately, all Latin American and Caribbean countries will, for the first time, meet with the European Union in Rio de Janeiro on June 28 and 29. So, the family is already growing although, in general, the Caribbean nations have been the last of the forgotten as we, Latin Americans, also were and still are forgotten.

The sum of all our cultures would make up one enormous culture and be a multiplication of our cultures. Integration should not adversely affect, but rather enrich, the culture of every one of our countries.

In this context, when we talk about unity we still do so in a narrow framework. But I'd like to go beyond that. I believe in the unity of all the countries in the world, in the unity of all the peoples in the world and in a free unity, a truly free unity. I am not thinking of a fusion but of a free unity of all cultures in a truly just world, in a truly democratic world, in a world where it would be possible to apply the kind of globalization that Karl Marx talked about in his time and that [Pope] John Paul II talks about today when he speaks of the globalization of solidarity.

We still need a good definition of what the globalization of solidarity means. If we take this thought to its final consequences we will realize that item 12 is a reality because I'm not sure that the capitalist system can guarantee the globalization of solidarity. No one speaks about the "globalization of charity," which would be very good in the meantime, but let us hope the day will come when charity is unnecessary. That will be the day when the sentiments of solidarity become universal and the spirit of solidarity goes global.

I say this to make it clear that I am in no way a narrow nationalist or a chauvinist. I hold humankind in a higher regards and cherish more ambitious dreams for the future of the human species, which has gone through so much hardship to end up being what it is today, and accumulated such knowledge as it has today, while still not deserving the description of a truly human species. What we presently have is still very far from that but, perhaps, the further it seems, the closer it actually is, since humanity is going through a colossal crisis and it is only from colossal crises that great solutions may come.

That is what history has been teaching us so far, up to this very moment when the real globalization, which was not even mentioned a few years ago, has been made possible and inevitable by the enormous advances in science, technology and communications. People communicate with one another in a matter of seconds, wherever they are.

Technological advances explain the accuracy of the famous satellites guiding the missiles and the smart weapons that are not so smart because they fail disturbingly often; that is, if their failures are unintentional.

The incident with the Chinese embassy [in Belgrade] seemed so strange, so bizarre; then in trying to explain it, they said the problem was some old, outdated maps. So, due to some outdated maps a bomb could have fallen here, too, in this meeting room!

Money moves rapidly, too, and speculative operations with currencies are carried out at great speed for a trillion dollars every day; and they are not the only speculative operations taking place, nor do they only speculate with currencies.

In Magellan's time, it took I don't know how many months to go round the world and now it can be done in barely 24 hours.

We have seen the world change in a few decades.

If you don't mind I will introduce an issue that I call "culture and sovereignty." I will rely on concrete facts and I am not talking theory or philosophy but things that we can all see, that even a near-sighted person can see: namely, that there can be no culture without sovereignty. [Cuban Minister of Culture] Abel [Prieto] outlined how a handful of brilliant personalities in Cuba succeeded in saving the national culture from U.S. neocolonialism and hegemonism.

Another country that has more merit than we do is Puerto Rico, which has been a Yankee colony for 100 years now, but where neither their language nor culture has been destroyed. It is admirable!

Of course, imperialism has today much more powerful means to destroy cultures, to impose other cultures and homogenize cultures — much more powerful means. Perhaps, at this moment, it can be more influential in 10 years than it was in the past 100 years. However, the example I gave you sheds some light on the peoples' capacity to resist and on the value of culture. The Puerto Ricans were deprived of all sovereignty and, despite everything, they have resisted.

Although it is possible to find examples to show that there can be culture, or that a certain degree of culture can be preserved without sovereignty, what is inconceivable in today's world or in the future is the existence of sovereignty without culture.

While you, congress delegates, ministers and government leaders of culture in Ibero-America, were here yesterday involved in your debates, a great battle was being fought at the United Nations for sovereignty and we would say a major battle for culture, too. Today, the means in the hands of those who dominate the world economically and politically are much more powerful than they ever were.

That great battle had to do with the Security Council meeting that discussed a draft resolution on the war unleashed against Yugoslavia, basically against Serbia. In my view, it was a historic battle because imperialism and its allies — rather, imperialism and those who support it against their own best interests — are waging a massive struggle against the principle of sovereignty, an awesome offensive against sovereignty.

We could see this coming. After the collapse of the socialist camp, the Soviet Union disintegrated and a single superpower remained in the world. It was noticeable that that superpower — of well-known origins whose diabolical methods and principles are also very well known — could not refrain from trying to use all its vast power to impose its standards and its interests on the world, carefully at first and then by increasingly stark means.

We are already looking at an imperialism that is using all its might to sweep away anything that stands in its way, and culture is one of those things very much in its way. They are the owners of the vast majority of the communication networks, that is, 60 percent of the world's communication networks and of the most powerful and unrivalled television channels. And, they have an almost absolute monopoly of the films shown in the world.

It can be said that France, which is fighting an almost heroic battle to preserve its culture as much as possible against the U.S. cultural invasion, is the only country in Europe, that I know of, where U.S. films shown account for less than 50 percent of the total. In the other countries of the Old Continent, it is above 50 percent. In some of them it can be 60, 65, 70 and even 80 percent. As for television series, it is 60, 70, 80 and 90 percent, so that about 70 percent of the television series shown and 75 percent of the video cassettes distributed are from the United States; you must have heard these figures before. It is an almost absolute monopoly.

There are major Latin American countries where 90 percent of the films and series shown come from the United States and you know the characteristics of what comes from there. Very little material comes from Europe, so in those aspects there is a total cultural colonization by the United States.

It goes without saying that, in our case, it is extremely difficult to find films of some moral and cultural value. How do we escape from films that show violence, sex and the Mafia almost exclusively? How do we escape from so many alienating and poisonous films that they distribute throughout the world? It becomes difficult for us, for our television practically without commercials, as I said to you, to find films to show on weekends; and people are often critical of what is shown. On the other hand, they are copies because we should say, in all sincerity, that as we were blockaded and all our imports prevented, we found ourselves forced to copy.

In the past there used to be more good U.S. and European films. They were worth watching.

The commercial spirit has so pervasively penetrated culture as to become overwhelming. Which country in Europe can spend $300 million or more on a film? Which country in Europe can make profits of $500 million, or even $1.2 billion trading on paraphernalia related to a film? Those are companies that exploit everything, and the sales of goods associated to an expensive and highly publicized film actually give them higher profits than the screening of the film.

Actually, those films can cover all their costs and produce high profits in the U.S. market alone. Therefore, as you can easily understand, they can sell the films much more cheaply anywhere in Europe or the world. Who can compete with them?

Some European countries are in a real cultural shock and others relatively indifferent to the phenomenon. With their unity and integration they expect to develop their economic, technological, scientific and cultural possibilities — practically as a necessity for survival — but still those countries support the imperialist policy. They are supporting a policy aimed at sweeping away the principles of sovereignty. And it is not the case of very small countries, small islands or very poor, underdeveloped nations whose per capita Gross Domestic Product (GDP) is $200 or $300 a year, but rather countries whose per capita GDP is $20,000, $25,000, $30,000 and even $40,000.

They, of course, are giving up national sovereignty to the extent that they are uniting, opening borders, applying the free circulation of capital, of workers, of technicians and creating common institutions that provide advantages only for the European countries. The South countries must arrive in little boats and enter illegally.

Those countries are giving up their national currencies, and with good logic, in order to adopt a common currency. That is different from adopting a foreign currency governed by the U.S. Federal Reserve system, which is tantamount to annexing the country to the United States.

What would become of us, who have, at least, demonstrated that it is possible to resist a double blockade and such a difficult period as we have gone through during these years? How would that have been possible without our own currency? To this I would add, in passing, that we have revalued our currency seven times. From 1994, when one U.S. dollar bought 150 pesos, to 1999 or the end of 1998 — let us say almost five years. Today, one U.S. dollar can only buy about 20 pesos. No country has done that, I tell you. None!

The formulas of the [International] Monetary Fund, all the recipes that it imposes and that you know so well, where do they lead? Sometimes, through privatization or savings the countries are able to accumulate major reserves to protect their currency. But then, in a number of days or weeks, they lose everything. We have seen that happen in a matter of days. We neither have nor need those enormous reserves. Other countries have them and lose them.

There is only one country — one single country in the world! — that does not even need a reserve because it prints the bank notes that circulate throughout the world. It is the country that, as we have said on other occasions, first converted gold into paper by unilaterally suspending the free conversion of its bank notes, and which changed the gold in its reserves for the paper currency that it printed — a currency accepted by everybody for its equivalent value in gold. Later, then, it converted the paper into gold, the miracle dreamed of by the alchemists of the Middle Ages. In other words, they print a piece of paper that circulates as if it were gold. I am explaining the phenomenon in a simple way although the procedure is more complicated than that.

They use treasury bonds and apply different mechanisms. But in essence, the fact is they can afford it because they print the currency that circulates worldwide, they print the bank notes kept as a reserve in the banks of every country in the world. They print the paper, they buy with it and the others keep the paper — a large part of it, not all of it, of course. Therefore, they are the ones who print the world's reserve currency.

That is one of the reasons for the emergence of the euro. Let us say that it is an attempt to survive against that privilege and against that monetary power so that no speculator can come along and do to any European country as they did to the United Kingdom, France, Spain and others when their currencies were devalued after they fell prey of enormous speculative operations. Actually, when some U.S. mega-millionaire wolves get together, no country can resist their speculative attacks. The pound sterling, a currency queen not so long ago, was brought to its knees in a matter of days.

That can give you an idea of what I mean. That country — well, there is hardly any need to say it — is the United States of America, the only one protected. Others, faced with the continuous and incessant devaluations, crises, catastrophes and flights of capital, in their desperation, begin considering the idea of suppressing their national currencies and adopting the U.S. dollar, which is governed by the U.S. Federal Reserve.

Now, could our country survive if we had such a system? If our currency were the U.S. dollar could this country exist, blockaded as it is and unable to buy the peasants' products in U.S. dollars? Based on what we have had to go through and what we have learned, we realize that in our conditions, if we did not have our very modest peso, which we have revalued, as I said, seven times, we would not have been able to revalue in the slightest. Practically all the schools would have been closed here, while not a single one has been closed. And all the hospitals, while not a single one has been closed. On the contrary, in this "special period," we have increased the country's medical staff, especially the doctors working in the community but also those working in the hospitals by a figure that comes to approximately 30,000 new doctors. All this despite our great economic difficulties, lack of resources and often even of medicines, although we have the basic ones.

Today, a newspaper reported that in a central province of the country, not in the capital but in Villa Clara, infant mortality in children under one year was 3.9 for 1,000 live births. If we consider Washington, the U.S. capital, for example, its infant mortality rate is four or five times higher than in Villa Clara province. There is one area, the Bronx, where it is 20 for 1,000 live births and other places in the United States where it is 30 for 1,000.

Our national average of infant mortality is lower than the U.S. national average by at least two or three percentage points. They are at perhaps 10 or 11 and our hope this year is to reduce it to seven for 1,000. Last year, it was 7.1.

Needless to say, it is due to the efforts made that not a single day-care center has been closed. Not a single family doctor's clinic has been closed. The number of doctor's clinics has increased by many thousands during the "special period." We have been able to do this, of course, because there is a revolution, there is a united people, there is a spirit of sacrifice and there is an extensive political culture.

WHEN WE SPEAK ABOUT CULTURE we don't forget the political culture. It is one of the sectors whose development is badly needed and which is very much lacking in the world. It is impossible to believe or imagine that an average person in the United States has a higher political culture than a Cuban or a European. I admit that Europeans have a higher political culture than Americans but, in general, Europeans do not have a higher political culture than Cubans. That is for sure. You could even have a contest to compare the European average political knowledge and the Cuban average, a contest between people who unfortunately live alienated by millions of things.

In our Latin American countries, sometimes necessity and poverty help develop a political culture higher than in those very rich countries that do not suffer the calamities that we do. That is why, in the Latin American teachers' congresses held in Cuba with thousands of teachers in attendance they constantly speak of the horrors of the neoliberalism that cuts their budgets; and, in the medical congresses they have similar discussions, as in the student congresses or any congress for that matter, because they see it every day and they are conscious of it. Of course, awful things happen in Latin America that have not been seen for quite some time in Europe.

Where none of that exists, people suffer much more. We have more fertile ground to become politically cultured. In our case, we also have the experience accumulated by our country in very difficult battles against imperial aggression and in very great difficulties; and difficulties make good fighters.

But all that notwithstanding, we could have done none of what I am telling you if we did not have a national currency that helps us to redistribute wealth, and also to maintain many free services.

Of course, you compare it with the U.S. dollar and there arises the misleading formula of the exchange rate between the U.S. dollar and the Cuban peso in the Exchange Bureaus. If they say that it is 20 to one, then somebody earning 300 Cuban pesos is said to earn $15. If it was in New York, to those $15 you would have to add $1,000 to $1,500 to pay the rent, another $500 to pay for public health services — this is about $2,000 already — another $500 or $1,000 for education, depending on the educational level because there are university courses there that cost $30,000 a year. Then add some $750 more for the free education given to children, adolescents and young people here and the total could be some $2,750, plus $15 that would be $2,765. All this is very misleading, is it not?

If you take into account that all children in Cuba up to the age of seven receive a liter of milk for 25 cents of a Cuban peso, then this would be a child or a family that is paying only 1.3 [1.25] cents of a U.S. dollar out of the supposed $15, for a liter of milk, and similarly for other essential food. Unfortunately, there is not enough food but there is a certain amount that, measured in dollars, is bought at a minute price.

If you go to our stadium, you can watch an important baseball match for 50 cents or one peso at most. If you go to Baltimore, where our team played the U.S. team, the 45,000 fans paid at least $10 and some paid $35. To watch a similar performance a hundred times, a Cuban pays a maximum of 100 pesos. An American must pay $3,500. The same applies to a lot of other activities and services. But our system, with all those characteristics, could not have had such achievements without a national currency.

Well, this is a long disquisition on the importance of a national currency and the delirious things crossing the minds of those considering the removal of the national currency.

IN EUROPE, WHEN THEY TALK about sovereignty, they cannot have the same concept we do. They are uniting and giving up many of the attributes of the nation state to a supranational state, to a supranational community. Other countries elsewhere in the world should do that; we, Latin Americans, should do that, too. If not, we will not advance even three meters. In fact, we will go backwards every year we do not integrate. In the light of what is happening in the world, it is not something to preach but rather to build an awareness about, to transmit a basic idea.

Actually, there is a very close, powerful neighbor who wants to integrate us into it. Of course, this is in order to have access to our natural resources and the cheap labor of hundreds of millions of Latin Americans producing jeans, shoes, T-shirts and handicrafts that are very labor-intensive. Meanwhile, they keep the cutting-edge industries and the brain drain continues. Right now, they are talking about hiring 200,000 highly qualified foreign workers for their electronic industries, preferably Latin Americans. And so, they take away those highly qualified people that you train in the universities, the most scientifically talented. They give visas to them all right. These do not need to become wetbacks or illegal immigrants.

If there is a good artist, an excellent artist who can be exploited commercially, they are coaxed to go there. They cannot coax a great writer like García Márquez because García Márquez might be coaxing them. At the very least with the high value of his works he might take a substantial part of the bank notes they print! Actually, a good writer can work in their own country, they do not need to emigrate; but in many areas of the arts it is not the same, and they are coaxing the best talents to go there. Someone like Guayasamín could not be bought, not with all the money printed by the Federal Reserve. There are men who cannot be seduced with any money, men and women — I'd rather add those two words than be accused of gender discrimination — and we have them here. We have them here! I don't need to mention names;

they are humble men and women who are worth more than all the gold in the world. That's a fact.

I am explaining all this because they can help us understand these questions of sovereignty, this battle. Because there are so many lies, so much demagogy, so much confusion and so many methods devised to disseminate them that an enormous effort should be made to counter them. If some things are not understood, the rest cannot be understood.

They talk about flight of capital, about volatile capital such as the short-term loans, as if those were the only kind of volatile capital. In any Latin American country, the volatile capital suddenly goes. But alongside the volatile capital goes all the money saved by the country's depositors because if some people withdraw their money for fear of a devaluation, the others rush to the bank, change it for U.S. currency and transfer it to the U.S. banks where the interest rate is higher or lower, depending on the situation.

So, all Latin American and Caribbean money is volatile capital. Let us be well aware of this. Volatile capital is not limited to those short-term loans with a high interest rate that are then quickly withdrawn by the owners when faced with a risky situation. Any money can become volatile, except for Cuban money; there is no way our money can become volatile. If they want to take it away we shall be delighted. The liquidity would decrease and the value of the peso would increase.

Now the Europeans are uniting. They do it to compete with their competitor. They talk about being partners but the United States does not want to be anybody's partner. At any rate, our neighbor wants to be a privileged partner. It constantly takes measures against Europe: banning the export of cheese for such a reason or other or whatever other meat products because they use certain fodder. They are always fabricating pretexts. Right now, because of the banana and a resolution from the World Trade Organization, which is not unbiased, they have punished European exports for a total of about $500 million. They take measures every day or threaten to take them. They are always wielding that weapon. Indeed, it is very clear that Europe must compete very hard with them.

We welcome this Caribbean and Latin American meeting with the European Union that I previously mentioned. I think that it is convenient for Europe, and it is convenient for the Caribbean and for Latin America, as well. And let us hope that the euro is strengthened. It has now dropped a little. It is enduring the consequences of that adventurous and genocidal war — to call it by its true name.

It suits us that there is another reserve currency, so that there are two and not just one in the world. If only there were three! It suits us that there is more than one strong and stable currency.

I hope that, among the many historical acts of madness committed in this hemisphere, we don't end up adopting the U.S. dollar as a circulation currency. It is a currency entirely managed from the United States by the Federal Reserve and they are not going to accept any Latin American representative there.

Obviously, that is a utopia. Of course, they are not going to welcome anybody, not even from the richer and more developed countries with a higher GDP, not even from Brazil, Argentina or Mexico, to mention the largest fraternal countries of Latin America. They are never going to accept our representatives in their reserve system. The Latin American and Caribbean destiny is in danger, but everything is not lost — far from it. We can still fight.

I hope you understand, European comrades, that the concept of sovereignty cannot be openly and shamelessly defended as it was yesterday by a European representative. Europe, in general, is quite committed to that anti-sovereignty doctrine promoted by the imperialism of the superpower.

This explains how a European country — whose ambassador spoke at the United Nations in a way nobody had ever spoken there — could regard as anachronistic the UN Charter and the principle of sovereignty and nonintervention, something fundamental in international law. Those who so express themselves have practically renounced sovereignty and will enjoy, in the near future, a simple national autonomy within a supranational state, with a supranational parliament and a supranational executive.

Even now, as a reward for his glorious wartime exploits — forgetting those who died and the millions who have suffered and will keep those wounds for life — they have created the position of European minister of foreign affairs; a prize for an outstanding character who seriously believes that he is something he is not and who acts like he really is. I mean the great marshal and secretary general of NATO.

Do you not know who that is? Have you ever heard of him? He was a minister of culture in a European country. He is Javier Solana. Did you not know that he was a minister of culture? I met him at an Ibero-American summit in Spain, he met me at the airport and I chatted with him for a few minutes as protocol demands. He was at the time a peaceful minister who actively participated in anti-NATO demonstrations. Today, he is the secretary general of NATO and a field marshal. He must really be at least a field marshal to give orders to the U.S. generals. Now, they are making him a sort of European foreign minister.

Our comrades are asked by the press: Are you not worried that they have named him Europe's minister of foreign affairs? We, in fact, don't tend to worry about anything, nor do we exchange principles for interest or convenience. But we might answer that we would rather have him as a minister of foreign affairs than as a NATO field marshal. I don't know what his power will be as a minister of foreign affairs but we know only too well the power that he claims as a NATO secretary general.

We have all the statements he has made, both before and during the war [in Yugoslavia], and I know few people as attached to the doctrine of violence, who use such a threatening style, with such a merciless and tough language. Obviously, he has a very great responsibility, which he assumed when he formally ordered U.S. General [Wesley] Clark, head of the NATO military forces in Europe, to start bombing. This was after the NATO countries had given their secretary general the power to start the war when, in his view, the diplomatic procedures had been exhausted.

In his capacity as secretary general he issued orders and made constant statements during more than 70 days of brutal bombings. They were all threatening, arrogant, abusive, almost cynical statements. Then, after the Security Council's meeting yesterday he issued the last of his assumed orders: the cessation of the bombings. All this with the corresponding theatrical overtones.

How obedient those U.S. generals are! A model of discipline such as history had never seen! They immediately attack or they immediately cease to attack because a distinguished ex-minister of culture gives the order.

Can the countries of the European Union have the same concept of sovereignty as Mexico, Cuba, the Dominican Republic or any small Caribbean island, like a Central American country or like Venezuela, Colombia, Ecuador, Peru, Brazil, Argentina or a Southeast Asian country like Indonesia, Malaysia or the Philippines? Can they have the same concept as the vast majority of countries in the world that are dismembered?

When we are all integrated in a Latin America and Caribbean union, our concept of sovereignty will be different. We will have to give up a lot of those principles to obey the laws and the administration or the decisions of a supranational state.

Moreover, a Marxist can never be a narrow national chauvinist. A Marxist can be a patriot, which is different, and love his or her homeland, which is different, too.

A long time before today, there were men who dreamed, like [Simón] Bolívar almost 200 years ago, of a united Latin America. There were men, like [José] Martí who, more than 100 years ago dreamed of a united Latin America. At that time, when Bolívar proclaimed his dreams, Latin America was not yet made up of free, independent countries.

In fact, the first independent country following the United States was Haiti. Haiti provided material assistance to Bolívar in his struggle for Latin American independence and also contributed, with its ideas and exchanges, to reinforce Bolívar's belief that the emancipation of the slaves, which was not attained after the first triumphant independence movement in Venezuela, could not be deferred.

As you know, there was in the United States a struggle for independence and a declaration of principles in 1776. But it was only after almost 90 years and a bloody war that the emancipation of slaves was formally declared. Of course, the slaves' situation was often worse afterwards since they were no longer any master's property, they were no longer their owners' assets, so if they died, the former masters did not lose a dime. Previously, if a slave died, his or her master lost what the slave had cost him in the infamous auction. Later, it was the case here, too, and everywhere. They were worse off practically.

In Latin America, slavery as a system disappeared at a much earlier stage than in the United States. There were men who dreamed about those things.

There were not even independent states when Bolívar dreamed of a united and powerful Latin American state based on our similarities, such as no other group of countries in the world have in terms of language, ethnic groups of similar ancestry, religious beliefs and general culture.

Religion is also a part of culture. When we see the invasion of Latin America by fundamentalist sects I wonder about this invasion that wants to divide us into a thousand pieces. Why is there this fundamentalist invasion, by hundreds, even thousands of religious denominations that are different from the traditional Christian religious denominations, which have an increasing ecumenical spirit?

When I was a student there was nothing ecumenical about them. Really, when the Pope visited us, in my welcoming speech, I praised the current ecumenical spirit of his church. I recalled that it was not like that in my early youth when I studied in Catholic schools. As a rule, I was a boarding student except for very short periods when I was a day pupil. Relations among the traditional churches have changed a lot since then.

Now I wonder, why do they want to fragment us with this invasion of thousands of non-unitary sects? As we understand it, in Latin America common religious beliefs constitute an important element of culture, identity and integration. It is not that there has to be a single church — far from it — but pro-unity churches, ecumenical churches. Such elements should be preserved.

We, Latin Americans, have many more things in common than the Europeans. For centuries until not long ago, they were warring against each other. There was one war that they called the Hundred Years' War, and wars of every kind: religious, national, ethnic wars. Those who know a bit of history know this only too well.

The Europeans have transcended all that because they have become aware of the importance of unity. It must be said, really, that the Europeans became conscious — their politicians, in general— of the need to unite and to integrate, and for around 50 years they have been working to that end. We have hardly even started. The UN Charter and the principles of sovereignty are absolutely indispensable and crucial for the vast majority of peoples in the world, especially for the smallest and weakest who are still not integrated into any strong supranational grouping in the current stage of extraordinarily uneven political, economic and social development of the human community.

The United States, captain and leader of the doctrines fostered by NATO, wants to sweep away the foundations of national sovereignty. It simply wants to take possession of the markets and natural resources of the Third World countries, including those that were part of the former Soviet Union, like Azerbaijan, Uzbekistan, Turkmenistan and others, while it is already virtually the master of the great oil reserves of the Caspian Sea. It wants to play the role of a new worldwide Roman super-empire, which, of course, will last much less than the Roman empire; and it will meet with universal resistance.

Nonetheless, it is preparing for the development, consolidation and exercise of a boundless empire. Some U.S. analysts and writers denounce the cultural invasion, the almost total dominion over the mass media and the cultural monopoly they are trying to impose on the world. The empire's most fervent theoreticians consider culture to be the nuclear weapon of the 21st century. This can be seen clearly in everything they do and in the way they do it.

The empire's pretexts? Ah, humanitarian reasons! Human rights is one of the reasons they give for which it is necessary to liquidate sovereignty; and internal conflicts must be resolved with "smart" bombs and missiles.

Whose proposal is this? Looking back, recalling what happened in our hemisphere in the past few decades, who fathered all the coups d'état? Who trained the torturers in the most sophisticated techniques? Who was responsible for there being relatively small countries where more than 100,000 persons were disappeared and a total of about more than 100,000 persons were disappeared and a total of about 150,000 were killed? Or the fact that, in other nations, tens of thousands of men and women had a similar fate? I am talking here only about people who were disappeared after horrible torture. Who trained the sinister culprits? Who armed them? Who supported them? How can they now claim that national sovereignty must be removed in the name of human rights?

A few years ago, they killed four million Vietnamese by dropping millions of tons of explosives on a country that was 15,000 or 20,000 kilometers away. They were relentless in their fierce bombing, with the result of four million people dead and a large number disabled for life. Now, they are asking that sovereignty be removed in the name of human rights.

In Angola, for example, who armed UNITA, which for more than 20 years massacred entire villages and killed hundreds of thousands of Angolans? We know very well who did it because we were there a long time supporting the Angolan people against the South African racists. They are still killing there and their favorite leader has hundreds of millions of U.S. dollars in the banks — I don't know who launders the money — part of which is used to buy weapons, much to the pleasure of arms manufacturers. He controls extensive areas that are very rich in diamonds and has a personal fortune of hundreds of millions of U.S. dollars.

Likewise, there has been no repressive government in the world that the United States would not support. How could the apartheid regime have seven nuclear weapons? They had seven when we were there, on the Namibian border and the U.S. intelligence service, which knows everything, did not know about it! Did it not know? And how did those weapons get there? This is one question that could be asked and one of the things that will be known in full detail one day when some documents are declassified, because the day will come when absolutely everything will be known.

One could also ask where those seven nuclear weapons are because their manufacturers say they have been destroyed. That is all the apartheid regime would say. The ANC leaders do not know. Nobody has answered that question. But again, there are still a lot of questions that have never been answered.

Who supported Mobutu [Sese Seko]? The United States and Europe did. Where are the billions that Mobutu took from the Congo? Which bank is keeping them? Who protected and looked after him or inherited his immense fortune?

I could go on offering many similar examples. Who supported the acts of aggression against the Arab countries? The United States did.

I am in absolutely no way an anti-Semite, far from it. But we have been very critical of the wars against the Arab countries, the massive evictions, the diaspora of Palestinians and other Arabs. Who supported those wars? And there are many other overt or covert wars and other similar incidents that I am not going to mention which have been carried out and continue to be carried out by those who want to sweep away sovereignty or the principle of sovereignty, in the name of humanitarianism. Of course, that is only one of the pretexts but not the only one as we see in Africa.

The Africans themselves are rightly concerned about tackling the problems of peace in their continent. They are trying to unite. They have a strong sense of unity. They also have their regional groupings and are trying to settle their conflicts. But who occupied and exploited Africa for centuries? Who kept it in poverty and underdevelopment? Who drew those borders that cut through ethnic groups?

With great wisdom, really great wisdom, the Africans, from the time they started emerging as independent states, set out the principle of the inviolability of the frontiers whereby the inherited borders were sacred. Otherwise, a huge number of conflicts would have unleashed in Africa.

The colonial powers created all that. They are responsible for centuries of exploitation, backwardness and poverty. Are we going to resort to a racist interpretation of the reasons for the poverty of those African peoples when it is a known fact that, in that continent, various civilizations had attained remarkable progress at a time when in Berlin, Paris and many other places of civilized Europe there were only wandering tribes? A thousand years before, there already existed a civilization in Egypt, Ethiopia and other parts of Africa.

The United States emerged as a nation only 20 centuries later. What is the cause of that poverty if not the colonialist, slaveholding, neo-colonialist, capitalist and imperialist system that reigned in the world in past centuries? Why could those peoples not benefit from the fruits of science and human progress? Those who exploited them for centuries are guilty of this.

At one time, they also semi-colonized and humiliated China. It is common knowledge that, in the past century, they used cannon fire to open up Japan's ports to world trade. It is a known fact that the British empire sent its troops to conquer a portion of Chinese territory and, in a coalition with other European powers and the United States, it sent troops as far as Beijing. Thus came invasions and wars to sell opium.

Now they want to invade countries where poppies are planted by hungry and sometimes desperate people. Impoverished nations, aware of the huge market for drugs in the United States — one that was not created by a Latin American country or any other nation in the world — plant poppies or coca for the colossal consumption of the industrialized and rich countries.

The question could be asked: How many drugs per capita are consumed in the United States and in Europe? Possibly much more than in Brazil or Argentina, Uruguay or Paraguay, Central America or Mexico, or even in Colombia itself. The market is up North. It was a disgrace for our countries, those where the crop originated, that there was such a high demand in the United States.

This is important because yesterday was hardly the first time that they publicly tried to promote the anti-sovereignty doctrine that they have been discussing among themselves and with other NATO members, the one they have been advancing little by little, step by step.

The so-called global threats are also considered enough reason to fully justify an intervention. We will quote three of those threats: drugs, terrorism and the possession of weapons of mass destruction. Of course, this has nothing to do with them! They can have all the weapons of mass destruction they want, thousands of nuclear weapons, as is the case of the United States. They can also have rockets that, with great accuracy, they can position anywhere in the world and a whole arsenal of laboratories devoted to producing biological weapons — they have used biological weapons against us — and any other kind of weapons. They have reached agreements among themselves to eliminate chemical and biological weapons. But at the same time, they develop other even more deadly weapons.

According to this doctrine, a Third World country could have a nuclear weapon and, for that reason, become the target of a sudden air strike and invasion. And what about all those who possess nuclear weapons? It is a matter of wars, either pre-emptive or punitive, to preserve the monopoly of nuclear weapons and other kinds of weapons of mass destruction that are very far from being humanitarian.

The fourth reason is the massive violation of human rights.

Up to now, the great promoter, the great patron, the great fatherly educator and supporter of those who committed massive violations of human rights has been the United States. The massive destruction of the infrastructure and economy of a country as has just happened in Serbia; genocide using bombs to deprive millions of people of crucial services and their means of life; genocidal wars like the one launched against Vietnam — they were the culprits. I am not even talking of the time when more than half of Mexico was conquered.

I am not talking of Hiroshima and Nagasaki, a terrorist experiment into the effects of nuclear weapons on cities where hundreds of thousands of people lived. I am talking about things that have happened since World War II. Who were their allies? Why did the Franco government in Spain remain in power for almost 30 years after the end of a world war against fascism that lasted six vicious years and cost no less than 50 million lives? Because he had the support of the United States, which wanted to have military bases there. Who supported utterly repressive governments in countries like Korea? They did. Who really supported the massive carnage of ethnic groups like the Chinese, for example, or of communists or left-wing people in Indonesia? They did. Who supported the horrendous apartheid regime? They did.

There has been no bloody and repressive government, no massive violator of human rights that has not been their ally and has not been supported by them. In the case of Duvalier — to give you an example closer to home — who supported him? They did, until one day when they intervened in Haiti to overthrow him, for humanitarian reasons.

Do you realize what I mean? It is the development of a whole philosophy aimed at sweeping away the UN Charter and the principle of national sovereignty. The doctrine can be divided into three categories of intervention: humanitarian intervention due to internal conflicts; intervention due to global threats, which we have already described; and intervention due to external conflicts, to which are added the very confusing Yankee concept of "diplomacy supported by force." This means, for example, that if Colombia cannot solve its internal conflict — a difficult battle, of course — if it cannot achieve peace, for which many are working, including Cuba, this could become a reason for intervention. At the same time, if it does not succeed in eradicating drug cultivation it could also be the target of an armed intervention.

I have tried to collect precise information about the extent of drug cultivation in Colombia. It has been suggested to me that there are about 80,000 hectares of coca alone. This has been increasing. And there may be up to one million people working in coca cultivation and the harvesting of the leaves.

Can you imagine the situation where one million people can earn $50, $60 or $70 in the coca fields, while other crops would bring them $10 at most? How much would our farmer earn after changing a hectare of coca for one of corn? Instead of $4,000, he would earn maybe $60 or $100. So, where are the possibilities for alternative crops?

The United States has already created a drug culture. They have alienated millions of people with their voracious market and their money-laundering. It has been the U.S. banks that have laundered the vast majority of the funds coming from drugs. They are not just a market but practically the financiers, the drug money launders. Moreover, they do not want to spend money to really eradicate the growing of coca or poppies, although they invest billions in repressive measures.

I think that, theoretically, there might be a solution but it would cost billions of U.S. dollars, even if those resources were rationally invested. What are they going to do with those who live on drug growing? Are they going to be exterminated? They could also invade that country on account of "a global threat" even if the drug problem cannot be controlled with simple repressive measures.

Of course, invading it would be madness because the heat in the forests of the Colombian plains would finish off their soldiers used to drinking Coca-Cola on combat missions, cold water every hour, ice cream of the best quality. Actually, Vietnam is a well known case in point and [U.S. soldiers] are more and more used to every kind of luxury and comfort. The mosquitoes and the heat would almost suffice to finish them off; but they could cause a real disaster if they intervened there to eradicate drugs. Certainly, that would not be the kind of war to use B-2 bombers because the coca crops cannot be fought with laser-guided missiles, smart bombs or planes. There, they would surely have to go in with ground forces, either to wipe out an irregular force in the jungle or to eradicate crops. On the other hand, since they describe guerrilla warfare as insurgency and terrorism — a global threat — we have a country with two possible pretexts for intervention: internal conflicts and drugs. Two causes for intervention according to the theories they are trying to impose.

Would an invasion or the bombing of Colombia solve the internal conflict? I wonder if NATO could solve that problem now that it is establishing the right of action beyond its borders. In principle, they agreed on that during the 50th anniversary celebration. How many potential cases would there be? Is there anybody who believes this could be the solution?

I know that in their desperation at the violence and the problems in the country, not a few people in Colombia itself have expressed support for the idea that, if there is no other solution to the violence, it be resolved through the intervention of an outside force.

Of course, the fighting and patriotic tradition of the Colombian people should not be overlooked. I am sure that such an act of madness against a country like Colombia, in the style of what they did in Serbia, would be a disaster, absolute madness. But no one knows, really, since international law, the principles of respect for sovereignty and the UN Charter no longer provide a reliable coverage. Such a decision could be taken on their own by some kind of Mafia armed to the teeth, which is what NATO has become.

The rest of the countries, ours included, cannot feel safe. Not at all! And there is the risk of insane actions that cost millions of lives. I am sure that an invasion of Colombia, that is, the implementation of this doctrine in Colombia would cause millions of deaths. That is a country where violence is rampant, where 30,000 people meet a violent death every year — a figure that is well above the average of violent deaths in the rest of Latin America.

Now, would an invasion by NATO forces solve the problem? No, but then, they would come and say as Solana did: "Diplomatic or peaceful ways were exhausted."

As Latin Americans, we should try to cooperate with Colombia, with the country itself, to help it achieve a fair peace, one that would benefit everybody.

There are formulas that, in my view, are so complex and difficult that I would tend to call them utopian, because there is not one war there but three or four. There are significant guerrilla forces with political motivation but divided into two organizations fighting on their own. There are extremely repressive paramilitary forces at the service of the landowners and there are the forces of the drug growers, people armed to shoot down the crop-spraying helicopters, for example.

Colombia's situation is really complex. We should all help! It should never be said that the diplomatic and peaceful ways have been exhausted; the discussions should never stop. A process has already begun. Venezuela wants to cooperate. We cooperate to the extent of our possibilities and so do other countries. Colombia's domestic problems have no solution other than a political and peaceful settlement. This is crystal clear to me. Let us help the Latin Americans find these solutions!

If one day we had a federation of Latin American states, if there were unity, we would give up many of the attributes of our sovereignty. Domestic order would then become the prerogative of a supranational state that is ours and does not belong to a foreign superpower that has nothing to do with us or to a powerful Europe.

We want to have friendly relations with Europe, in trade, scientific and technological development. But this has absolutely nothing to do with the domestic problems of our countries. We would surely be capable of politically solving our domestic problems ourselves, without bombing, destruction and bloodshed. We don't need anyone to do it for us.

Why are they going to demolish the principles of the United Nations? I could begin by exploring some examples. It occurs to me to ask how the NATO doctrine would apply to Russia, for example, if a conflict broke out there like the one in Chechnya or various other conflicts that might arise from the fact that the state is made up of numerous different ethnic groups that also have different religious beliefs. Also, an internal conflict might arise among the Slav Russians themselves because some are communists and others are liberals or neoliberals or some position in between. And then what? Would they invade Russia? Would they unleash a nuclear war?

Russia was a superpower. There used to be two superpowers. Today, there is one superpower and one power. What makes the difference? That the power can destroy the superpower three or four times over and the superpower can destroy the power 12 or 14 times over. In other words, quite a few more times over. But just once is enough, isn't it? Can they go about applying such theories?

At the UN Security Council they have had intensive discussions. A draft resolution has been passed by that body.

I will ask another question: If there is a conflict in India, it might be a border conflict — right now, there is artillery fire on the Indo-Pakistani border — so can the doctrine be applied there? Would it apply where there are more than a 100 million Pakistanis and, on the other side, almost a billion Indians, from many different ethnic groups? Can such a deranged theory be applied in countries that, moreover, possess nuclear weapons? I don't know whether they have 50, 100 or 20 nuclear weapons. But just 20 would be a huge amount and the war could become nuclear. How many would die enforcing this U.S. formula inexplicably supported by Europe? Total madness!

I will go a bit further: What if the conflict is in China, where there are different ethnic groups, in a country with a population of more than 1,250 million and with an extraordinary war experience, courage, fighting spirit. This is the case with every people, of course, but the Chinese have been forced to confront many acts of aggression and difficulties.

We also remember that during the Korean War as [General] MacArthur's troops were approaching the Chinese border and some were already talking about attacking the other side, a million Chinese combatants crossed the border and reached the present demarcation line. One million! Of course, the number of fatal casualties could have been perhaps, up to 200,000 Chinese soldiers. The United States already had all sorts of bomb and other weapons but the human masses could not be contained and they would not have been able to achieve victory, not even with nuclear weapons.

How would the doctrine apply in China, a country they are constantly harassing with campaigns about human rights as they do with our own country? There have been some significant problems there widely exploited by Western propaganda. Imagine how confused those young people were who took as a symbol the Statue of Liberty, in the port of New York, which has become a symbol tainted by the hypocrisy and voracity of an empire that suffocates and insults every idea of justice and true human freedom.

It is striking that this happened in a country with a culture thousands of years' old and a much more solid identity than that of any of us. [China] is a more integrated country, more distant from the West in terms of language, culture, traditions and many other things. It is not a country like ours, which has a lot of elements of Western customs and culture, but a country that has often been humiliated and where an extraordinary social revolution eradicated age-old famines. It is a country that in barely 50 years was raised to its current prestige and the impressive place it occupies in the world.

How would they solve it? If they feel like it, the imperialists and their allies could declare any incident that occurs in China — and that become a bone of contention — a massive violation of human rights. Buddhist Tibet, for instance, is mentioned and certain Muslim minorities in the northwest. We closely follow, through the international press dispatches, China's constant harassment by the West. Any domestic political problem could be considered a massive violation of human rights. They constantly go to great lengths to provoke it, moved by petty propaganda purposes and the stupid attempt to do with China what they did with the Soviet Union. They simply fear that great nation.

Of course, the Chinese are wise politicians — that is why people talk about the Chinese wisdom — and they do not easily make the mistakes that a team of serious and skilled leaders should not make. They would not invade a country to take it over. They are, indeed, very zealous in matters relating to their own affairs. They strictly follow the principle of noninterference in the internal affairs of other countries. For many years, they have been demanding the return of Taiwan to Chinese territory, but they are ready to wait peacefully for 100 years. Their mind set is that of a millennia-old patience, so they talk about what they intend to do in the next 50 or 100 years as if it were tomorrow or the day after.

Any of these problems might be an excuse to send in B-2 bombers, all sorts of missiles and laser-guided bombs. Some of the principles of their absurd and arrogant doctrine could serve as an excuse to attack China. Is that not an insane proposition? I am no longer talking about Colombia, I am talking about China, I am talking about Russia or India or the conflict between India and Pakistan. We will see if those in

NATO and their marshal — their leader or Marshal Secretary General — are really excited enough to solve the conflict in Kashmir with a "humanitarian intervention."

I ask: What is that doctrine for? Why think about such methods? Whom are they going to apply them to? Only to smaller countries that have no nuclear weapons and to the rest of the world, wherever there might be a problem among the many that constantly arise.

Such formulas do not apply to us, just in case anyone thinks that we are concerned by what might happen to us. Putting aside all conceit or boastfulness, our country, which has endured such hard trials, can sing The Pirate's Song: "And if I die / what is life? / I already gave it up / when the slave yoke I shook off / as any brave man ought."

We, Cuban revolutionaries, can say: "And if we die, what is life?" And there are a lot of us Cuban revolutionaries. We know that no true revolutionary, no true leader of the Cuban revolution would hesitate to die if our country became the target of aggression.

I will say more, because we deeply analyze all their technology and their tactics — there is no war, big or small, and no criminal and cowardly bombing that we have not studied well, aside from the fact that it will not be easy for them to find an excuse.

THEY ARE ALWAYS INCITING AND scheming against Cuba, trying to stir up conflicts inside our country. They go to great lengths to create any kind of internal conflict that would justify monstrous crimes like they have just committed against the Serbs.

Those irresponsible people who in our country put themselves at the service of the United States and receive a salary from the U.S. Interests Section are really toying with sacred things. They are toying with the lives of our people and they should be aware of that. The empire, knowing that Cuba would not give in, longs to accumulate enough forces with its blockade, its propaganda and its money to create internal conflicts. We are not talking of family remittances; we are talking of U.S. government money. It has been publicly recognized there as well as in its own laws or amendments. They have recently declared that any U.S. citizen can send money to any Cuban. They have practically said: "Let each American buy a Cuban." So I said to myself: "We should raise the price since there is one Cuban to 27 Americans."

They authorize family remittances but no more than $300 every three months. Cuba is the only country in the world with such restrictions. No, they do not raise by a dime the amount authorized for people of Cuban descent to send remittances to their relatives, but they invite Americans to send remittances to any Cuban. Perhaps, they will work through the telephone book, I don't know. They also give money to whatever small group or faction, to anyone. In their eagerness to stir up conflict, they have so declared and they have passed legislation about sending money. It is a serious matter. Extremely serious!

In their arrogance and disdain, they do not accept that Cuba is resisting. It is so hard for them to accept that — they would like to wipe us from Earth, like they tried to do with Serbia. It is just that here it is different. I would absolutely not question the Serbs' heroism and courage. Absolutely not. A country is not braver than any other; what makes people brave are their convictions and certain moral values. It can sometimes be a religious conviction that leads a person to martyrdom, or it can be a political conviction served with religious fervor.

If it occurred to them to carry out one of those mad actions against us, they would not only find the people I have described but one with a sound political culture and important, sacred values to defend. This fight has been going on for many years and I can tell you that we will not ask for a truce. No truce! The people in charge of this revolution would die rather than make a single concession of principles to the empire.

Rather than relinquishing a single atom of our sovereignty, those of us responsible for leading our people in peace and in war, in every endeavor, we would not survive capitulation. We are deeply committed to what we have done all our lives and because we feel it very intensely, because our commitment rests on convictions and values, we would stand right under the bombs rather than surrender.

In such an adventure it is not difficult to die. There is no greater glory! At least we would be setting an example for others! The Yugoslav people set an example. They resisted the most unbelievable bombings for almost 80 days, without hesitation. We knew about the spirit of the people there through our diplomatic representatives. I don't intend to criticize anybody. I respect the decision that any government might take and it does not escape me that decisions are difficult under certain circumstances. But for us they will not be at all difficult because we solved that problem a long time ago. If they were to do that here, they would be defeated, as simple as that. Not even a genocide would give them victory because there is a limit to their killing capacity, and I firmly believe that, if the aggressors had had to extend those bombings for 15 or 20 more days, the world and the European public opinion would not have accepted it. A few days before the famous peace formula was imposed on Yugoslavia, the world opinion was increasingly turning against the aggressors.

Of course, nobody would have been able to impose that on us because we have been here alone, all by ourselves, all alone for a long while, near the mightiest power that ever existed. So, who could come here to impose it on us? Nobody could. And we do not need any mediator. Honor is not negotiable! Our homeland is not negotiable! Dignity is not negotiable! Independence, sovereignty, history and glory are not negotiable!

There would be no negotiating with us for a cessation of bombings. I will assert that if they started bombing some day, they would have to continue for a hundred years if it was a war from the air they wanted to make; or they would have to stop dropping bombs because as long as there were a few combatants still alive in this country, they would be forced to send ground troops. I would like to know what would happen if they did that.

We don't do anything foolish that they can use as an excuse. You can see how patient we have been with that [Guantánamo] base. It is a small piece of Cuban land and we have every right to have it back. The people here have had quite a radical view of the issue. Not us, we are patient. We say: "No, it is much more important to liberate the world than to liberate that beloved piece of land that we will never give up." They would have loved it if we had started a strong national movement claiming the base in order to have an easy pretext for their adventures, to deceive U.S. and world public opinion, to say that we have attacked them. But they have never had the remotest chance of saying that Cuba has been hostile or aggressive toward the U.S. military personnel stationed there.

What can they say about us on humanitarian issues? That we have not a single illiterate, that we have not a single child without a school, not a single person without medical care. That there are no beggars here although there are sometimes irresponsible families who send out their children on errands. That is associated with tourism and it affects, if not our identity, at least our honor. There is nobody abandoned in the streets.

What can they say? That we have a massive number of excellent doctors. What else can they say? That we can save hundreds of thousands of lives each year in our hemisphere and in Africa.

What did we tell the Haitians? That we are willing to put forward a plan to save some 30,000 lives a year, 25,000 of them children's lives.

What was our proposal to the Central Americans? A plan to save, every year, as many lives as the hurricane took — about 30,000, maybe less because many who were missing began to show up later. We were ready to contribute the required staff and we asked that any industrial country, no matter which, contribute the drugs. Why is it that all those spending so many billions on bombs and genocide do not use a little money to save lives?

I mentioned the loathsome things they attributed to us. But not a single person is tortured in this country! Not a single political assassination! Not a single disappeared person! Forty years have already passed since the triumph of the revolution despite all the conspiracies and all the efforts made to divide us, to subvert the revolution. They have confronted our people's iron-like unity and patriotism, their political culture, and all this under extremely difficult circumstances.

I am absolutely certain that very few people would resist the almost 10 years that we have resisted after losing all our markets and supply sources and with a tightened blockade. They underestimated us.

Also, if they carried out one of the acts of madness mentioned, they would be underestimating us and I don't think they underestimate us quite that much.

I already told you that we have no need for that kind of new specialist — those mediators — who emerged from this war in Yugoslavia. They can come only to report that they will suspend the bombing or withdraw troops or to cease all hostilities. This much we dare say: No weapon has been invented that can conquer humankind! We are not afraid of those repulsive and cowardly wars where they do not risk a single life! They are nauseating, disgusting, but they only make us better socialists and better revolutionaries. That is all.

WE HAVE BEEN READING A lot of background information on the so-called ethnic wars that broke out [in Yugoslavia] in the 1990s, the people who helped — certainly not on purpose, since I don't attribute it to a premeditated and cynical concept but to irresponsible acts. Anyway, they unleashed the disintegration of Yugoslavia, beginning with Slovenia on June 25, 1991, when avoiding any legal procedure Slovenia declared its independence and its leaders took command of the troops in that republic, about 40,000 men; every republic had its self-defense troops. As I understand it, some 2,000 young draftees from the neighboring Croatian republic left for Slovenia. There was practically no combat.

The disease began to spread. Another republic, Croatia, did the same. In that case, more violent conflicts broke out.

What happened? These republics could very well have followed the constitutional procedures. Yugoslavia was no longer a socialist country. It was a country that had established all the capitalist and market standards. It was not the old Yugoslavia of [Marshal] Tito. It was a capitalist country with a Western-style multiparty system.

A very influential factor was that in 1981, 10 years before this happened, Slovenia's GDP was five times the per capita GDP of the rest of Yugoslavia. They began to feel that the poorer republics were a burden and they were encouraged to move toward closer economic integration with the West. Some supported them, some gave them weapons at that stage, even before they had declared independence. One of their leaders has admitted this much.

On June 21, 1996, in a program on the Ljubljana television specially devoted to the fifth anniversary of independence, President Kucan conceded "Slovenia was already building up its army before 1990 in anticipation of a war." In the same interview, the Slovene president added: "The European Union played a great role in making possible the breakup of Yugoslavia."

This is real history. I don't want to offend anybody nor do I mean to hurt anyone. I stick to the facts, the historical facts. It was irresponsible and truly criminal to encourage and support the disintegration of that country which had achieved the miracle of living in peace for 45 years.

There were different factors bearing on the situation, both economic and of a nationalist character, and there were a lot of people in Europe who understood the potential consequences. I have spoken with European leaders who understood that this was very risky. However, one day two countries, specifically Germany and Austria, officially recognized Slovenia and Croatia and, immediately, the rest of Europe followed, thus beginning all sorts of conflicts that we now know about.

There were difficulties in Kosovo where there was a strong nationalist movement. The Albanian Kosovars or Kosovar Albanians were already a large majority. I remember that even when [Marshal] Tito was alive, many Serbs had migrated to Serbia because they felt unsafe there. In 1974, the constitution was amended and Kosovo was granted autonomy in what is precisely the Serbs' birthplace. There are many historical sites there that they value highly. Some of those sites have suffered with the bombings. But I don't know whether that constitution, which granted autonomy to the Kosovo province, gave it the right to secession, as it did with the republics. Anyway, it was not declared a republic but an autonomous province. I assume that it did not have that right recognized and that, in any case, there would have been a process, like in Macedonia.

What began in 1991 has continued until today and nobody knows when it will end. There were many wars and blood was unquestionably shed on both sides. That is the truth, as I see it.

Now then, instead of starting to supposedly straighten out those countries, it would have been better if they had not been disrupted, if they had not been disorganized. Of course, living standards were largely different in Macedonia and Slovenia, very different. There was a constitution by virtue of which the Socialist Federal Republic was established. It had the word "socialist" before but more or less after perestroika it was removed; that much is clear. Its present name is Federal Republic of Yugoslavia. That is, the name of what is left because what remained was Serbia and Montenegro since Kosovo was not a republic. The word "socialist" was removed long ago.

The government may call itself socialist because you know that there are many governments where there are socialist parties but the countries are not socialist. There are socialist parties in many places and in the government, but this does not mean that the country is socialist or that it plans to be so. They are countries with free enterprise, neoliberalism, pure capitalism.

As for Yugoslavia, our position is based on principles, both with respect to Serbs and with respect to Kosovars. We defend their right to autonomy. Moreover, we defend not only their right to have their own culture, their religious beliefs, their national rights and feelings but also if one day the Kosovars or all ethnic groups and the rest of Serbia decided to separate peacefully and democratically, once an equitable and just peace has been achieved and not one imposed from outside by means of war, we would support them.

No one knows what will happen with Montenegro. During the war Montenegro behaved the best it could to appease NATO. It volunteered some criticisms, some opposition, and perhaps that is why its quota of bombs was much lower than Serbia's. I have read many messages sent by the aggressors to Montenegro encouraging it to secede and it was accorded special treatment during the war. All the bombs were for Serbia.

When the agreement reached by the Group of Eight refers to substantial autonomy for the Kosovars, one could ask: Does it mean the kind of autonomy that Macedonia used to have? In that case, there would be a peaceful road to independence. There are many aspects on which Serbs and Kosovars can agree. It is beyond question that most of the Kosovo population are not Serbs. The Serbs constitute a minority and it is very likely that after this dreadful war Serb civilians will follow the Serb troops out. It is obvious. News has come that they were exhuming their dead because it is part of their tradition to migrate with the remains of their ancestors.

I don't know what they will do. Messages are being sent discouraging a massive migration and violence against the Serbs living there. Those risks exist at the moment. Many are claiming victory but who is accepting blame for all the factors that led to this situation and all the ethnic conflicts? A horrendous crime they are calling a victory. A victory they would have to be ashamed of because from the moral point of view if we are to talk about victory and defeat, the morally defeated were those who waged a cowardly war and dropped 23,000 bombs over Serbia, some of the most sophisticated, destructive and technologically advanced bombs. What a victory!

Our UN ambassador estimated that the NATO countries' GDP is 1,013 times greater than Serbia's and that the Alliance member countries have 43 times more regular troops. But regular troops are useless in an air war like that which was waged there. The difference was zero to infinite. Bomber planes arriving from the United States were able to drop bombs from great distances without running the slightest risk. It was a war that lasted 80 days and in which 23,000 bombs were launched against a country while the aggressors did not have a single combat casualty. It was the first time in history that something like that happened.

It must be said that this war, of which nobody can be proud, is a cowardly war, the most cowardly of all wars ever waged. The alleged victory was morally pyrrhic and the war genocide.

Why was it genocide? What is genocide? The attempt to exterminate a population: you either surrender or face extermination. How long were the bombings going to last? They were talking of up to October or November but that was idle talk. We know very well how many European leaders felt. Many newspaper articles were published on the growing discontent and opposition to the bombings in Europe and even in the United States. And there was even greater opposition to ground troops involvement. In my view, NATO was in no condition to continue that bombing much longer. Neither Europe nor the world would have tolerated it. NATO would have broken apart if it had persisted on that path.

As I said, we had three comrades [in Yugoslavia] with a cell phone, working day and night, round the clock, under the bombs and with the air-raid sirens, even when there was no electric power. We always asked them about the morale of the population, about the prevailing spirit. The people crowded onto the bridges; men, women and children went there so that they would not be destroyed. That was the case with the last bridge standing in Belgrade.

The NATO planes attacked all the bridges and there were times when it mostly attacked the electricity network. It destroyed virtually all the power plants leaving millions without light and energy. Imagine a house, if they had something to cook, how could they if there was no fuel, no light, no water? All those pumping systems operate with electricity. Take away the electricity and the cities are left without water. Destroy all the bridges and the cities are left without any supplies whatsoever.

When the electrical service, for example, is rendered useless a whole lot of basic services become useless, too. Imagine intensive-care units without electricity or water; hospitals without electricity or water; schools without electricity or water; households, medical and educational facilities, all facilities and supplies cut off. So, it was not a war against the military, it was a war against the civilian population.

Then it occurred to Marshal Solana to make a solemn statement, that "electric facilities were absolutely military objectives." No one should be so arbitrary with words, ideas and concepts to justify genocide. All means of life were under attack. The main workplaces were destroyed so half a million Serb workers were left jobless and it is not known how many more will be. Hospitals, schools, embassies, prisons, Kosovar convoys were attacked. They said that these had been failures.

I remember reading a dispatch about a general in the British air force who, after 15 or 20 days of bombing, said: "Well, it is just that our pilots have been very restricted up to now. Now, each plane will simply go hunting a target." They went hunting targets, whether it was a convoy of Kosovar refugees mistaken for Serb troops or a prison where they killed 87 people. In addition, they attacked maternity and pediatric hospitals. There is a very long list of such incidents. Above all, admitting that a bomb might have been dropped by mistake, the destruction of all the bridges and electricity systems could not be, and was not, a mistake.

What would have happened if the Serbs had continued resisting? How long could they have prolonged such barbarian actions?

The UN Security Council adopted a draft resolution. Of its 12 sponsors, seven belong to NATO, another is a neocolony of one of the seven NATO cosponsors and another one triggered the disintegration of Yugoslavia in 1991. There is also Japan, a member of the group of the seven richest countries — and this draft was by the Group of Seven — and the Russian Federation. The meeting of the Group of Seven plus Russia agreed on a peace plan and sent its emissaries to Belgrade to submit it. Ukraine, a Slav country separated from Russia although it keeps normal relations with it and very good relations with NATO, also sponsored the resolution. These are the 12 sponsors of the draft resolution submitted to the UN Security Council and produced, in this case, by the Group of Eight.

The chronology of what happened can be seen clearly. Marshal Solana gave the order for the attack and the disciplined U.S. generals, who were leading the operation, began the attacks on the night of March 24. They were completely certain that the attacks would only last three days. Look at how senseless, shortsighted and irresponsible they were, as well as poor calculators. They estimated that Serbia would immediately surrender after three days of bombings. The fourth day went by, then the fifth, the sixth, the seventh...

We have some interesting documents that might be published some day with various messages going in different directions, showing how events unfolded exactly as we predicted. We were familiar with the Yugoslav traditions: they fought against 40 of Hitler's divisions and among the countries that took part in that war it was Yugoslavia that had the highest percentage of dead compared to its total population. The Soviet Union had about 20 million out of a population of about 250 million. Higher figures were given later but 20 million was the one always reported, a round figure. The Serbs must have had some 1,700,000 dead in that war. It was the country that suffered the highest number of dead with relation to its population. At that time they fought using irregular warfare and a concept of fighting with the involvement of all the people.

Right now, the Serb troops are withdrawing from Kosovo with almost all their tanks, cannon and armored vehicles. It is amazing! It is amazing that complete units are being withdrawn, as shown on television, despite the density and the intensity of the attacks launched against them. They were in perfect condition for ground combat.

I really believe that they should have developed other concepts. I say this in all sincerity. This is an issue to which we have given a lot of thought. They had complete units, although this was not a war of conventional Serbian war units against NATO units. They could have used tanks, cannon and whatever they wanted but with the units organized in unconventional ways. Perhaps, or almost certainly, they had them deployed in a way that was absolutely appropriate for the type of war they might have had to wage. We have no information on what they did and how they did it.

We knew beforehand what was going to happen, namely, that they were going to resist. If it had not been for the pressures they came under from friends and enemies alike, which seems to have been enormous, possibly the Serb leaders would have continued to resist. I will say no more. The people would surely have resisted indefinitely. NATO would have had to decide on a ground campaign or else suspend the bombing, and in a ground war it would not have been easy for NATO to overcome the growing political obstacles nor would the war ever have ended. That is my point of view.

Well then, the draft resolution by NATO and the Group of Eight was adopted and the bombings stopped. In one of its sections, the resolution adopted reads that the UN Security Council:

"Decides on the deployment in Kosovo, under United Nations auspices, of international civil and security presences" — the words seem so harmless — "and welcomes the agreement of the Federal

Republic of Yugoslavia to such presences." Well, it does not say what presences. International security forces, but it does not say whose.

It later reads that it: "Requests the Secretary General to appoint, in consultation with the Security Council, a Special Representative to control the implementation of the international civil presence." The question is, who is in command there? The United Nations leads the civil presence, "and further requests the Secretary General to instruct his Special Representative to coordinate closely with the international security presence to ensure that both presences operate towards the same goals and in a mutually supportive manner."

It asks its man to coordinate with the leaders of those troops while still not saying which troops — a civil leadership which is the one under the orders of the United Nations — and it asks the civil representative to coordinate with the security forces, in case they pay any attention to him.

"Authorizes Member States and relevant international organizations to establish the international security presence in Kosovo as set out in point 4 of annex 2 with all necessary means to fulfill its responsibilities under paragraph 9 below."

It *authorizes*, although they are not under its command. It *invites*, knowing beforehand who were *invited*. It is said that many are called but few are chosen.

"Affirms the need for the rapid early deployment of effective international civil and security presences to Kosovo, and demands" — a terribly strong word — "that the parties cooperate fully in their deployment." In other words, that the different countries cooperate fully. We are also ready to cooperate if they want doctors, but not one soldier because that is not an internationalist or a peace mission. It is an imperialist mission with very specific objectives. We are ready to cooperate to save lives. As for the rest, the decisions taken by each one do not concern us.

It is known, however, that the British will have 13,000 troops in Kosovo — the main forces — with a British general in command. The number of Americans is unknown. Some marines have already landed in Greece — they will probably arrive in the thousands. The French, too, and all the aggressors. The figure of Russians is not public although it is known more or less how many Russians are already there; a press dispatch has brought the news that somebody said that there could be between 2,000 and 10,000. Who is commanding them? We will see, because this is a bone of contention.

Concerning the possibilities for the presence of Russian soldiers, a statement was made yesterday by the current Russian prime minister [Stepashin] that reads: "The armed forces are in such a catastrophic state that the military-industrial complex and the army are barely surviving. We must remember this in next year's budget." What will be next year's budget? Nobody knows. Even if it is catastrophic, they would have to cover the costs of the troops, which will come to 4,000 or 5,000. If they get to 5,000, they would only be 10 percent of the so-called security forces.

What is well known is that regardless of who accompanies NATO, it will be NATO that will have 90 percent of the occupying troops under its direct command, and not only its own troops but also the accompanying troops. There will be countries, such as Ukraine, that will offer some soldiers. A Latin American country might offer a small group of soldiers, some young draftees. But NATO will have everything there in addition to the thousand planes that took part in the bombing.

The Russians will, at most, have a helicopter, a light aircraft to fly from one place to another. The Ukrainians might have some jeeps and maybe even a helicopter. NATO will have everything on air, land and sea and command over everything. The discrepancy now is with the Russians who are embittered, humiliated and threatened, that is the truth. Actually, with that precedent anybody might think that any day now missiles, laser-guided bombs and millions of other things could begin falling on them, especially when it has been admitted that "the armed forces are in a catastrophic state." This does not exclude the fact that the strategic missiles do work and they have thousands of them. Yes, they have thousands of strategic missiles. They are a nuclear power and, of course, all that is expensive.

The UN Security Council: "Welcomes the work in hand in the European Union and other international organizations to develop a comprehensive approach to the economic development and stabilization of the region affected by the Kosovo crisis, including the implementation of a Stability Pact for South Eastern Europe with broad international participation in order to further the promotion of democracy, economic prosperity, stability and regional cooperation." The adopted resolution does not say: The international community should contribute to rebuilding everything destroyed there, whether Kosovar or Serb. No, what the NATO leaders are declaring is that the government that made an agreement with them, and yielded to the advise or the pressures of the Group of Eight's mediators, must step down now and appear before the International Tribunal for Yugoslavia where it has been accused.

Not a word about building anything in Serbia. About Montenegro, they do say that it will receive suitable treatment, that it has behaved very well and accepted refugees. But nothing about Serbia. Before, they dropped bombs on them for having such a government and now, for the same reason, they will not help them to feed themselves after all that destruction. Look how noble, how generous and humanitarian the United States and NATO are! What is the fault of children there aged from zero to one, 10, 15 years' old? What is the fault of the old people? What is the fault of the pregnant women, the retired, ordinary men and women who have lived through such a traumatic experience?

Often, the most traumatizing consequence of bombing is the explosions, the noise. The Nazis, who have been quite well imitated in this merciless war — and I say this from my heart — used some terrifying sirens in their Stuka planes when dive-bombing their targets. I remember that war. I had just turned 13 when it began but I was interested in all the news. I remember the war almost as if it were yesterday. In their combat planes, they had sirens that made a hellish noise aimed at sowing fear, panic and disarray while they dropped their bombs, which were not at all like those of today. They were toy bombs compared to those dropped by NATO over Serbia.

The terror of bombings produces lifelong trauma, much more so in a child of three, four, five, six, seven, eight years, who remain day after day and every night hearing the noise of the sirens and the explosions. Would any doctor, any psychologist dare say that those children and millions of people will not endure a lifelong trauma with the terror they lived under for 80 days from the air-raid sirens plus the hellish roar of the combat planes as they flew at ground level, which is much more deafening than the Stuka sirens and with much more powerful explosions than those of the Nazi bombs?

Yet, they must now be punished: not one dime to rebuild a school, which they say was mistakenly destroyed, not one hospital, not one power plant. What are they going to live on? Well, now it is a hunger bombing. An agreement was signed with certain leaders who will handle things and they know what they are doing. But I consider it a crime to deny even a handful of wheat to the Serb people after dropping 23,000 bombs and missiles on them. Then, if the man presiding Serbia remains in government for three months or six or if he simply stays longer, a year — I don't know, nobody can foretell — the people will be subjected to a genocidal war for a year, all the civilians, all those who are in no way responsible for any ethnic cleansing or for the masses of refugees.

There were 20,000 refugees but when the massive bombings began people withdrew for many different reasons: out of fear or because they were afraid of being evicted or suppressed, or maybe because they were terrified by the bombings or afraid of dying. You can never say it is only one reason. What is the fault of the children, the civilians, the hundreds of thousands who were left jobless and other workers, the peasants, the farmers, the pensioners, the civilian population in general? What is their fault, really? It is a crime to keep them waiting until the government changes. To make them wait for a month is 30 times more criminal and a year would be 365 times more criminal. Each day that they are denied food is a crime.

I remember that during our liberation struggle we had an enemy force under siege, with no water or food because we had cut off their water supply and they had run out of food. Our combatants handed their cigarettes and their food to the exhausted soldiers who surrendered because a sense of chivalry had been created in the revolutionary troops and there was a policy in place for treating the enemy. If a policy like that does not exist, a war cannot be won. If you mistreat your enemies, if you torture them, they will never surrender. They will fight to their last bullet.

We had a strict policy in that sense: after 24 or 48 hours, they were set free. At the beginning, they fought very hard. Later, when they realized they were lost, they parleyed and the officers were allowed to leave with their pistols. We did not want to make them go hungry nor could we give them what little food we had. At times, we called in the International Red Cross, as we did during the last enemy offensive when we took hundreds of prisoners in two-and-a-half months of combat. During the war, we ended up with thousands of prisoners that we had taken in combat. Entire units were besieged and we treated them gently because they were our arms suppliers.

We did not receive arms from anybody during our short but intense liberation war while fighting against quite powerful forces but it did not occur to any of us to surrender. Our supplier was Batista's army, organized, equipped, trained and also advised during all that time by U.S. officers. It was not an army to look down on, not at all. They believed themselves to be the masters of the world. We had to endure great needs but we gave our enemy prisoners our food and even our medicine.

WE HAVE THE RIGHT TO ask ourselves about Serbia, destroyed by NATO, that the West is going to refuse a handful of wheat to a pregnant woman in a country that is said to have surrendered and accepted every condition and still more conditions than those demanded by the Group of Eight. Is that correct? Is that fair? Is that humanitarian?

I already told you that they were arguing over who was going to lead that security force. Actually, the Security Council agreement does not say under whose command the security forces are going to be. It only calls for them to go, knowing already who can and will go.

Now the Yankees are interpreting the agreement. Here comes the time for interpretations! This resolution establishes an international security force in Kosovo. Now here is the catch: In his speech yesterday [at the United Nations], the U.S. representative says, among other things: "The authorities of the Federal Republic of Yugoslavia accepted that KFOR... The Kosovo International Security Force will operate with a unified NATO chain of command, under the political direction of the North Atlantic Council, in consultation with non-NATO force contributors."

It is NATO and under the direction of the North Atlantic Council, in other words, the NATO Council. Who gave them permission? The Security Council? No. This demand was contained in the agreement of the Group of Eight meeting of May 6. On May 6, when they saw that the bombings were continuing through March and all of April, 40-odd days had passed and there was not the least sign of capitulation, they began to worry. Many of those in NATO began to make up things and they held a Group of Eight meeting on May 6 where they adopted certain agreements.

There was not yet a new Russian prime minister but somebody had been appointed as special envoy of the Russian government for the so-called peace efforts. I am not criticizing that, of course. I think it was very appropriate that the Russian government did everything possible to try to find a political solution to the conflict. That conflict could not have a military solution and they were not in any condition nor had they any possibility to help the Serbs militarily, except with nuclear weapons and that is out of the question. Nobody would agree to that. That form of support would have seemed to us absolutely insane and impossible and it would have been a world suicide.

But it was obvious that the Russians did not even have the possibility of sending a plane with ammunition to Serbia. Nothing could be sent by land or sea. Hungary, a new NATO member, is there on the border. There are other similar countries there. Nothing could be sent by land; nothing by air; nothing by sea. They had nothing but their nuclear weapons left and, let us say, political support.

There was the Agreement of the Group of Eight under which a peace plan was adopted on May 6 and accepted by the Yugoslavs on June 3, that is, almost a month later. After its approval in May, many efforts were made: [President] Ahtisaari, from Finland, comes and goes, the same as Chernomyrdin. There were U.S. envoys and Russian envoys until June 3, when during a visit to Belgrade the Russian envoy and the president of Finland convinced the president of Yugoslavia to accept the formula.

It has been said that the president of Finland left and the Russian envoy, once alone, was finally able to convince the president of Yugoslavia. Some day we shall know what they said and how they said it. So, I am not criticizing the Russian peace efforts; that is quite different from the question of Yugoslav leaders accepting the conditions imposed on them. I have my personal view of the different things that might have happened. I will just say that in spite of its immense power, NATO's position was already weak because you cannot go on bombing and killing every day before the eyes of the whole world. There comes a moment when the killing becomes too scandalous and intolerable.

But nobody there talked about who was going to command the troops. That would be discussed later. Until the last minute, when the resolution was about to be submitted to the Security Council, the Russians opposed the idea that the troops taking part in the aggression be allowed there — that was also the Yugoslav position — and that there should be a single command under NATO. The mediators had to consult the Chinese, and the Chinese had reasons to be irritated by NATO because of the attack on the Chinese Embassy.

The Russians agreed to discuss the draft first in the Security Council and then discuss the organization and distribution modalities, the question of security forces in Kosovo. Giving in first to something and then discussing another important issue is not good tactics. You give in and when you start discussing they then ask for more. No, sir, take a few more minutes to get things straight before supporting the agreement, before renouncing the right to veto and voting in favor.

I know of Russian leaders who have made serious and honest efforts to find a solution to a really complicated and dangerous situation. They have weakened themselves a lot politically and people do not respect them like before. That is why nobody knew who was going to lead the troops.

But the Americans rapidly found a solution in the speech delivered by the U.S. representative in the Security Council. Look, they were talking in Macedonia with the representatives of the Serb troops in Kosovo. They discussed for a whole day but did not reach an agreement. They returned for a second day of discussions and used the situation to request a false permit. And now a new disclosure yesterday: that the role of NATO had already been authorized.

It was not the Group of Eight or the United Nations or the Russians who agreed. In the discussions in Macedonia, the authorities of the Federal Republic of Yugoslavia had accepted that KFOR operate with a unified NATO command under the political leadership of the North Atlantic Council; that is, the Yugoslavs gave them permission. There is evidence that they have made fools of the Russians. A cable revealing this was broadcast today showing that the Russians did not like it at all.

They solved the problem. Who? The vanquished. Nobody else authorized the Americans and NATO and the British generals who discussed with them, of course, following strict orders from Marshal Solana, with due respect to the new minister of foreign affairs of Europe, the pre-united Europe. He is a pre-minister of a supranational pre-authority. These are his titles, more or less.

Right away, the United Kingdom takes the floor saying: "The authorities of the Federal Republic of Yugoslavia and the Serb parliament have now accepted the principles and demands set out in the G-8 statement of May 6 and in the Chernomyrdin-Ahtisaari paper."

"This resolution and its annexes clearly set out the key demands of the international community." NATO is the international community to which Belgrade must now oblige.

"They also provide for the deployment of an international civil presence, led by the United Nations, and for an effective international security presence to reestablish a safe environment in Kosovo (...) That is why NATO has made clear that it will be essential to have a unified chain of command under the political direction of the North Atlantic Council" — not the United Nations — "in consultation with non-NATO force contributors. This force, with NATO at its core, will be commanded by a British general. The United Kingdom will provide the leading contribution, at least 13,000 troops."

"To have come this far, to have secured Belgrade's acceptance of all our demands, required a huge diplomatic effort. My government pays tribute and expresses its gratitude to Mr. Chernomyrdin, President Ahtisaari and Mr. Talbot for their outstanding contribution. The positive engagement of the Russian Government, via its Special Envoy and in the preparation of this Resolution by Ministers of the Group of Eight has been vital." They start by saying that the Yugoslavs authorized NATO to lead the security forces.

Were the Russians happy? Ah, no! Today there was news from Europe that a Russian force of about 500 paratroopers who were in Bosnia moved forward in over 20 armored vehicles, trucks and some tanks, crossed over Serbia and were marching towards the Kosovo border to await the entrance of different forces; that is the solution of the problem of how forces were going to be distributed. Of course, they have said that Russian forces will not accept NATO command.

They must have been disturbed when, without saying a word to anybody, 24 hours before the resolution and the U.S. interpretation, they sent a column of paratroopers in armored vehicles to the border. Undoubtedly, this is an answer to all these interpretations. They hate accepting the idea and I suppose that domestically, where all this has been very traumatic, it must be very difficult for the Russian leaders to accept that their troops there are under NATO orders, whether they are 2,000, 4,000, 5,000, with or without a salary. It is only tricks and more tricks on the part of those who unleashed that dirty war.

The two main leaders, of course, are the United States and the United Kingdom. They are also the two countries bombing Iraq every day. Nobody remembers this, but it happens every day. It has become a habit, a daily shooting exercise to preserve their right to bomb every day. That is something they do on their own, and with all these problems nobody even notices.

We had denounced that Yugoslavia had been turned into a shooting range.

In a declaration on June 1, that is, just nine days ago, before the government of Yugoslavia accepted the Group of Eight plan, Cuba issued a declaration. Among other things, Cuba made reference to what was going on there day by day, each target, the attacks, saying:

"Yugoslavia has become a military testing ground. Planes taking off from the United States drop their deadly load on the Serb people, refuel in mid-air and return to their bases non-stop. Missiles are air-launched at a distance outside the range of anti-aircraft weapons. Unmanned aircraft are bombing hospitals with patients inside, homes with people inside, bridges full of pedestrians and buses with passengers."

It could be considered an uncalled-for denunciation on our part. But it so happens that yesterday — June 10, about nine days later — in Washington, an [Agence] France Press cable by Benjamin Kahn, reported:

NATO bombings in Yugoslavia against military targets and civil infrastructure allowed the U.S. Air Force to test several high-tech weapons, upgraded since the 1991 Iraq War.

Intelligent bombs designed to set their trajectory in flight were used in the Gulf War but the new upgraded versions were used in Yugoslavia and in a greater number than ever before.

Computer-guided bombs allowed the United States to kill thousands of Yugoslav soldiers from far away, without risking their pilots or ground troops...

Analysts affirm that the massive use of new cruise missiles and other state-of-the-art weapons will continue growing as a result of the search of the U.S. military to upgrade their capacity to attack beyond the reach of enemy defense.

Another breakthrough since the Gulf War was the building-up of missile noses with titanium to allow them to run through thick layers of cement and explode causing greater damage.

The new generation of B-2 stealth bombers — the most expensive of all — also made their debut in Yugoslavia.

At a cost a $2.2 billion each, B-2s of a super-sophisticated technology, manufactured by Northrop Grumman, Boeing and General Electric, flew from a base in the state of Missouri and eluded the Yugoslav anti-aircraft defense and dropped many satellite-guided bombs in each flight.

Today there are new facts. A dispatch reported that in three sorties such bombers hit 20 percent of their targets; 20 percent of the targets hit by bombs and missiles.

I believe that Mr. Clinton went today to this air base to congratulate warmly and fraternally the super-heroes who, always out of reach of enemy weapons, killed hundreds or thousands of persons or caused who knows what sort of destruction. An exercise in new technology, and by air. They did not land midway. B-2s, flying straight from U.S. territory, dropping tons and tons of bombs. They had to be tested using real fire against real targets.

"Bombs dropped by B-2 JDAMs — also new — use a GPS orientation system weighing 450-900 kilos and costing $18,000 each." Rather cheap for an aircraft that, according to the Washington reporter, costs $2.2 billion. With $2.2 billion you can estimate how many hundreds of thousands of lives of children, and people in general, in Haiti, in Central America and similar places could be saved in a few years. You can almost estimate how many lives can be saved in one year. This could be more than 400,000. Saving a child's life never costs more than $500: from the child who dies for lack of a vaccine worth 25 cents to another who dies from lack of rehydration salts, etc. Let us say $500, an exaggerated figure. With $500 million you could save almost one million people, if there are doctors and medicines.

With $1 billion, two million children can be saved; with $2 billion, four million children; with $2.2 billion, you could save the lives of 4.4 million children. Everyone knows, including the World Health Organization, that about 12 million children die of curable diseases, 10 to 12 million children.

Almost half of those dying in one year could be saved with the cost of a single aircraft. It would really be humanitarian to invest the cost of one of these planes in saving the lives of almost 4.5 million children by conservative estimates! In the programs we are designing doctors work for free. We pay our doctors here, with our currency. We do not have to spend U.S. dollars because they are paid in our own currency and recently all doctors' wages have been raised. As for NATO, it is surely setting a humanitarian record!

It is very sad the way they manipulate people with lies and demagogy. Actually, you should not leave without these few facts I still have here to share with you.

I say that there are three basic ideas. I have spoken of the Group of Eight. But what is the Group of Eight? The Group of Eight is a company, a small club of the super-rich. On account of their major influence and money, the United States, Japan, Germany — tremendously rich countries — are there and all the others, and they set monetary policies for the International Monetary Fund. They dictate measures for coping with crises and make certain arrangements if there is a crisis in Southeast Asia or in Russia or if there is any danger that it may spread to Latin America.

The Seven Rich meet annually. But with the collapse of the Soviet Union and the improved relations with Russia, once in a while they invite it. From Russia alone, the West — mainly Europe — has taken out $300 billion. Of course, they did not do this at gunpoint. It was not necessary either because such skilful business people have cropped up there that they have become multimillionaires in a few years.

UNDER THE REFORMS INTRODUCED BY the West, Russia has suffered terribly. Its economy was cut by half; its defense considerably weakened. In return for a $20 billion credit, the West imposes restrictions and demands many conditions that Russia cannot meet, some of them humiliating. What are $20 billion in Russia, which is so badly in need after the August crisis? And spread throughout a whole year even if it is only one fifteenth of the hard currency that wound up in the West.

But not only that. The ruble has been devalued twice. Before, a ruble equaled a U.S. dollar and had a higher purchasing power in Russia than a dollar. In a few years its purchasing power was 6,000 times lower; that is you needed 6,000 rubles to buy one U.S. dollar. All those who had savings, pensioners and others, lost them. As a result of devaluation, an entire nation lost its money.

They set a new parity and a new ruble. They took off the zeros, divided it by 1,000 and then, with six rubles you bought one dollar. Therefore, when the crisis began, those who had saved rubles found that their rubles instead of being rated six to one dollar were worth only 24 to one dollar, one fourth. Once again those with savings had lost their money. This has happened not only in Russia but in many other countries as well. Latin America is tired of living through these experiences, through the repeated devaluations. The currencies become volatile capital.

Where is the person who, having lost all their savings in their own country twice, would want to have their cash in the national currency again, even if it pays a 40, 50 or 80 percent interest rate? On the other hand, no economy can withstand that. It is impossible, because the mechanism recommended by the theoreticians of neoliberalism in the International Monetary Fund to the countries is an increase in the interest rate, so that people do not take away their money. Which budget can withstand 80 percent rates?

It is impossible. Besides, even if interest rates are raised to those levels, there can be a 400 to 500 percent devaluation, incomparably higher than the increased rate. What do savers or people with revenues do? They exchange their money for dollars. No bank can resist that. How much money would a country need to keep the ruble-foreign exchange convertibility? An endless amount of dollars.

How many years will pass before the nationals of a country suffering this problem can have confidence in their currency again? And there goes the IMF demanding free conversion and lots of other unpractical things that cannot be implemented. A few estimates suffice to identify the problem; they change everything to dollars, stuff them inside a mattress and take them out of the country.

So the country is now very impoverished and heavily dependent on foreign credits. Yet, I don't believe it must necessarily be like that. A country like Cuba that has gone through a hard experience — without fuel, steel, lumber, anything and has survived without a dime from any international agency — knows that with its huge resources that country would not need any credits. If we had those resources we would be growing at a double-digit rate. Without anything and despite everything, including the blockade, we are growing and this year we shall grow from three to four percent, approximately.

We have the right to imagine what could be done. The revenues of most of our exports are spent just in fuel alone.

We do not have the immense Siberian forests, oil and gas fields. We do not have a significant steel industry and machinery either. If we only had raw materials and today's experience, because we must add that we have learned to be more efficient and make a better use of our resources, the Cuban economy might grow perhaps 12 or 14 percent.

It is my conviction, and this is the first time I say this in public, that Russia can save itself. It does not have to depend on Western credits; sooner or later its leaders will understand that. But undoubtedly, today it depends on credits.

The group of the seven richest countries in the world except Japan, which is not a NATO member, took part in the attack on Serbia. The eighth country, Russia, is ironically the country that has become poorer in less time. Its per capita GDP is at Third World levels.

It is now an impoverished, indebted country depending on Western credits. Still, I am not suggesting at all that these were the reasons for the sad role it played in the Group of Eight. I believe that they were genuinely concerned about the crisis unleashed, the danger of this adventurous war and the impact on its own population, a mirror image of what might happen to them some day. They must have grown aware of all the influence and strength they have lost.

Actually, I would admit that their position is right in as much as they advocate a political solution of conflicts and defend the UN Charter. Their speech in the Security Council was critical and positive.

The rapid advance of a column of Russian paratroopers heading for Kosovo caught NATO by surprise; in fact, it caught everybody by surprise. It was an irrefutable answer to the deceit of negotiating permission with the Yugoslavs so that NATO would head security forces in Kosovo. It was not a UN decision; it was not discussed with Russia. That was the humiliation, deceit and trickery.

In short, NATO attacked and got stuck. They invented a meeting of the Group of Eight and fabricated a peace plan. The peace plan that provoked so many differences with the Russians was finally adopted and taken to the Security Council while the issue of who was in command of that force remained unresolved. Right there in his speech, the U.S. Representative said that they already had permission from the Yugoslavs to take command of the Yugoslav province of Kosovo.

I want to say something else. We started delving as deeply as possible in the history of that region, its past and recent history. Yesterday our UN Ambassador pointed out that when Hitler invaded Yugoslavia he set up a fascist government in Zagreb, which included Croatia, Bosnia, Herzegovina and a great part of Voivodina, almost on the doorstep of Belgrade.

The fascist regime of Ante Pavelic enforced the so-called Three-Thirds Doctrine. What did that mean? One-third of the Serbs were to be deported, another third assimilated and forcibly converted to Catholicism — the official religion of Croatia, because the others, the Serbs, were Orthodox Christians. The Orthodox Church is rather close, in general, to the Catholic doctrine although with evident tensions between them. The last third would be annihilated. That doctrine became the political orientation of the state machinery that started organizing all three things with unequally effective results.

Many of the converts were finally annihilated since deportation was not easy. Thus, physical extermination became the most general practice. Amazing! For us this was a discovery: a holocaust, a true holocaust of huge magnitude.

In terms of the total Serb, not Yugoslav, population at that time it is possible that they annihilated a higher percentage of Serbs as compared to the total Serb population living in Croatia, Bosnia and Herzegovina than the percentage of Jews annihilated during World War II, vis-à-vis their total number. A more detailed study would be required. This holocaust has been hidden. The West never wanted to mention it.

Now what do Croat and Serb writers say? Croat writers acknowledge that there were 200,000 victims; that is, those who were killed under the fascist Three-Thirds Doctrine.

What do Serb writers say? They speak of one million people killed. What do more reliable sources say? That there were 400,000 to 700,000 [people killed].

What does one of the admittedly most reliable sources, the British Admiralty Archives, have to say? Do not forget that the United Kingdom was an ally of Yugoslavia at the time taking part in operations in the Balkans; their archives are considered important, serious sources. Raising this issue may perhaps awaken interest so that better-informed people can speak up on it. The British Admiralty Archives set at 675,000 the number of civilian Serbs killed, including many peasants and people of all ages and gender, who were coldly murdered in concentration camps or where they lived. Whole villages were wiped out. I suspect the number of victims might have been higher.

There is a population analysis based on 1941 population data of three territories — Croatia, Bosnia and Herzegovina — their different cultures, ethnic groups and nationalities living there. Among Bosnian-Herzegovinians, Serbs and Croats one cannot actually speak of ethnic differences because the three nations are ethnic Slavs. There is even a Serbo-Croatian language. The difference is rather cultural, religious and national. A single ethnic group may have several nations. In Latin America, besides the language we share many ethnic traits. The Dominican Republic and Cuba — just to mention an example — belong to the same ethnic group and are two independent nations.

According to statistics, in 1941, the [Croatian] population was 3.3 million. Forty years later, according to the 1981 census, how many Croats were living there? 4,210,000, that is, an almost one million increase.

Muslims, who are Slavs, too, but of the Muslim religion: In 1941, there were 700,000; in 1981, there were 1,629,000 (more than doubled).

Serbs: how many Serbs were living in that same territory in 1941? 1,925,000. How many after 40 years, according to the 1981 census? 1,879,000, that is, approximately 45,000 less. Based on these facts, people who have analyzed population, customs, habits, growth, etc. have estimated that in that holocaust 800,000 to 900,000 Serbs died.

All of us have heard of Auschwitz and other concentration camps. Some of us have had the possibility of visiting them and having a terrifying vision of what those concentration camps were. Now we find out, or we are told, that there was an extermination camp called Jasenovac, the equal of Auschwitz in Poland. In Jasenovac lie the remains of hundreds of thousands of Serbs as well as thousands of Jews, gypsies and people of all ethnic groups. People say that the biggest Serbian city after Belgrade lies there, below the ground.

The fact that Croatian writers themselves, such as Josép Palau, acknowledge the figure of 200,000 is significant. Since 1982 he has been involved in many international activities linked to European peace movements and has been a representative of various nongovernmental organizations. He has also been a UN consultant.

It is understandable that Yugoslav leaders avoided digging into the issue. It is hard to do so when such a horrible thing has happened. When there have been century-old conflicts, undoubtedly digging into this type of problem would have run counter to the aim of building a solid federation, a united and just state, a peaceful society.

One could ask why the West does not speak of this holocaust. It is particularly important now when they have been dropping thousands and thousands of bombs on that same nation. To this we would have to add that these are only those who died in the territory of Croatia, Bosnia and Herzegovina because the fascist government imposed by Hitler covered more territory, including part of Voivodina. However, there doesn't seem to be any information about Voivodina.

We need to calculate the number of those who died in the territory ruled by that government and those who died in parts temporarily occupied by Italian fascists or Hungarian fascists. I don't mean in combat but in concentration camps and killed in cold blood.

A holocaust and no one talks about it, why? There are sad and painful stories of the more recent massacres and ethnic cleansing, and I don't doubt that they did take place. I have not been there or seen it, nor am I going to ask for the papers. It is enough to know a little of the history of hatred and real conflicts.

But I know, too, that during the 45 years that the Socialist Federal Republic of Yugoslavia existed there was peace among all those ethnic groups. Tito himself was an ethnic Croat but he knew how to win the love of the Serbs and the Serbs were actually the backbone of the resistance. It is understandable that in Tito's time there was not much talk about the matter. Today, in a split-up Yugoslavia, when in one part of the country a crime such as this has been committed, it is worthwhile making these truths known.

I must say that it is not my intention to incite or blame anybody, least of all the people in that country. I do not intend to blame Croats for this. It would be like blaming the Germans for Hitler's massacres of Jews, gypsies and many others who died in concentration camps, in his systematic efforts to coldly exterminate an ethnic group, a nation, a multi-ethnic population or a single ethnic group.

But a holocaust of such magnitude is tremendously important. Blaming the Croat people would be like blaming the Italian people for the crimes of that clown named Mussolini. (I cannot think of calling him anything else because that is what he was to a great extent and he killed many people, invaded, waged war and sent troops to the Soviet Union.) It would be unfair to blame any people for the crimes committed by a fascist system. I want to make this clear, honestly. I am not blaming anybody; I simply rely on historical facts.

Something else must be said: The Jews who suffered the holocaust in Germany and elsewhere were very friendly to the Serbs and very grateful to them, because the Serbs saved the lives of many Jews. It is even said that the U.S. secretary of state, on her way from Czechoslovakia, sought refuge in Serbian territory and there she received help and support from the Serbs. They played a role, fighting heroically against Nazism.

Our position [on Kosovo] is based on principles and is very clear. Not only now, but 12 days after the bombings began, when as a direct or indirect consequence of the bombings, all sorts of conflicts must have been triggered or worsened, we offered 1,000 doctors to a religious Catholic community involved in assisting refugees. Twelve days after the conflict began! Not just a week before Cuba spoke in the United Nations. We did not say it publicly, leaving it to them, until several weeks ago.

Likewise, when the Americans who occupy a base in our territory informed us — they usually do not request permission — that they would bring 20,000 Kosovars, in violation of the terms of the agreement, an agreement that has been violated by all possible means. At least this time they had the decency of telling us, perhaps because they thought that we would say that they should not bring the Kosovars. But we told them: "We absolutely agree that you bring them. We are ready to cooperate in everything. We can offer our hospitals, water services, all the help we can give them."

Later, perhaps they thought things over. Because it was really disgusting to unleash a war which, in its turn, would unleash a colossal migration, a human drama and bring those people from Albania to a naval base in a tropical country, a long distance away. I believe they finally brought 2,000 to a camp in their own territory. Out of the one million, with a generous and humanitarian spirit they have assisted a little over 2,000 refugees; Britain took another handful. The two countries combined assisted some 0.8 percent of the refugees — a rather negligible number.

We said that we agreed, that they would be welcomed in the occupied Cuban territory. We offered medical care and we reiterate it now. That was our clear and categorical position: respect for their cultural, national and religious rights and support for their autonomy. We went even further, and possibly many Yugoslavs do not understand this, or many Serbs do not understand this well; but we admitted the idea of independence provided all Kosovo ethnic groups attained a fair peace and the Serbs in other territories of that republic reached agreement peacefully. Yes, I say that it has to be peacefully and mutually agreed upon.

I believe that such a possibility exists. Yet, I don't think we should interfere with this delicate issue. We have stated our position. We have done our duty. We do not do things to make friends or enemies. Sometimes we hurt friends and make enemies at the same time. But there is something much more important than any temporary advantages: seriousness and honesty.

I have criticized the Europeans with the words I have used without having any feelings of animosity against them. But one day I will be able to demonstrate that I warned them very precisely what was going to happen, only seven days after the attacks began. I apologize for preserving and not declassifying this material.

One of the big European mistakes was that instead of working with moderate forces, they worked with the extremists, whom they called fearful terrorists just a few months ago. It was only in 1998 that the movement went from a few hundred armed men to over 15,000 to 20,000 armed men. Now we have to find out what the famous CIA did, how many it trained, with which weaponry and what tasks it gave them. What nobody doubts is that this war practically had a timetable. I believe that the greatest chance for peace was in supporting moderate groups and not extremist groups.

THIS IS THE LAST IDEA I want to share. Why should we be so concerned about this policy, this onslaught on sovereignty, this attempt to do away with the principles of the UN Charter? Why are all these theories invented, so many pretexts used for humanitarian intervention or against global threats? As I was saying, there is something called diplomacy supported by force which is another concept. What else will follow?

We have had bitter experiences with the behavior of U.S. political leaders. Once in a while they elect someone with a religious ethic. I would dare mention a case in point: President James Carter. I cannot think of Carter waging this type of genocidal war. But we have known a few U.S. presidents of whom the same cannot be said.

We have just sued the United States for $181 billion. In our lawsuit we said: "The unquestionable historical truth about these events and the cynicism and lies that have invariably accompanied all U.S. actions against Cuba can be found in the original documents of the time, produced by those who, from within that country, planned the policy of aggression and subversion against Cuba."

The plots against Cuba and their actions began as soon as we passed the Agrarian Reform Act because U.S. companies owned here estates of 10,000, 50,000 and even 150,000 hectares. We passed a land act that logically and inevitably affected their properties and as of that moment their crimes against Cuba began. By August the first terrorist actions were carried out, the first plans to assassinate Cuban leaders, and it was an honor that they devoted a good number of them to me. They started in November 1959.

Nobody here had spoken of socialism. We talked about socialism on April 16, 1961, when we buried the combatants who fell as victims of the attacks by U.S. warplanes piloted by Cuban mercenaries and deceitfully displaying painted Cuban flags. They even had Stevenson lie at the United Nations when he was an ambassador, the same official explanation they gave when they said that they were rebel Cuban Air Force planes.

Actually, it served as a warning about something we were expecting. We foresaw an imminent mercenary landing in the attempt to destroy our small air force, which they were unable to do because our fighter planes were scattered and the base was defended by antiaircraft batteries. They destroyed part of it, but we still had more planes than pilots and the ones left operational were enough for the time the adventure lasted.

The lawsuit reads: "By this token, it may be illustrative for this Court that, on March 17, 1960, at a meeting attended by Vice-President Richard Nixon" — an angel — "Secretary of State Christian Herter" — who was later not elected president — "Secretary of the Treasury Robert B. Anderson, Assistant Secretary of Defense John N. Irwin, Under Secretary of State Livingston T. Merchant, Assistant Secretary of State Roy Rubottom, Admiral Arleigh Burke of the Joint Chief of Staff, CIA Director Allen Dulles, the high-ranking CIA officers Richard Bissell and J.C. King and the White House officials Gordon Gray and General Andrew J. Goodpaster, the U.S. President approved the so-called 'Program of Covert Action Against the Castro Regime'." A number of brutal actions are mentioned in this CIA document.

Among other things, that program enabled the creation of a secret intelligence and action organization within Cuba, for which the CIA allocated the necessary funds. In a recently declassified memorandum on that meeting, General Goodpaster noted: "The President" — it is President Eisenhower — "said that he knows of no better plan for dealing with this situation. The great problem is leakage and breach of security. Everyone must be prepared to swear that he [Eisenhower] has not heard of it. [...] He said our hand should not show in anything that is done."

Serious things were already taking place here. In August 1959, pirate attacks and bombings began, sugarcane fields were set on fire by planes coming from the United States and the ship *La Coubre* was blown up resulting in the death of 101 Cubans. The [Washington] meeting had been held a few days before. Actually, that was a formal meeting, especially because the CIA had already suggested my assassination before the end of 1959, on December 11. Not even one year after the triumph of the revolution! There are other more revolting things and they are here for those of you who have not read it.

This is another declassified document. Nixon was no longer vice-president nor was Eisenhower president. Kennedy was president and it was after the Bay of Pigs invasion.

On March 7, 1962, the Joint Chiefs of Staff stated in a secret document their belief that a credible internal revolt would be impossible in the next nine to 10 months, requiring a decision by the United States to develop a Cuban 'provocation' as justification for U.S. military action.

On March 9, 1962, under the title "Pretexts to Justify U.S. Military Intervention in Cuba," the Office of the Secretary of Defense submitted to the Joint Chiefs of Staff a package of harassment measures aimed at creating conditions to justify a military intervention in Cuba. See this? They were always looking for pretexts. Some of the measures considered included the following, which were taken to the Joint Chiefs of Staff by the Office of the Secretary of Defense:

A series of well coordinated incidents will be planned to take place in and around Guantánamo [naval base] to give a genuine appearance of being done by hostile Cuban forces.

The United States would respond by executing offensive operations to secure water and power supplies, destroying artillery and mortar emplacements threatening the base. Commence large-scale U.S. military operations.

A "Remember the Maine" incident could be arranged in several forms.

We could blow up a U.S. ship in Guantánamo Bay and blame Cuba.

We could blow up a drone (unmanned) vessel anywhere in the

Cuban waters.

We could arrange to cause such incident in the vicinity of Havana or Santiago as a spectacular result of a Cuban attack from the air or sea, or both.

The presence of Cuban planes or ships merely investigating the intent of the vessel could be fairly compelling evidence that the ship was taken under attack.

The United States could follow up with an air/sea rescue operation covered by U.S. fighters to 'evacuate' remaining members of the non-existent crew.

Casualty lists in U.S. newspapers would cause a helpful wave of national indignation.

We could develop a Communist Cuban terror campaign in the Miami area, in other Florida cities and even in Washington. The terror campaign could be pointed at Cuban refugees seeking haven in the United States.

We could sink a boatload of Cubans en route to Florida (real or simulated).

We could foster attempts on lives of Cuban refugees in the United States even to the extent of wounding in instances to be widely publicized.

Exploding a few plastic bombs in carefully chosen spots, the arrest of Cuban agents and the release of prepared documents substantiating Cuban involvement would also be helpful in projecting the idea of an irresponsible government.

A "Cuban-based, Castro-supported" filibuster could be simulated against a neighboring Caribbean nation.

Use of MiG-type aircraft by U.S. pilots could provide additional provocation.

Harassment of civil aircraft, attacks on surface shipping and destruction of U.S. military drone aircraft by MiG-type planes would be useful as complementary actions.

An F-86 properly painted would convince air passengers that they saw a Cuban MiG, especially if the pilot of the transport were to announce such fact.

Hijacking attempts against civil air and surface craft should appear to continue as harassing measures condoned by the government of Cuba.

It is possible to create an incident, which will demonstrate convincingly that a Cuban aircraft has attacked and shot down a chartered civil airliner en route from the United States to Jamaica, Guatemala, Panama or Venezuela.

The passengers could be a group of college students off on a holiday or any grouping of persons with a common interest to support chartering a non-scheduled flight.

It is possible to create an incident that will make it appear that Communist-Cuban MiGs have destroyed a U.S.A.F. aircraft over international waters in an unprovoked attack.

"Five months later" — of these sinister, truly sinister variables suggested by the Joint Chiefs of Staff — "in August 1962" — mark the year — "General Maxwell D. Taylor, chairman of the Joint Chiefs of Staff, confirmed to President Kennedy that no possibility was perceived whereby the Cuban government could be overthrown without direct U.S. military intervention, which was why the Special Group-Augmented was recommending the even more aggressive approach of Operation Mongoose. Kennedy authorized its implementation as 'a matter of urgency'."

1962: October [Missile] Crisis. Some information simply came to our and the Soviets' attention. Not this document I just read — we did not know about it.

But Khrushchev was totally convinced. For us, it was something we were used to. We were always mobilized on news of a possible invasion. We were not interested in having strategic missiles here. Actually, we were more interested in the image of our country that it would not look like a base of our Soviet friends.

The decision was made based on our sense of solidarity because before the Bay of Pigs invasion they had sent us many weapons. We had hundreds of thousands of weapons. We had already bought them from the socialist camp and the Soviet Union since that March 4, 1960, when *La Coubre* was blown up, bringing weapons from Belgium. In the 13 months before the Bay of Pigs invasion in April [1961], we received dozens and dozens of ships with weapons from the Soviet Union through Czechoslovakia: tanks and cannon, antiaircraft artillery and rifles.

We learned how to use them very quickly. So that when the Bay of Pigs invasion was launched we had hundreds of thousands of men trained and armed, thousands and thousands of artillery men to operate those weapons. They were not very experienced but they could handle them and had a fighting spirit.

The Soviets were very, very concerned because they got news of a possible invasion. They gave us the sources, not the most important, not to me. Possibly the information they received was incomplete but they did give us the information they extracted from their talks with Kennedy and other high-ranking personalities.

By the time of the Bay of Pigs invasion they had sent us not only weapons but they had also made very strong statements and even spoken of the missiles. At that time the Cuban Revolution was like a miracle. They could never have imagined it. It was not imported or promoted by anyone from abroad. It was truly and fully ours.

The only thing we imported, actually, were the books from which we got a revolutionary political culture. To this we added some Cuban notions and tailored it to the Cuban reality.

We had to build our revolutionary consciousness when there were planes, tanks, cannon, communications and many things unimaginable in Engels' days. Since we believed in a number of principles and had a tradition, we conceived the idea of an armed struggle, the strategy and tactics to be pursued.

No Russian had anything to do with it. No Soviet. Nobody. Nobody sent us guns, either. Nobody gave us a dime. Later, there were revolutionary movements in this hemisphere that had tens of millions of dollars. One day I estimated the cost of the assault on Moncada, the *Granma* and the Sierra Maestra warfare — perhaps I am not too wrong if I put their cost at $300,000. So, we can score another point and say that we carried out the cheapest revolution ever.

I was telling you about the [Missile] Crisis. We knew that the United States had some missiles in Turkey and Italy, medium-range missiles that are faster than strategic missiles and bombers. There is no doubt that the presence of 42 missiles here gave the Soviets a certain strategic balance. So, for us, who received weapons, support and even the hope that they might fight for us, no matter how much we wanted to preserve a certain image of the revolution, it was not fair or honorable to refuse an agreement on the medium-range missiles. Actually, for us it would have been better to run the risk of not having them, although based on what we know today, the invasion was a sure thing.

By that time, the number of weapons and trained people we had was considerable. We would have been another Vietnam and paid a very high price.

Why did the attack not take place? The Soviet thesis proved its value. We received additional news but we did not pay attention because we were used to such hazards. We had no fear of imperialism. And we had had the experience of our war that was short but intense, therefore, it was the best of schools to enrich that experience. The Soviets were fully convinced, a conviction that could not come out of the blue, without access to documents or other sensitive sources of information.

Looking back at those times, I see that the recommendations to fabricate a pretext date from March 9, 1962.

It is known that the Soviets had some friends or sympathizers in many U.S. institutions taking part in meetings with a lot of people, meetings resulting in lots of papers. Now I don't have any doubts that what they knew came from very reliable sources. I discussed the problem with the revolutionary leadership. In those days Che, Raúl and other comrades were the main leaders.

The Soviets asked me a question: "What do you think would prevent this invasion?" I told them, and I still believe it: "A Soviet declaration stating that an attack on Cuba would be tantamount to an attack on the Soviet Union." They said: "Yes, yes. But how do we make it plausible?" That was when they suggested deploying the missiles. Then we started thinking and analyzing among ourselves, and we analyzed it from the angle I told you, in terms of honor and solidarity. The answer was "Yes." That was weeks after instructions had been given to fabricate the pretext for an invasion.

The moment we signed an agreement on that, we began working really fast. By August [1962], Kennedy had accepted the plan as a matter of urgency."

We probably prevented a direct invasion at that time. Later, there were rumors of movements of arms and ships, and so on. In July and August there were some rumors because the missiles were arriving — land-to-air missiles — and a large amount of weapons, modern planes and many other things. The crisis really began after October 20. The Soviets were absolutely right. Khrushchev was absolutely right, his certainty based on access to the documents and activities in which the Unites States was engaged. And they had many more resources than we did to obtain that information.

We had enough hard information, I think, and, above all else, intuition — we outguessed them. On the other hand, we had a rule: An attack should never take us by surprise. It is better to mobilize 20 times, even if nothing happens, than not mobilizing once and be attacked. We might say that a mobilized troop or country is 20-25 times stronger than when taken by surprise.

That was what happened to the Soviets in June 1941, when Stalin behaved like an ostrich, sticking his head into a hole while the Germans concentrated three million troops near the border, tens of thousands of vehicles, thousands upon thousands of tanks, thousands upon thousands of planes. They attacked on a Sunday, when many officers and soldiers were on leave and they destroyed almost every plane on the ground. That story is incredible and we know it very well because we have read a lot about that war and it has helped enrich our experience in many fields.

It was only when the Americans decided to declassify these documents that we learned the details of those sinister plans and their unbelievable lack of scruples. All this is useful today. Other documents will be declassified. Something like the Bay of Pigs is definitely easy to prove. But there is a whole story, from the first to the last man recruited, who did it, where he was sent, the weapons he was given. We took 1,200 prisoners here and swapped them for baby food and medicine. That was the compensation they paid.

Through the declassification process they have put in our hands documents, precedents and facts. Now, we are engaged in this legal battle. I hope that they do not invade us because they consider us a global threat.

I can certainly speak of another global threat, namely, ideas. Clear ideas, such as those you have analyzed and adopted. We should all help globalize ideas, help them expand. We should all work the miracle of sending them everywhere, as I have said. Those are indeed global threats: speaking, reasoning, thinking, explaining, demonstrating. If in your opinion I have been too extensive, in my opinion I have not.

10

The Empire is Unsustainable

Rio de Janeiro State University

T he summit was not an easy meeting for me. We are demons; Cuba is hell. This has been said so many times, so many millions of times, by our neighbors in the North... Although it would be incorrect to call them our neighbors in the North, it would be better to call them the adversaries among our neighbors in the North, neighbors who have been fooled for a long time. The U.S. people are not guilty of the many historical crimes committed by that empire, even before it became an empire.

As a matter of principle, we have never blamed the U.S. people. The most that we can say, recalling Lincoln's famous quote, is that you can fool all the people some of the time, or some people all of the time, but you cannot fool all the people all the time. Today the world has globalized and the globalization of the world has brought about the globalization of lies. We could say the same thing: you can fool some of the world all the time, or all the world some of the time, but you who are here today are demonstrating that it is not possible to fool all the world all the time. This means the beginning of global truth and the beginning of global victory.

I read the wire services every day, a great many press dispatches, maybe 200, 300; it is an old habit which allows me to know what is being said in the world, and even some of what is happening in the world. You can become practically an expert in identifying the many

---

Fidel Castro gave this speech at Rio de Janeiro State University, June 30, 1999, while visiting Brazil for the Summit of Heads of State and Government from Latin America, the Caribbean and the European Union.

lies said in the world and the many truths that are hidden as well as the mechanisms they use.

Quite often, while reading the press dispatches we see a headline that has nothing to do with the content [of an article]. These are techniques used to manipulate certain news so that all of the world's newspapers, for example, print the headline, and then add a text.

On the other hand, it is true that many people read only the headlines in the newspaper, nothing else. It is sad but true. The habit of reading has largely been lost in this world while there are other major media for spreading ideas such as radio and television. But radio and television have also globalized. There are major networks that broadcast their message to every corner of the world, audiovisual media that have tremendous influence and, in most cases, these audiovisual media are in the hands of our neighbors in the North. They own the majority of the mass media and the means of communication, almost all the satellites that will one day block out the sun. They are the owners of the most powerful film industry and of the most powerful television and videocassette industries.

Some have studied this phenomenon and we must be aware of what is happening. Which of our countries could spend $300 million on a movie, a single movie, recoup its cost on the domestic market, and then, after having earned so much money, circulate the movie around the world at any price?

The statistics are available on the percentage of U.S. movies seen by Latin Americans, the percentage of television series coming from the United States, the percentage of the videocassettes originated in the United States circulating around the world. To a greater or lesser extent, there are countries in this hemisphere where 90 percent of what is shown in movie theaters and on television is produced in the United States, all of it developed and designed with a commercial intent and aimed at spreading what we could call the worst that society has to offer, such as violence.

I read once that 65 percent of these materials contain violence. No other country in the world produces movies, television programs, etc, with such a high percentage of violence, sex and extravagant life-styles. Then, what they produce on a fundamentally commercial basis they use to poison, confuse and fool a large part of the world. This is perhaps one of the most serious problems we face today.

A $300-million movie not only makes profits through screenings but is also tied in with commercials, product sales, to such an extent that some of them exceed a billion dollars in earnings. They have mixed everything together, and these large communications syndicates, film studios and other major companies tend to merge.

We are not trying to say that there are not some good productions — and some are really very good — but it is very difficult for us to choose the movies we show in the theaters and on television. Every week we have to show two or three movies.

Europe, which produced a lot of good movies 30 or 35 years ago, with few exceptions has been practically overwhelmed by U.S. cultural aggression.

There are some countries, like Britain, where almost 80 percent of what is shown is produced in the United States, and in many other cultured European countries there is an average of 70, 65, perhaps 60-odd percent of U.S.-produced material. Perhaps France, as an exception, receives less than 50 percent, but it is the only one. It is trying to defend its culture against this invasion and it seems to be making a special effort.

Several months ago at a congress of Cuban writers and artists, which we could call a cultural congress, the point on which all of the hundreds of delegates unanimously agreed was the cultural aggression afflicting Latin America and the world. All of this material serves a particular ideology and a model of consumption that if applied worldwide would accelerate what would truly be the end of history. Not the end of history that some euphorically talked about after the collapse of the socialist bloc; the end of history, in this case, means the point that we would be led to following the road traveled by the world today, that of the consumer society.

Somebody spoke about the number of undernourished people, the number of poor people. They do not number in the hundreds of millions but in the billions. Eighty percent of the world's population today is poor, not including the Chinese, who are poor but who eat every day, and have clothing and shoes, and homes, and medical care and education. Learning Chinese is not at all easy and I have a theory that the Chinese are highly intelligent, winning almost all of the math and physics Olympics everywhere, because they develop their intelligence learning their language.

One of our sister nations, Venezuela, once had the good idea of creating a ministry called the Ministry of Intelligence. Many people laughed at the ministry and the minister. I think I was one of the few people in the world who did not laugh at either. I even had the opportunity to talk with the minister and he maintained that intelligence is developed in the first years of life, during a certain period. There are researchers working to develop techniques to raise the IQ, because these human beings, meaning us, have considerable mental capacity. At least, the equipment is installed in our heads but they say that humans only use about 10 or 12 percent of their intellectual capacity. And, of course, the tests that have been carried out demonstrate that certain teaching methods help us to use 15 percent, 16 percent, or even more. Let's hope the day comes — and woe betide the pretenders, the liars, the exploiters — when humans come to use 50 percent of their intellectual capacity!

We know — and it is not sacrilegious to say so — that we are the product of natural evolution. This was discovered in the middle of last century, approximately 150 years ago, and the theory was very controversial and highly criticized. But I say that it is not sacrilegious because I recently read that Pope John Paul II had declared that the theory of evolution was not incompatible with the doctrine of creation; I believe that everyone accepts this reality, believers and non-believers alike. But humans can no longer continue evolving in the same way they did for hundreds of thousands of years. In the future, the great asset of the human mind will be the enormous intelligence potential that is genetically received but that we are unable to use. That is what we have at our disposal, that is where the future lies.

WE MUST UNDERSTAND THAT WE are living in a world where events are happening more rapidly than our awareness of just how unsustainable this world order is, and of the imperative and inevitable need to replace it with another, if humanity is to survive.

We must sow ideas, many ideas. What can those of us who do not control huge mass media networks do about it? We use some of their electronic media. There is, for example, the internet, but it is difficult to transmit ideas to the countries of the Third World through the internet. Why is that? Because only two percent of Latin Americans, for example, have access to the internet while between 70 percent and 75 percent of Americans have access to it.

Well, we cannot depend on the internet to transmit ideas and messages to you but it serves, at least, to provide those with access to the internet with messages, ideas, reasoning and arguments on just how insane, fragile and unsustainable their world is. These messages need to reach not only the victims but also the victimizers; that is, the many people who think but who have never come across a viewpoint other than those they see in movies or television or read in their newspapers, all of which are instruments that serve an economic and social system of exploitation and domination. It is with these media that they invade the world carrying the rotten ideology and lies of imperialism.

We have a good deal of proof because many people visit us in Cuba where they learn about our modest country, its sacrifices and limitations, especially in these times of the so-called "special period," after the socialist bloc collapsed and we were left subjected to a double blockade. We lost our markets and the guaranteed supplies, which we were not able to acquire in other places because they would not sell them to us. All that was gone and the blockade was opportunistically tightened as it befits the actions of that great empire. It seemed to be saying: Now is the time to squash those insolent people on that little island like bugs; that little island that should be ours, the one we have dreamed about for 200 years, where they have had the nerve to disrespect us and rebel against the dogmas of imperialism and the neocolonial established order.

Forty years have passed and they keep trying; but the more time that passes, the more puzzled they are. They undoubtedly think that we are a special kind of bug. But no, we are exactly the same as all the other bugs; it is just that we have become bugs with a consciousness. That is the only evolution that has taken place in our country. It is with this consciousness that we have defended ourselves throughout all this time, and even more so when we were left completely alone in terms of our economic relations with our basic markets and sources of credits and supplies, and without access to any of the international financial institutions.

Every once in a while we hear in Cuba about an institution called the International Monetary Fund. We have also heard that there is an Inter-American Development Bank and another called the World Bank. We ask, "What is that?" Although some of us know very well, the immense majority of Cubans have not heard very much about the International Monetary Fund and the World Bank, fortunately.

It may sound strange to you but we have learned to live without a Monetary Fund, without a World Bank, without an Inter-American Development Bank, without the many credits they talk about, the export credits, etc. We must pay about twice the interest paid by other countries for all our loans, which are always short-term loans, because due to so much blockade and so many Torricelli Acts and Helms-Burton Acts, plus a mountain of amendments that are not even known, many take advantage of the situation to charge higher interest.

Every now and then, after the U.S. Appropriation Act is hurriedly passed — it is a 5,000 pages long act — by many lawmakers, quite a few who are friendly with Cuba suddenly send us messages expressing their regret for not having realized that there was a paragraph that constituted a new measure to tighten the blockade. Many members of Congress do not even read many of the bills approved by the U.S. Congress! It is lobbying that determines in a game of give and take: "Go along with this wording for me, I need it for my state, and I will go along with this one that you need."

That is the way it is; an endless exchange and in the end nobody knows what is in these laws. That explains why in such a democratic country the legal profession is so prosperous and there is work for so many lawyers, because there is no way to understand that. I imagine that a wise man from ancient Rome would go insane by simply reading one-tenth of the laws approved in that country, and its laws function in the same way, as do its judges and its courts.

In that absolutely perfect and ideal democracy, everyone knows how money is raised on the eve of every campaign. They have gone so far as to rent out Abraham Lincoln's room during election periods because some people have certain whims. They admire Lincoln, or they have heard about that bearded figure, the lumberjack who first became a lawyer and then a president, whose lot it was to live in that moment of history after a great internal war influenced by agricultural and industrial interests and sectors leading to a change in the form of slavery and its formal abolition.

The cruel and true historical fact is that in Cuba, after slavery was abolished in 1886 and the slaves were transformed into supposedly free workers, they ended up living in even worse conditions, because capitalism is the continuation of the slave system under an equally inhuman and merciless form of exploitation.

FORTUNATELY, WE HAVE BEEN WITNESSING the world's growing awareness of certain realities. After the stunning blows dealt to the progressive and revolutionary movement, many people are meditating and thinking things over.

The changes are visible, and we are doing everything we can to spread ideas, and if we need to distribute millions and millions of booklets, we will do so. Solidarity groups often take charge of reproducing them; they sell some and use the money raised to print more, and so on. A lot of information is being spread that way and it is like the guided missiles used in Yugoslavia. They are aimed directly at certain individuals, intellectuals, outstanding personalities, media directors, and members of parliament, political and social leaders. We spread these ideas to all those who can have an impact on the destiny of their nations. If these ideas are clear, righteous and objective, then conditions are ideal in the world today for them to spread. We cannot allow ourselves to be crushed by the immense power of the mass media owned by those currently in control of the world.

The importance of this meeting lies in the fact that those in the North want to swallow us up whole, and if we allow ourselves to be swallowed up, they will digest us faster than that whale in the Bible digested the prophet I believe they called Jonah. It appears that the whale delayed a while and the prophet managed to escape from its belly; but if this whale swallows us, it will digest us really quickly.

They can buy everything, thanks to a mechanism created over the course of this century, which can be traced back to World War I. The dollar began to replace the pound sterling as the world's reserve currency and they invented fixed-interest bonds to finance the war effort; but when they least expected it they were hit by a huge crisis that lasted from 1929 until 1940. And there is nothing to guarantee that this will not happen again.

They are constantly inventing things to avoid being hit by another huge crisis, while the value of their stocks keeps climbing, sometimes doubling, tripling and quadrupling in barely 10 years, thus creating fabulous artificial fortunes and inflating a balloon that can and must inevitably burst. In 1929, only five percent of the people in the United States had their savings invested in the stock market while today 50 percent of the Americans' savings are invested in stocks, in addition to their pension and retirement funds. Therefore, such an explosion would be truly catastrophic.

In recent months, they were very frightened that this very thing would happen, so they switched from anti-inflation policies to anti-recession policies amidst great confusion. One cannot believe all they say, but one needs to know what they are thinking and what they are saying quietly among themselves. The fact is that they have created such privileges for themselves that the country whose people save less of their net income than any other in the world is precisely the one that spends, invests and buys the most.

It is said that the Japanese are the champions of personal savings, that they save more than 30 percent of their personal income. In Europe the average is around 20 percent; thus there exist various different parameters. The Americans have been the ones to save the least for some time now. They sustain the growth that they boast so loudly about on the basis of a domestic market of 270 million people who spend unrestrictedly. If they own a car, they change it for a new one every two years, some of them every year; they buy everything that is produced and preserve employment on this basis.

Of course, the raw materials cost them nothing: whether it is iron, nickel, petroleum, whatever, they pay for it with papers. Those who receive the papers store them away, for the most part, thus creating monetary reserves in the central banks or even the private banks while taking the risk of suffering the same as many so-called emerging countries: losing in a matter of weeks the reserves accumulated over dozens of years.

I am explaining all of this in a simplified manner because they really use different mechanisms. In essence, they print the bank notes, buy things, and those who receive the bank notes store them away. They give nothing in exchange for this. Or perhaps it would be more correct to say that this is what happens with a significant part of these bank notes; another part, as is only natural, is spent by their owners on goods and services.

Actually, at Bretton Woods the United States assigned itself the task of issuing and protecting the international reserve currency, but it failed to fulfill its duties and turned the country into a privileged monopoly that has access to all the money it wants through its bonds and bank notes. They allow themselves to have a trade deficit of $200 billion, $300 billion, but no one else. Naturally, they import everything they want. They will never lack a gallon or a liter of fuel, and there, where there are more cars than anywhere else, a liter of gasoline is cheaper than in any other country.

Look at all the privileges they have come to accumulate, resulting in personal savings being less than zero level last year; that is, on average they spent more than they earned. There may be some that saved part of what they earned and others who spent much more, but the average savings of U.S. citizens was under zero. This is something unprecedented in the history of capitalism; still, everything remains so very calm. They talk about a buoyant economy, but who is paying for it and how long can they keep paying for it? Also, what will happen when this system and these enormous balloons burst and everything collapses?

This is absolutely true, and we understand that it is our duty to help the masses — the billions of poor people in the world and even the middle class — recognize these realities since the world must be prepared for the moment such disaster hits. I assure you that in recent months they had a close call. All it took was a crisis in Russia, whose Gross Domestic Product accounts for two percent of the world economy, and the suspension of payment of a few short-term obligations. Suddenly, there was panic and the Dow Jones dropped a huge number of points, practically overnight. It seemed that disaster was already on its way, if the crisis extended throughout Latin America.

It was pandemonium when the government, the U.S. Treasury and the Federal Reserve realized that if the Latin American economy burned, the fire would reach the U.S. stock markets. They tried to head off the crisis by lowering the interest rates, or rather injecting money into circulation to prevent a serious depression. However, they have merely postponed it and the longer it is put off, the greater the disaster will be. Later there was renewed euphoria, more spending, another increase in stock values on the market and more speculation.

The problems are not all that complex. I would even say they are relatively easy to explain. These are the pillars that sustain the empire. It will collapse and not by work of our good wishes. It will collapse because they are building on unsustainable foundations, and the day could come when disaster strikes; and the peoples and the world are unprepared to deal with this and draw from it the necessary lessons. This would lead to all kinds of crises, everywhere in the world.

I believe that, rather than weapons, the peoples need ideas. They need a change from an inhumane, unsustainable global world that threatens life on the planet, to a just and humanitarian social order that offers humanity an opportunity to survive. The peoples need a world with a bit of drinking water and air to breathe, where the necessary food is available and advanced technology can be used to produce housing, schools to educate the children, medicines to preserve human health and medical care indispensable to all, children, adolescents and the elderly.

Why do they talk to us about the 21st century and fill our heads with illusions that last less than the bubbles in the champagne with which the world's privileged minority will celebrate the arrival of the new century? We already know that billions of people in our world, where there are already six billion of us, will be celebrating with a sparkling drink — let's hope it is not Coca-Cola!

I say this because in this globalized world we also see the strange phenomenon of countries with cultures dating back thousands of years, such as India — with all due respect, it is a country we greatly admire — where the people drink U.S. Coca-Cola and eat hamburgers. Of course, the owners of the fast-food chains of restaurants say that those hamburgers are made with buffalo meat, or lamb but not beef, given that the centuries-old traditions there allow for the consumption of the cow's milk but not its meat. Anyway, who knows what those gentlemen from the transnational mix in there? They are quite capable of mixing the meat of cows found dead along the roads. We know how unscrupulous those gentlemen are when it comes to human health. But even in countries as extraordinary and with as much merit as China, the foreign multinationals are attempting to introduce all of these consumption habits. This is a good example of Yankee cultural globalization.

And if only it were just Coca-Cola and hamburgers! What is really awful is that they are introducing into the human mind, which has so much potential, the idea of living the way people live in Paris, London, New York or California. It is an idyllic world about which I once heard the U.S. president speaking at a WTO meeting in Geneva. Of course, they need to tell the world something, so they say that everything they are doing is aimed at a future when the whole world is middle class.

I jokingly told some journalists that, after Karl Marx, Clinton was the only one to have conceived of a classless society. For Marx, it would be a society of workers, for Clinton a bourgeois society. The former was thinking about the exploited workers; the latter dreaming of the middle class in the elite suburbs of California and other wealthy U.S. cities with contented owners of inflated stocks who have two cars, electric power, one or two telephones, cable and satellite television, the internet to order anything they want, any movie, even to shop in a supermarket without having to leave the house, buying whatever they want, paying with a credit card or whatever, since they do not even need to bother carrying money around. Good heavens! They have achieved what Karl Marx once dreamed about: the removal of money based on a formula that never occurred to Marx: that of first gaining control over all of the money in the world, then working the alchemist's miracle of changing paper into gold and becoming the real or potential owners of the world's entire natural resources.

Do you think that is enough for the empire? No! The Persian Gulf, with a few exceptions, is theirs, all theirs. The Caspian Sea, with its immense reserves of oil and gas, that entire region belongs almost completely to them or to their transnationals. Wherever they go, in Africa or any other part of the world, either on land or in the sea, they try to control all of the raw materials in existence. They hope to buy all of the gas in Russia, which has the largest reserves, and all of the oil so that these reserves become the property of their companies; it is never too much for them. They do not want to leave anything for the Europeans.

The Europeans wanted to make some investments in Iran, Libya and a few other countries, so the Yankees passed another law according to which they cannot invest in those countries. That was how we became a sort of exchange currency. They were seeking an "understanding," so that if the Senate agreed to moderate one of the articles in the Helms-Burton Act regarding the European investors' interests in Cuba, the United States would be tolerant of some of the investments made by the Europeans in Iran, Libya and elsewhere. That definitively internationalized the infamous law and made them all happy in the end.

Europe will be a powerful and wealthy supranational state; it is moving in that direction. This powerful and wealthy supranational state has contradictory interests with those who want to keep everything and be in control of everything. By this token, it is unquestionable that this immense territory made up of the Latin

America and Caribbean countries, with a population of almost 500 million and vast natural resources, must adopt the most intelligent tactics. Likewise, it should recognize the contradictions between two very wealthy and highly developed areas, which have conflicting interests in the economic field and others.

Europe does not want to see its cultures swept away. That same Europe would not be able to survive economically today if it were isolated and divided. Thus, after centuries of warring they have worked the miracle of coming to an agreement, uniting, integrating, agreeing upon a single currency, to defend themselves and their markets from speculation, or to put it simply, to survive.

We Latin Americans mostly speak the same language, share the same culture and are descendants of more or less the same ethnic groups; here there is no basis for so-called ethnic cleansing. We are a group of peaceful nations who have managed to live in peace for a long time, with few exceptions. We have many more factors that unite us and you can even see how those in the North are attempting to destroy the integrating elements of our culture, such as the language, a major element. We are a combination of Europeans, indigenous peoples and Africans, and according to the laws of biology hybrids tend to be more vigorous, stronger and even more intelligent, more creative. There must be some reason why they seek us out to win championships.

You can see that many of our European friends' teams are made up of Third World people. They have gathered them together, and they win games and even championships, and then they boast, "This is real racial unity; this one came from Algeria, this one came from Nigeria, this one came from here, this one came from there." I don't understand why there are not more pure Aryans in their teams.

WE BELIEVE THAT OUR NATIONS have all of the potential talent needed and something more: all the potential for kindness and generosity. You can see it if you have the privilege of taking a short trip — it has happened to me here in Rio de Janeiro and in Niteroi. I have seen it in the streets, speaking with the workers who take care of us, or those in charge of security, services in the conference centers, the hotels and everywhere — you see nothing but kindness, friendliness, decency, modesty. I have not found a single arrogant Brazilian, not one! Nor have I found a Brazilian who is not friendly and helpful. In other places, in highly developed countries, it is hard to find the modesty, the courtesy you see in Brazilians, in Venezuelans.

We recently visited the Latin American Medical School [in Havana], which was established in only a matter of weeks, after the hurricanes hit [Central America], using an old naval school with great capacity. There are currently around 1,800 students there, and its total capacity will be around 3,400. It is a truly excellent school that we, a blockaded and poor country, have managed to open in a very short time, not because we have money, since our monetary resources are scarce, but because we have a great human capital, a great human capital!

While they were turning paper into gold, we were turning ignorance into science, ignorance into knowledge, selfishness into solidarity. We have lots of evidence on this. I think I should give you a few examples: Over the last 30-odd years, 26,000 Cuban doctors have provided free services to the Third World, far from home and family, in the most remote places, saving lives, many lives, tens of thousands and hundreds of thousands, perhaps millions of lives. Not a word about this will ever appear in those media monopolized by our neighbors in the North.

Ah! If we arrest a spy, the world comes tumbling down! If a few individuals — who shamelessly operate at the service of the U.S. Interests Section in Cuba paid by that country's treasury attempt to divide the people and support the criminal blockade — receive a relatively light sentence, in a case where they should receive five times the sentence, there is a formidable uproar.

I want you to know that simply for visiting Cuba, a constitutional right, a U.S. citizen can be punished with a fine of up to $300,000 and 10 years' imprisonment. And woe to anyone working for another country as a foreign agent in the United States! Countless years in prison await them.

They define everything, from who respects human rights and who does not, to who is helping in the fight against drug trafficking and who is not. They are the world's moral judges, not only the material owners, but also the supreme judges. If one day they felt like saying that Brazil is a global threat because of a potential for drug cultivation, they would say it. It has happened in other places, unfortunately. Whatever they call a global threat can be subject to a NATO military intervention.

There is absolutely no need to give tougher sentences to the petty traitors who sell out for their gold or their greenbacks. What we must do is demonstrate that we do not fear their masters, that we are not willing to allow impunity for its agents and for those who betray their nation, and that our people will never accept pressure or blackmail from anyone. But there is no need for severe penal sanctions. There will always be a greater sanction, that of history: watching powerlessly as their every plan is thwarted, seeing how this small and heroic country stands firm. That was said here today. Yes, perhaps our country has a small merit: for 40 years, it has been capable of resisting the siege and the aggression by the most powerful imperial forces that history has known.

IDEAS ARE THE KEY AND they must be stated courageously. I was telling you that the meeting recently held in Rio was important, due to the common interests shared by European, Latin American and Caribbean nations. But there may also be interests not held in common. In any case, the mere fact that they met is historic. Fortunately, Cuba — the Cinderella — was not excluded. Some time ago, at a meeting held in Guadalajara, Mexico, we had the honor of being included. It was the first time that a meeting was held in the absence of the United States.

In the past, Latin Americans would meet every time Washington convened a meeting. [All they would need to do is] move their index finger [like this] to call them; that's all, and everyone, without exception, would rush to Washington.

Since the inception of the Ibero-American Summits, we are meeting without a notice from Washington. This time Latin American and Caribbean nations — the latter usually neglected — met with the European Union countries here in Rio de Janeiro. This has been a conference of historic significance. It was not easy to produce documents because there are many conflicting interests, and while these countries may have disagreements with the United States they are its military allies.

I was listening carefully to everyone here and I heard certain statements on the genocidal war that has just been waged in the heart of Europe.

No crime or ethnic cleansing can justify genocide against an entire people, the genocide of millions of children, pregnant women, other women, men and elders who will for ever live with the trauma of the terrifying clamor of the bombs, the wailing of the sirens and the deafening roar of low-flying jet fighters. Those children, now three, four, five, six, seven or eight years' old, who were forced to rush to the shelters every night will never forget. When exposed to someone afraid of thunderstorms, some children will experience that same fear for a lifetime. Just imagine 80 days of bombing, low-flying jets and wailing sirens. What will be imprinted in the minds of millions? All the wealth of a country was destroyed in a matter of minutes.

Claiming that a country's power grid is a military target is like saying that this theater can be bombed because it has a number of lights on. Depriving millions of people of electricity in the midst of winter — no lighting, heat or energy for cooking — is definitely an act of genocide. It is an attempt to force a people to surrender to weapons and methods of mass extermination. If every bridge is blasted, if all communications are destroyed, if vital services, including the hospitals' intensive care units, maternity and children's wards are rendered useless, what is that if not genocide?

There is no need to go any further. In our view, to blockade a country forcing it to yield through hunger and disease, particularly when its people are honorable, worthy and patriotic enough not to surrender, that blockade is an act of genocide. Let's call a spade a spade once and for all!

The issue at hand was extremely serious for it was associated with the sovereignty of all our countries, and the problems and conflicts, social turmoil and upheavals of all kinds that hunger will bring to the world as a result of the order that has been imposed on it. Apparently, they are afraid of this; they understand it and intend to be ready to quell any peoples' attempt to rebel. At least, they try to sow terror but they will not be able to avert the inevitable.

The war in Yugoslavia has been the most cowardly war ever waged, for it has been the only war in history where the aggressors did not lose a single life. It was a technological war, practically conducted on the internet, by using and abusing the technologies they have developed, often using minds from the Third World where laboratories or resources are unavailable, so they hire those minds and take them away.

Coincidentally, while this genocide was being committed, at a time of much frustration, NATO celebrated its 50th anniversary. One month of bombing had already passed and they had initially estimated three days, or five at the very most. They had encountered the will of a truly heroic people who had fought against fascism, held back 40 Nazi divisions during World War II and endured a holocaust.

Much research on that matter is required, and much writing needs to be done. Hypocrites must be exposed, quite a few lies must be disproved and quite a few facts that have been kept hidden by the West must be brought to light.

On April 24, in the midst of the champagne-splashed celebrations of its 50th anniversary, NATO proclaimed its new strategic concept for the next 50 years, and therein lay the threat. This military bloc was originally designed as a defensive alliance that, according to its statutes, could only take action within the boundaries of its member countries; in Yugoslavia they went beyond that limit.

I must say, in all honesty, that not all the positions [of NATO members] are the same. I realize that possibly the majority of them are genuinely ashamed of what happened in Europe, of that war calculated to last for a maximum of five days but which stretched to 79, a war in which they had already been defeated. The country had been destroyed and had nothing else to lose.

Then they exercised all their influence to impose on the Serbs a political formula that contained virtually all the demands and objectives of the NATO aggressors. The matter was strongly debated at the UN Security Council in early June [1999]. Our ambassador took the floor twice, and I think his statements were truly brilliant while the other parties did not have a case.

By then we were extremely worried that for the first time certain theories and doctrines were being launched as setting a precedent. A European member of NATO went on record there to declare that the UN Charter was anachronistic and all the other rights enshrined in that charter were subordinate to the Alliance's new and noble humanitarian sentiments.

Those who starve tens of millions of people to death around the world have suddenly found that they hold the deepest and loftiest humanitarian sentiments.

Those who killed four million people and maimed millions more in Vietnam, who poisoned the land and forests, and used chemicals whose eventual consequences are yet unknown, now proclaim the revocation of the countries' right to sovereignty and security, the anachronistic nature of the UN Charter and the right to global intervention.

Here are bizarre and coincidental events: a 50th anniversary and a new doctrine for the military alliance; debates at the UN on June 10 and a country that openly proclaims — right there in the United Nations and for the first time ever — things that were hitherto only rumored or quietly discussed. The announcement did not come from one of the larger countries but from a relatively small European country closely connected with the big boss in that military alliance. They had come to an agreement. Our ambassador figured it all out and prepared some quick notes when he realized that a debate was about to take place.

Curiously enough, another country of this hemisphere, not the United States but also a NATO member — a country which was never a metropolis and had always treated the Latin American and Caribbean countries with respect and discretion, never showing any imperialistic or interventionist pretensions — immediately and unashamedly supported that proclamation of the right to intervene and the subordination of the UN Charter's most sacred principles to NATO's impudent interpretation. Let me mention four causes. Firstly, drugs; secondly, terrorism; thirdly, massive human rights abuses — put forward by those who kill so many people and commit massive human rights violations every year, or every day — and fourthly, internal conflicts. Humanitarian intervention, as determined and decided by them.

One may think of a country like Colombia, for example, that has been a victim of the development of the drug industry. The source of its tragedy is in the large U.S. drug market that has made millions of Colombians socially dependent on drugs. There are also internal conflicts in Colombia. These could be interpreted as two reasons for NATO to decide at any time to launch thousands of bombs and missiles on Colombia.

Admittedly, all throughout this century now coming to an end, our northern neighbors have never needed any Atlantic alliance or any new strategic approach to intervene anywhere they pleased. They gained possession of Puerto Rico, which has heroically defended its culture, quite similar to ours; they occupied the Isthmus of Panama and before that they had seized more than half of Mexico. They intervened in Central America; they have intervened in Haiti and the Dominican Republic several times and not on account of global threats but rather to collect interest and debt repayments amounting to tens of millions of dollars. They seized control of customs, collected their debt from Haiti and left Papa Doc, of the Duvalier clan, in control. They did the same in the Dominican Republic. They occupied the country, collected their debts and left the Trujillo clan in power. Caamaño rebelled with a group of military officers in 1965, and immediately 40,000 troops were dispatched by President Johnson to occupy the country and crush the uprising.

They intervened in Grenada with the pretext that some students from a U.S. school were in danger there, but these students were never safer. We can certify that because we were in Grenada building an airport and know everything that happened there.

One fine day they invaded Panama, without there being any agreement, treaty or doctrine whatsoever. They have done as it has pleased them and the Security Council did not even issue a condemnation.

You are familiar with what they have done to Cuba for many years. Declassified documents attest to that. A legal claim has been filed by the people of Cuba against the U.S. government for human damages and compensation for the amount of $181.1 billion, for the death of 3,478 Cubans killed at the Bay of Pigs, in the explosion of the *La Coubre* ship, the bombing of a Cubana airliner off Barbados or the fight against [counterrevolutionary] bandits organized and supplied by the United States. The case is supported not only by our own evidence but also by secret U.S. documents, which have been declassified.

A few months earlier, they had made a decision to freeze the funds owed to Cuba as payment for telephone services between the two countries. Each country receives a share of the payment for such services. Last December, around $19 million in payments to be made by U.S. telephone companies under agreements and contracts executed with the involvement of the U.S. government were blocked to pay a $187 million compensation claimed by the relatives of three U.S. nationals born in Cuba.

For years, these people had been committing violations and taking part in provocations in our territorial waters and air space. After our many warnings and expressed concern over a potential incident, their acts and provocation went so far that finally, one day, an unfortunate incident happened. The event then became a pretext to pass the Helms-Burton Act, which Clinton himself had qualified as absurd since it would cost Cuba the unbearable and unheard-of sum of $100 billion.

But this incident did not happen near Washington, Miami or New York. It was an incident in the vicinity of Havana provoked by an organization [Brothers to the Rescue] that was tolerated and encouraged to provoke such incidents. Three people were killed while directly taking part in illegal and provocative actions against our country, and for each of them $62,542,637 were claimed. Right after this lawsuit was filed the funds were blocked awaiting a court ruling by a judge, one of the many they have. Never in 40 years has one of their judges ruled in favor of Cuba. People who have committed brutal murders, hijacked a vessel and taken refuge there are released almost immediately.

There is something else exclusively applicable to Cuba. Ours is the only country in the world whose nationals, if willing to emigrate, only need to set foot on U.S. territory to be entitled to resident status. This was always part of their harassment plans. While consistently displaying their wealth and after dividing families, the privileges granted to those who decided to illegally migrate to the United States not only served as propaganda but also served the interests of certain politicians and certain lobbies.

Immediately after the triumph of the revolution, the large landowners and the wealthiest people in the country who carried their money off with them were the ones who left Cuba. Many war criminals also took millions of dollars with them, as well as their managers and technical personnel, which is why these immigrants were among those who prospered the fastest. Since they have a lot of money, they finance political campaigns, even for the presidency and not just for members of Congress, mayors and senators.

I insist that our claim was filed for the death of 3,478 compatriots, including those killed at the Bay of Pigs, as I previously said.

Around 5,000 acts of terrorism were committed in just two years following U.S. government plans, and it is not simply our word. Well-informed ex-CIA officers have written about such acts either after they were committed or while involved in each of these plans; after 30, 35 or almost 40 years these documents have been declassified. Not everything has been declassified though, since they keep confidential some of the most compromising or embarrassing, and some declassified documents are edited with deletions; but certain institutions are dedicated to chasing down and collecting documents of this nature.

Our lawsuit demands $30 million in human losses for each Cuban killed and $10 million in damages. In other words, $40 million, a lot less than they claimed and for which Cuba was indicted by a U.S. judge.

We have demanded much less. Do you know how much we would have demanded had we used the same basis for calculation as they did? Let me explain briefly. As the claim was against the Cuban government and its air force, they calculated that the air force had 100 MiG fighters, each worth $45 million. We wish we could sell each of those alleged MiGs for $45 million in the marketplace! Then, they multiplied the $45 million by 100 and the product was $4.5 billion. The judge ruled a payment in damages amounting to one percent of the total value of the air force, and one percent of $4.5 billion is $45 million. That was the basis of their calculation: $45 million for each death, and there were three. This figure represented the bulk of the claim, to which further amounts were later added.

Do you know what would have happened had we used the same basis for calculation? We might estimate that the U.S. air force is worth $500 billion, including of course its B-2s, worth two billion each, its B-52's, its aircraft carriers and thousands of other sophisticated aircraft. We might work out our calculations based on this figure and not on its actual value, which must be a lot more than twice as much, leaving out the navy and the army, although U.S. battle ships escorted the Bay of Pigs invaders. Also, it was the army that supplied the tanks brought by the invaders and the aircraft that bombed our country disguised with false Cuban markings were the property of the U.S. armed forces. If we had added all of that up and sentenced them to pay one percent, just calculate the resulting figure!

But I will restrict myself to the U.S. Air Force, which I estimate is worth $500 billion. Now, one percent of $500 billion is $5 billion. We could be petitioning close to $2 trillion, an amount that may sound exaggerated but is rather conservative. And if we had based our calculation on the actual value of all the equipment of the U.S. armed forces, then the resulting figure would be higher than the U.S. Gross Domestic Product in one year, all in full compliance with the law and on the basis of available evidence.

They set a precedent. But our legal claim summarizes in just 30 to 40 pages the outrageous history of U.S. aggression against Cuba and the repugnant pretexts proposed to the U.S. Chiefs of Staff, which were once endorsed by the U.S. president to justify a direct aggression. These are contained in three shameful pages. All of this was discussed and agreed to by the U.S. administration and led to very serious threats to the world. The measures we adopted in the face of imminent danger gave rise to the famous Missile Crisis in October of 1962 that came close to developing into a thermonuclear world war. That was one of the consequences of their absurd and incredible recklessness.

Concerning the total number of assassination plots against me that were investigated by the [Cuban] Ministry of Interior, I knew there were many, and the U.S. Senate had recognized a certain number of them. Do you know how many, both major and minor, direct or indirect, plots there were? They use three methods: one is to make up a direct plan to remove a person; another is to organize groups that bear their own names and are apparently independent but perfectly trained who acquire an international status and the right to go on a hunting spree on their own account. What kind of right is that? The right to kill any of us. And the third is the induced approach: "The demon must be killed, the demon must be killed, the demon must be killed." They repeat it and many heavenly angels hear the call to kill the demon.

In summary, do you know how many assassination plots were investigated and known about in various degrees? A total of 637. They made me a champion, no doubt about it! If they want to give me any award for it, I would receive it more readily than the undeserved honors bestowed upon me this evening.

What am I a champion of? I hold the Olympic record for plots prepared by the United States and its henchmen to put an end to my revolutionary life. I am also a champion of the happiness and pleasure produced by their failure to eliminate me. They might eventually succeed by making me laugh myself to death!

I greatly admire the men who have worked to prevent it from happening. I have been the most carefree of all, I tell you frankly. Inevitably, when I have to travel abroad, I am accompanied by a larger security detail than other visitors. Coordination is always made and close cooperation established with the authorities of the host country whose rules and functions are strictly abided by.

Do you know how many aircraft I must use? Two. Admittedly, they are Soviet-made and the Soviet Union is long gone, but we have some spare parts left. I jokingly tell my colleagues, "I consider myself braver than you because I am the only one who still flies in an old Soviet aircraft with relatively few spare parts." The fact is that our pilots, mechanics and technicians are real champions.

I have to use two aircraft because they always have a plan in the making. They may, for example, use a Stinger missile that can be placed kilometers away from the airport. The United States has spread these weapons around the world while supporting the forces involved in its dirty wars.

At the time of the Ibero-American Summit held in Venezuela, an assassination plot was being hatched. While the perpetrators were traveling from Miami, a U.S. Coast Guard cutter involved in drug-interdiction operations stopped them in the vicinity of Puerto Rico. The Coast Guard seized two 50-caliber automatic rifles with a 1400-meter range that could pierce an armored car 400 meters away or shoot an aircraft during take-off or landing, equipped with a telescopic sight, infrared night vision and the ammunition to shoot semi-automatically as many bullets as required. They were arrested and brought to court in Puerto Rico.

Now, who organized this plan? The chairman and ringleaders of the Cuban American National Foundation, many of who have proudly appeared in photographs with the president of the United States. The amount of money they contribute to candidates in both parties is not negligible. On trial are those directly involved but not the chairman of the distinctive foundation and other chief culprits; we will have to wait for the outcome of that proceeding.

On many occasions they have been close to meeting their goal. In Chile [in 1971], to give you an example, accredited journalists with Venezuelan passports and documents issued by venal and corrupt officials and agents had a machine gun built into a camera. They were standing a few meters from me but, fortunately, they were not fanatics so they got scared and did not shoot. They have been awfully close more than once. Then again, apparently I have been a bit lucky.

Anyway, I have tried to use my luck as best I can because every year, month, week, day and hour in my life has meant struggle, and not out of revenge, but in loyalty to my convictions. I have forgiven them in advance for their attempts to kill me. After all, they have paid me a tribute by regarding me as much more important than I really am — infinitely much more important. But their methods are simply repugnant.

While working on the material for the claim, we could look at all their misdeeds together, all their crimes against the Cuban people in 45 years. Believe me, if I felt contempt for the empire before [this recent lawsuit against the United States], if I had an extremely low opinion of its absolute lack of scruples and morality, it is not an exaggeration to say that we felt 30 percent or 40 percent more revolutionary. This was not because we were unaware of such actions. But it is really shocking and it has an impact to see all these materials put together in a few pages. Personally, I have been through the events of all these years; yet, I was shocked. Not a single word is exaggeration. It is all irrefutable evidence and official U.S. documentation. We know them only too well.

Why the attempt to publicly declare, simultaneously with the Yugoslavian war, the doctrine of the right to global intervention for any reason? That attempt had to be forestalled. That was what made me say what I said. I don't mean that I was not planning to speak and write about those things. Rather, I was worried about the need to do so precisely at that meeting, at the risk of sounding impertinent or impolite to the European personalities taking part in that constructive exchange. But I had no choice. I read my [speech] for three minutes and I firmly believe their blood ran cold. There was absolute silence. A private meeting was supposed to take up the matter. I made a special effort, I focused and I said what was indispensable. I am sure that if I had returned to Cuba and had not done that, I would have felt ashamed. It was like crossing the Rubicon because those four paragraphs and three questions addressed sensitive issues and interests held by highly powerful forces. Above all, it was a frank and necessary denunciation made public at that important forum about the new NATO strategic approach that has been impossible to conceal, since many wire services have already disclosed it.

A second sensitive issue: The draft document of the summit adopted by the 15 European Union countries expressly recognized that "this strategic partnership is based on full compliance with international law and the purposes and principles contained in the Charter of the United Nations, the principles of nonintervention, respect for sovereignty, equality among States and self-determination." Does that mean that the United States, as the chief and main ally of the EU, will agree to such principles? If that were not the case, what would the European reaction be if the United States, at any time and under any pretext, began to launch bombs and missiles against any of the Latin American and Caribbean countries gathered there?

As I said, the United States invaded Haiti and the Dominican Republic to collect unpaid debts amounting to tens of millions of dollars. At some point the United States might conclude that a debt such as Latin America's, amounting to more than $700 billion, could never be collected — because the more it is repaid, the more it grows — thus constituting a global threat, and therefore, a sufficient reason for a "humanitarian intervention." Then the United States might begin to launch bombs left and right and by the tens of thousands over our region or any country in our region.

The third delicate issue: For the first time, it was necessary to make open reference in an international forum to the fact that the West, particularly the United States, has helped the state of Israel to develop hundreds of nuclear weapons, a fact that has always been kept under a strange and hermetic silence. This is closely related to the serious and arbitrary nature of NATO's new strategic approach. I did not raise this fact to even remotely suggest that NATO should inflict bomb or missile strikes against Israel, as it did on Serbia. That Middle East state is home to Israelis, Palestinians and citizens of various ethnic groups, religions and cultures.

I strongly defend everyone's right to life and peace. Such a case, in which there has been a massive and clandestine proliferation of weapons of mass destruction, one of the causes for military intervention under NATO's new approach, demonstrates the absurd, unrealistic and contradictory nature of this doctrine.

That small territory is afflicted by internal conflicts, a proliferation of weapons of mass destruction, ethnic cleansing and the constant danger of war, all them cause for a NATO military intervention. However, no one could ever think that such a complex issue may be solved by launching tens of thousands of missiles against power grids, distribution networks, factories, roads, bridges and vital services without which millions of innocent people would not survive, innocent people who are not in the least to blame for the problems that have built up there. Anyone can understand that these issues cannot be solved using the NATO methods without the risk of causing certain and colossal disaster.

This stupid and criminal doctrine, whom has it been designed for? Solely to be applied to countries that do not have nuclear capability, who are not members of powerful military blocs or cannot give rise to overly serious complications. Latin America, the Caribbean, Africa and most of the Asian countries would be included in the risk area. No country of real worth that is ready to fight can be intimidated. We know for a fact that such an aggression can be defeated.

That U.S.-led military alliance has just waged a merciless war and committed genocide against a European people of great historical merit, who are not to blame whatsoever for the mistakes made in the Balkans by the European and Yugoslavian governments over the past 10 years. Actually, the government that ruled over the remains of

Yugoslavia was not socialist; it had not been so for more than 10 years. It had repealed the name of Socialist Federation of Yugoslavia for the simple Federal Republic of Yugoslavia, and it complied with all the Western requirements of a free market economy and the kind of bourgeois-capitalist political structure that the United States and Europe are trying to impose as a universal formula. However, socialist Yugoslavia, where peace had prevailed for almost half a century, was dismembered and the West is responsible for that disintegration which almost immediately led to all sorts of ethnic, cultural and national conflicts. All the peoples in the former federation had to suffer the consequences.

The conflicts were not always ethnic, since the Croats, Serbs and Bosnians are all ethnically Slavs, except that some are Roman Catholic, others are Orthodox Catholic, and others are Muslim; and the fact was that cultural, religious and national conflicts broke out. In Kosovo, the conflict did have ethnic ingredients as well. No reference is made to anyone responsible.

No reference is made to the Serbian holocaust lasting from April 6, 1941, until the final years of the war, when hundreds of thousands of Serbian men, women and children were coldly and systematically executed in concentration camps with the Nazi methods of Auschwitz, Dachau and others, under the doctrine applied by a fascist installed in power by Hitler after his invasion of the Yugoslavian region then encompassing Croatia, Bosnia, Herzegovina and a portion of Voivodina.

A true holocaust! The West has kept absolute silence about it and concealed this holocaust. Why? Is it because they were Serbs? Is it because the Serbs were part of a socialist republic after the war? Why, really? Some mysteries need unraveling and it is possible to do it.

WE MUST NOT ONLY SOW ideas but also expose truths and enlighten the world about the immense hypocrisy of the West.

Some European politicians have spoken out against Cuba's tightened laws and have specially criticized the fact that our Criminal Code provides for capital punishment. Now, what laws have been tightened? The sentences meted out to the rapists of minors have been made more severe and cases of extremely serious and repugnant crimes may carry the capital punishment.

Our country is already being visited by nearly two million tourists. In general, these are respectable people, mostly Canadians and Europeans with exemplary behavior. But there are always visitors, from various places, who travel for sex. Our people, particularly our children and teenagers must be protected, all the more so since the outbreak of diseases such as AIDS has led unscrupulous people seeking safe pleasure to believe that 11, 10, eight or seven year-old boys or girls pose a lower threat than an adult. And there is always someone willing to push such services. We have also hardened our sentences against procuring, particularly against the corruption of minors. All the gold in the world is worth less than the purity and dignity of a Cuban boy or girl.

We have also toughened our sentences against drug trafficking to include capital punishment. What does that mean? As our country has opened up to millions of visitors, including Cuban nationals and tourists who enter and exit the country quite easily, and in many cases without a visa requirement, some international criminals have attempted to use these facilities to carry in small drug shipments. At the same time, some foreign firms in partnership with Cuban companies have been provided with the facilities needed to import or export raw materials or finished goods. We discovered that one of these companies had made an investment in the country with the idea of shipping significant quantities of drugs between Colombia and Spain.

Fortunately, we detected their plan in time. We could have caught the alleged European businessmen, if certain Colombian authorities acting under effective agreements between our two countries had forwarded the information they already had before going public for the sake of publicity following the murky advice of U.S. officials. Sheltered in their home country, the false businessmen have not yet been arrested.

Cuba cannot tolerate such things. It is an outrage to our country that compromises its prestige and even its national security. For this indisputably valid reason, the National Assembly decided to establish capital punishment for large-scale drug trafficking that uses the Cuban national territory. For less significant cases the applicable prison term was extended.

Our Criminal Code does provide for capital punishment. However, in its latest amendments, the National Assembly adopted the life sentence as an alternative to capital punishment, so that the latter is applied only in exceptional cases. On the other hand, Cuba has a Council of State whose 31 members hold their individual and independent views. Any sentence to capital punishment ratified by the Supreme Court is automatically referred to the Council of State, which carefully reviews the case — and generally the crimes that carry this sentence are horrible and repugnant — and unless an almost unanimous consensus is reached, the death sentence endorsed by the highest body of justice in the country is not applied.

That is the procedure. It is not like in the North, where capital punishment is administered only to Hispanics, Native Americans, mestizos and blacks.

Europe, which for a long time has not known the terrible social problems experienced in our countries, has introduced a policy aimed at eradicating capital punishment, but for 129 countries in the world this is not a viable choice. We dream of the day when we, too, can repeal such a severe sanction.

I said to a European leader who was concerned about this issue: you Europeans are concerned about capital punishment. It is a view and a sentiment that I respect. But there are two causes for capital punishment: one is the penal sentences that may take the lives of several thousand people a year, people whose actions could take the lives of many innocent and destitute people, or cause considerable damage to society. I don't feel it is ignoble for any country, or any man or woman, including many friends of Cuba and many noble and good people around the world, to oppose the death sentence for religious or philosophical reasons.

In our own National Assembly, three Christian deputies stated their views and objected to the passage of these sentences for the crimes just mentioned. They are honorable people who feel that way and they deserve all respect. But hypocrisy and lies do not deserve respect. There is another truly terrible cause of capital punishment: the hunger and poverty that kill tens of millions of people in the world every year.

As I have said to these European leaders, we must not wait until the conditions are created in the world for the court-issued death sentence to be removed. Instead, let us get to work immediately in order to save the lives of tens of millions of people in the Third World who die every year.

I tell them that we are ready to cooperate. Look, we know that in Latin America alone, more than one million people die every year who could be saved by simply sending doctors where none is available. We have promised our cooperation, and we are ready to send thousands of doctors.

This is the human capital I was telling you about. There would be no point in having the highest number of doctors per capita in the world unless, as a general rule and under sacred principles and established traditions, each of our doctors was not willing to act as a missionary, a crusader, a pastor, a priest, a martyr for health and human life. This is why our doctors set off with determination to places where they trudge through mud for days, and they go to these places alone — and sometimes they are women, for almost half the doctors in our country are women — places where there is no electrical power, where letters from their families take a long time to arrive, where there are mosquitoes, snakes and all of the calamities that can be found in jungles and rain forests. That is where our men and women doctors are stationed.

I have mentioned that we offered 2,000 doctors to Central America. I don't know, but I wonder if Europe and the United States combined would be able to pool 2,000 volunteers to work where our doctors are stationed. We have offered the free services of 3,000 doctors to northern sub-Saharan Africa alone, where the infant mortality rate in some countries is as high as 200 per 1,000 live births every year, and where hundreds of thousands of lives, mostly children, can be saved at a cost of pennies. These are the poorest countries and the ones with the highest mortality rates.

We have said to the rich countries, "If you contribute the drugs, we will send in the doctors." And not only that. We have begun sending the initial teams even though no industrialized country has pledged to deliver drugs. The medicines that are coming in are the result of efforts made by the governments involved or by some nongovernmental organizations that are truly humanitarian. The fact is that there are already a large number of Cuban doctors saving lives, in the hope that the more affluent countries will make some drug contributions, which represent the lowest cost.

I have talked to quite a few European leaders, and I intend to keep on working along these lines in order to send up to 6,000 doctors where they are most needed in various parts of the world. I do not quote a higher figure because 6,000 is the number that we can sustain ourselves by covering their wages and other benefits to them and their relatives.

We are pleased by having widely achieved this spirit of solidarity and sacrifice. When we raised this issue in our country, virtually all the health professionals volunteered, including nurses, technicians and other skilled workers. Each doctor can become a mini-school to train nurses and ancillary personnel by working with local youth with a minimum sixth-grade education. With the theoretical and hands-on teaching they receive here, these doctors can train them perfectly well in a short time.

I said 6,000, for I have to be cautious. In addition to salaries, we have to cover certain other expenses for each of the doctors we send abroad. In many cases, we have had to cover the airfare or send them in our own airliners, bearing all the costs involved because their host countries could not afford the airfares for these doctors. Often, we have had to cover the cost of bringing the students enrolled in the Latin American Medical School to Cuba, at no cost to them or their relatives.

Each year, we will receive 500 young Central Americans and 750 from the rest of Latin America. A small group of Brazilians from various states in Brazil have arrived. It is not that this large country is in need, but rather because we wish this school to have students from all the Spanish- and Portuguese-speaking Latin American countries that have many things in common. In addition, around 120 young Haitians have enrolled in the Medical School in Santiago de Cuba. They must first take Spanish lessons. Thus, we will receive between 1,350 and 1,400 Latin American medical students a year. I am not counting the Caribbean students, who have the right to a scholarship in any field, also for free, in our universities.

We had 21 medical schools and now with the Latin American School we have 22. The latter will provide the first two years of premed and basic science studies, which are the toughest. Later, the students will be distributed throughout the country because starting in their third year all our medical students work in teaching hospitals. Thus, their education is not just theoretical.

Before the revolution, doctors would graduate as surgeons without ever practicing surgery. Today's Cuban medical students get acquainted with hospital care from quite early. We hope that these young people from distant regions of our America, who are generally of very humble background and are anxious to study this noble profession, come to do better than our own students. What is most important is the willingness to undertake any mission or task anywhere. This is what has given our country its tremendous medical potential.

I am pleased to add that, when it comes to choosing a place to go, our compatriots, acting out of honor will choose the worst and most difficult location. Thanks to the effort and human capital we have built, we can now render such services and we are inviting the countries with large resources and a Gross Domestic Product 20 or even 25 times that of Cuba to contribute medicines that will save who knows how many lives. We know where people are dying, in which slums, in which distant locations where no doctor has ever been.

11

Globalization is an Irreversible Reality

Message to the Ministerial Meeting of the Group of 77

Allow me to extend a fraternal greeting to all of you. I had very much hoped to be able to attend this meeting personally, but it was not possible. This message is intended, above all, as an expression of Cuba's deeply felt honor and responsibility as host of the South Summit to be held in Havana from April 10 to 14 next year.

This important high-level meeting is being convened by our country, in compliance with the decision reached at the Ministerial Meeting of the Group of 77 and China just one year ago, in September of 1998. It will be taking place at a moment in history of crucial importance for the world, and particularly for the most disadvantaged part of the world, namely the countries represented here.

The Group of 77 needs to collectively reflect on ways to face the new world realities in order to achieve development, eradicate poverty, defend the cultures of its member states and occupy the place it deserves in making global decisions that affect everyone.

Since its inception in 1963, the Group of 77 has played a major role in representing the South and defending its interests in numerous negotiations. We make up a group of countries characterized by diverse geography, culture and degrees of economic development. Such diversity should be an asset not a liability.

Actually, only a calm reflection and an honest exchange of ideas will show us the way to better consider the legitimate interests of all member countries in the Group of 77 regardless of their size, region or

---

Fidel Castro sent this message to the Ministerial Meeting of the Group of 77, September 19, 1999.

culture, or whether they are continental or islands.

Over and above this diversity there is a common element of unity and cohesion: we are a group of countries that benefit very little — and often not at all — from the advantages of the current world order with its dazzling technology, market expansion and financial bubbles.

As we stand on the threshold of a new millennium, we face the enormous challenges arising from a unipolar world order and a globalization process that advances imperiously, shaping a world with greater technological potential than ever before but also with greater inequalities and exclusions.

Globalization is the historical process that is defining the world scenario as this millennium draws to an end.

Globalization is an irreversible reality characterized by the growing interaction of all countries in the world, their economies and peoples. The major scientific and technical advances have shortened distances and allowed for direct communication and transmission of information among countries located anywhere on the planet.

With its impressive technological achievements, globalization holds tremendous potential for development, the eradication of poverty and fostering well-being in conditions of social equality for all humanity. Never before has the world commanded today's formidable technological resources.

However, the world is still very far from materializing the potential of globalization. It develops today under the aegis of neoliberal policies that impose unregulated markets and unbridled privatization.

Far from promoting the expansion of development throughout an increasingly interdependent world badly in need of sharing the progresses achieved, neoliberal globalization has aggravated existing inequalities and raised to inordinate heights social inequities and the most disturbing contrasts between extreme wealth and extreme poverty.

In 1960, the difference of incomes between the wealthiest 20 percent of the world's population living in the developed countries and those of the poorest 20 percent living in the Third World was 30 to one. By 1997, that ratio was 74 to one. The cult of deregulated markets had promised a progressive convergence of development levels. However, the last two decades have brought an even greater concentration of revenues and resources and a wider gap between developed and underdeveloped nations.

The OECD member countries, with 19 percent of the world's population, account for 71 percent of the international trade in goods and services, 58 percent of direct foreign investment and 91 percent of all internet users.

It is obvious that the opportunities offered by globalization are distributed very unevenly in the conditions created by the cult of market competition and the reduction of the role of governments to passive recipients of decisions taken by the financial power centers.

In order for globalization to realize its enormous potential to benefit humanity it must be accompanied by a just and sustainable new world order. This new order must include the participation of Third World countries in global decision making and a profound transformation of the international monetary system currently dominated by the privileges enjoyed by the U.S. national currency. Likewise, a comprehensive approach to development is required in order to avoid the separation of trade, investments and finance, thus facilitating control by the developed countries. It is essential to reduce the widening gap between the group of wealthiest countries and the large majority of poorest countries, as well as to bring an end to protectionist practices, which clearly contradict the often-repeated rhetoric of liberalization.

Globalization's potential for progress and development for all, and not just for a privileged minority, will elude full realization in the absence of a dialogue between the developed countries and the Third World. This must be a wide-ranging and responsible dialogue based on a full understanding of the shared responsibilities imposed by globalization, of the different degrees of development that make it both unfair and absurd to demand equal contributions from such profoundly unequal parties.

Above all, it must be a dialogue on an equal footing and not a monologue in which the Third World is assigned the role of listening to a lecture on what it should do to earn a certificate for good behavior.

Many items should be included on the agenda for this dialogue. New conflicts and growing inequalities create the need for negotiations, in which our capacity for cooperation as the Group of 77, combined with an intelligent, flexible and strongly principled stance are indispensable to achieve a renovated North-South dialogue. Such a dialogue should be capable of approaching the enormous global challenges facing humanity and, in particular, the need to globalize development on a sustainable basis through environmental preservation and social equity.

It is of prime importance for our countries to work out an agenda, define our priorities and concert our negotiating positions. A number of issues demand close study and coordination, such as the Third World external debt and the heavy burden imposed by interest payments, which are truly suffocating for many of our countries; the international monetary and financial system, frequently shaken by financial crises that destabilize the world economy and hit the poor countries with particularly brutal force; the multilateral trade system, currently dominated by extreme liberalization measures imposed by developed countries and which they themselves violate on a daily basis through selective protectionism; and the unfavorable trends in the price of commodities, in a world market increasingly controlled by large transnational corporations whose annual sales exceed the GDP of many of our countries. The inequalities and dangers contained in the prevailing rules for trade in services and intellectual property, as well as the reduction of official development assistance to levels that fall increasingly short of the commitments made by the developed countries, are equally relevant issues that call for an analysis.

The South needs the South. Cooperation among our nations is one of the areas to which the Havana summit should make the greatest contribution through concrete action and innovative mechanisms. The promotion of South-South cooperation is instrumental in sharing our experiences and capabilities.

The issue of technology and expertise should take a preferential place on our agenda since it touches upon the problems that will largely decide the future of our countries. We urgently need to confront the extreme poverty of our group of countries in the global information networks, the internet and all the state-of-the-art means for disseminating information and images — that shining world where knowledge and images are thus exchanged remains unfamiliar and out of reach to our countries.

To use the internet it is indispensable to be able to read. Then, to have access to a telephone line and a computer, and be fluent in English, the language used in 80 percent of the material on the network. Any one of these requirements, and certainly all of them together, would be difficult to meet by many countries in the Group of 77. The truth is that with less than five percent of the world's population, the United States and Canada are home to over 50 percent of internet users, and there are more computers in the United States than in the rest of the world.

This extreme inequality rests on the meager opportunities for development-oriented research. A mere 10 countries account for 84 percent of worldwide spending on research and development.

The new communications technologies have divided the world into those who are and those who are not connected to the global networks. Being connected to this knowledge and participating in a true globalization of information that amounts to real sharing as opposed to exclusion, and that puts an end to the widespread "brain drain," is a strategic imperative for the survival of our cultural identities in the coming century.

For Cuba, it is vitally important that the 133 countries that make up the Group of 77 discuss their views on these decisive issues and adopt common strategies to defend their interests in this unipolar world, characterized by increasingly obvious attempts by a small minority to wipe out the principles of international law enshrined in the Charter of the United Nations, which has presided over relations among all countries for over half a century. Actually, not only the principles of international law are in jeopardy but also the very existence of small and medium-sized states. They are even demanded to stop breathing, so that huge transnational companies and a few over-powerful states under the aegis of one of them, can make all the decisions. Such a philosophy is inadmissible and unsustainable.

The South Summit in Havana will provide a favorable environment to coordinate our positions with a view to the Millennium Assembly and Summit and in defense of a world where social justice and real possibilities for development are available to all the peoples on Earth.

Cuba can offer the Group of 77 its experience in the area of cooperation. Just in health care, over 25,000 Cuban doctors have provided their services in dozens of Third World countries. There are currently over 1,200 doctors and other health care specialists offering those services free of charge in Central America, Haiti, and northern sub-Saharan Africa. By the same token, several thousand more are ready to take on the same task. They do not work in national capitals or big cities but rather in villages, townships and isolated settlements, where they are most needed. Millions of lives can be saved with this modest yet sincere gesture of solidarity by contributing the necessary human resources. At present, a total of 2,000 students from 18 countries throughout the region are already studying in a Latin American Medical School recently established in Havana. That figure will grow to 3,000 within a few months, and in three more years, the number of Caribbean and Latin American medical students in Cuba will reach 6,000. In Africa, we are cooperating in the creation and development of higher educational institutions in the medical field. We are also working tirelessly in the development of vaccines against AIDS and a number of lethal tropical diseases. A new concept on the role of doctors in human society is developing with irrepressible force. A similar plan to encourage the development of physical education and sports in the Third World is already in progress. It includes both sending highly specialized trainers to other countries and the establishment of a high-level school in Cuba to train young people from other countries as physical education and sports instructors. Cooperation in the training of scientific and technical personnel is expanding to other sectors as well. We have almost completed and will soon be trying out a system to teach reading and writing by radio. Thus, with an extremely small number of teachers and a low commitment of financial and material resources, it would be possible to bring the gift of literacy to hundreds of millions of people in the Third World living in isolated areas. To do so in any other way would require millions of teachers and billions of dollars a year, something completely beyond reach.

I hope you will forgive me for referring to these data. I simply wanted to point out how infinite our possibilities are and how much can be achieved with a bit of international cooperation and a spirit of solidarity. Cuba is but a small country, which has endured 40 years of uninterrupted, rigorous and relentless economic warfare. What would we not be able to achieve if our countries worked closely united? We would not only be able to preserve our current civilization, but also ensure the very survival of the species.

The only way to succeed in making ourselves heard, in fighting for our interests, and in defending our right to life, development and culture is to stand united.

We hope that along with my sincerest greetings and respect, each one of you will pass on to your heads of state and government these reflections, as well as Cuba's sincere wishes to welcome them all in Havana next April, as promised when we agreed to host that meeting.

12

Today's Dreams are Tomorrow's Realities

Congress of the Federation of Latin American Journalists, Havana

The ultimate dream of reactionary forces in this century, throughout the development of capitalism, has been to demonstrate that the state serves absolutely no purpose, although they know very well what purpose it serves.

According to the philosophy of these reactionary sectors, the state is inefficient, the state is a disaster, the state must be discredited; and I would even agree, depending on which state it was.

The state, responsible for playing a fundamental role in an era of historical transition, is an indispensable institution, absolutely indispensable. Actually, what we would like to do away with are the inefficiencies of a state that we revolutionaries have not been able to construct in a better way. The old state of the capitalists and exploiters is the state that we would like to see removed once and for all.

Therefore, there are two kinds of state and two different concepts of what the state is, which are diametrically opposed: that perverse state of theirs and this inefficient state of ours. In the end, when each has fulfilled its purpose, may they both disappear, as Marx dreamed.

One of the things about Marxism that I found most appealing was the idea that one day there would be no state, that once its mission was completed, this instrument that was needed to create a new society would have no reason to exist any longer.

Marxism is full of dreams, and I am not here to lecture you on Marxism or even to defend it. I am simply reflecting on a dream, not a

Speech at the closing session of the Eighth Congress of the Federation of Latin American Journalists (FELAP), Havana, November 12, 1999.

utopia. There is a difference between dreams and utopias, while there are many similarities between them.

Martí once said that today's dreams are tomorrow's realities. We must always start out dreaming, we must always start out creating utopias, and I am speaking as someone who started out as a utopian. When I first became a utopian by meditating on the problems of the society I lived in, I don't think I had even heard of utopians. But the truth is that I started out as a dreamer, a utopian. Today I believe I am a realist, a dreamer and a utopian. Everything begins with faith, faith in humankind. If you have faith in humankind, then you have the conviction that dreams and utopias can be made a reality.

How far we seem to be from communism, and how far we really are! How far we are from the distribution formula that goes, "From each according to their work, to each according to their needs." How far we are from that beautiful formula! And how wise was Marx when he spoke of two stages: one socialist and the other communist, the first governed by the formula "From each according to their ability, to each according to their work." It is a very simple, extremely simple formula. He was wise, because today this is practically the only formula that can be fought for, a necessary path that cannot be avoided and one that seemed an unjust formula to those of us who had fallen in love with the communist formula.

For me, the socialist formula is a necessarily unjust formula, but it is far better than the repugnant capitalist society where those who really do contribute according to their work receive almost nothing, while the laziest members of society get almost everything.

These reflections could perhaps serve to explain my rejoicing at the congress held in the first half of this year where I was able to see more clearly than ever what a decisive role the press can play in socialism, how the press should function under socialism, and the immense, infinite possibilities of the press in socialism. Many years of revolution have passed but it is like one of those things that you suddenly see so clearly.

Forty years of revolution were necessary, all kinds of experiences were necessary, the "special period" was necessary, a colossal ideological battle was necessary, it was necessary to end up in this so-called global world where, among other things, it is disinformation and lies that are the most global.

Perhaps, there are no better circumstances to understand the value of the media when it is at the service of capitalism and imperialism. Imperialism and capitalism have largely subsisted thanks to subjective factors, and one gets the impression that the capitalists discovered this before the Marxists.

As for me, I also feel that subjective factors are of major importance, and that history itself does not move in a straight line; there are advances, and setbacks, and then further advances that are always interspersed with greater or lesser setbacks.

I recently spoke at length about these matters with our [Cuban] journalists. The capitalists discovered the value of subjective factors, and discovered that the mass media were the perfect instrument to exercise an overpowering influence on these subjective factors that constitute indispensable ingredients of history, of historical progress, or of the continuation of systems that are wicked, exploitative, monstrous, inhuman, and that subsist until a crisis, which we could call nuclear, definitively destroys them.

I say nuclear, because it is only when such a huge quantity of problems builds up in these countries and they become absolutely unsustainable that they finally explode cutting across these subjective factors. This is despite the overpowering control that a system may have over the media, which it uses to inhibit these subjective factors, and which could contribute more to speeding up the course of history and the removal of a world full of injustice, full of misery, full of monstrosities.

What I mean to say is that progressive people, people who want to change the world, must understand the importance of these tools that are used to build awareness, and that can turn these subjective factors into decisive instruments in the course of historical events.

At the meeting I was referring to, these truths were made evident. Of course, they were not discovered on that particular day. It was the result of the battle we have been waging, the product of many years of reading a growing number of news reports about all of the things happening in the world, in this highly globalized world where a cat dying in a corner of Cairo features in a press dispatch. Those who are used to being informed, to spending two or three hours every day gathering information about what is going on in the world, have an idea about the functioning of the mechanism for spreading lies and disinformation.

I am recounting precisely what I have experienced more than ever in this era of crisis, of unipolar hegemony and the globalization of reactionary ideas and lies, which used to reach a country, and then a continent, and now reach every corner of the world, in fractions of a second.

In fact, the socialist bloc and the Soviet Union were not destroyed fundamentally by their own errors; this infernal machinery of lies, deception and disinformation destroyed them. They were led to believe, and no one was unable to counteract it, the illusion that these consumer societies, this Western world, were the most wonderful things that could ever be imagined. Just think of those magazines, which use as much paper as would be needed to teach the current population of the world to read and write 10 times over, and which are devoted to gossip about what this or that celebrity did, enough frivolity to send the current population of the world to hell a hundred times over. The [socialist bloc countries] were destroyed by all these things, all this propaganda, which those acting on behalf of progressive ideals were unable to counteract.

I know that the immense majority believed in these ideals, but they were not able to discover or develop the means, ways and procedures for combating the ocean of lies and illusions. They were not fools, those who devoted their energies to radio broadcasts like the Voice of America, and others by its allies, aimed at reaching every corner of the world and the heart of socialist societies with all of the illusions and all of the lies that alienated millions of people in these countries.

Of course, none of us Cubans deserves special credit for having discovered these things and for seeing them much more clearly. Some of these countries were enormous, and there were such things as narrow-mindedness and dogmatism there, to the extent that doctrine was practically turned into a religion and bureaucracy and a great many other things made possible a setback in history. They should have been perfected — and needed a great deal of perfecting — but were instead destroyed. The basic element continued to be that instrument so skillfully and efficiently used by capitalism and imperialism.

I already mentioned that immense amounts of resources were invested in this. I talked about the frivolities, gossip and foolishness that poisoned the people's minds in the same way that some of these extremely frivolous soap operas can tantalize, conquer and hold captive the minds of millions of people. This is the way they have manipulated and continue to manipulate today more than ever, the minds of billions of people.

Take, for example, the enormous amount of paper, of the highest quality, used simply for advertising, and the millions of hours invested every year in advertising. We ourselves have not had advertising on radio or television or in publications for quite a while, but in recent times we found ourselves obliged, in order to broadcast a major sports event, for example, to put some advertising on television. Suddenly, in the midst of an emotional, tense game, our television broadcasts and our people, especially those who are interested in these things, had to deal with an abrupt interruption to advertise some sort of merchandise, perhaps this or that make of car, or some other thing that the immense majority of the population does not have the slightest possibility of acquiring.

Finally, as a result of the recent Pan American Games in Winnipeg, where the banditry and corruption in sports, as in so many other things, became more evident than ever, we decided — even if we had to cut off a hand, or as they say, even if it cost us an arm and a leg — to put an end to commercial advertising during sports competitions.

Sometimes foreign television networks have interviewed us, and I have had the opportunity to see the broadcasts. It is really exasperating, and is only tolerated out of habit, when what someone is saying is interrupted every three minutes to advertise who knows what — some sort of ointment, some oil or cream to make your skin look more or less suntanned, or softer, whatever, some kind of cosmetics, or some gadget to do exercises at home, all kinds of crazy things — and I, at least, find it extremely exasperating.

I would say that today, people in the United States would not be able to live without these interruptions, because they have practically become a conditioned reflex; if a show is not interrupted for a commercial, they would find it lacking in suspense or interest, because they need to experience the anguish of waiting to see what happened next, or what else the guy talking had to say.

Just imagine how we, who have a little newspaper with only eight pages and have had just one daily newspaper for years now, feel to see a newspaper from some of our Third World countries with 80 pages of advertising. These countries where there is so much hunger and poverty and so many children on the streets who do not attend school, who go by begging and washing windshields. Think of all the paper used, the printing presses, all of the other things. And I am only talking about the press.

You want to find a piece of news and you have to go through three pages full of advertisements of the craziest things in the world to find something you are mildly interested in. When you do find it, there is a caption reading, "continued on page so-and-so" and you have to go over 40 other pages to follow up what has interested you.

So, taking into account the enormous poverty in many of these countries, perhaps the only benefit would be receiving every day, together with their colossal venom, a huge amount of toilet paper.

I only want to mention some ideas on the importance of the press or, better still, the importance of journalists, or of those that nowadays we call communicators

The truth is that communicators may save the world. At least in this country, communicators are engaged in the task of saving a small nation fighting against the most powerful empire ever, the mightiest power in every field, whether economic, military, or technological, with the added inconvenience of being not only our closest neighbor but also our most stubborn enemy. Apparently, fate has wanted to give us that "privilege."

This is the only country in the world against which that nation wages a direct economic war. It plunders the others, it robs them, it is rapidly taking them over, at a good pace we can say, using paper they print treasury bonds and U.S. dollars. It is the country in the world whose citizens save the least — less than zero right now — and spend more than their average individual income. They are the ones who spend the most and buy the most in the world.

At the emergence of capitalism, it was assumed that the financial monetary resources required would come from the savings that the bourgeoisie, the petty bourgeoisie, would make, because poor people have usually been unable to save. Resources would come from the savings of the capital invested at home or abroad. Today, capital flows from the printing presses of the U.S. reserve system.

Take a look at this planet, at the world economic order and see why, when those things happen, inevitably there will be not nuclear wars, but nuclear social explosions, the crisis that will put an end to all this. Let no one doubt it: this is unsustainable, regardless of how you look at it.

When I talked about the significant role of communicators, about their role here, fighting against those people, I was not trying to praise you, but rather to express a deep conviction. Cuba has the immense honor — in a world full of such great political cowardice, in a world where there are so many politicians who are so weak — of being the only country not only blockaded as everyone knows, but also of being the only country to which that powerful empire, in its desperation to reach the impossible objective of making us surrender, bans the sale of food and medicine.

See how low that system has fallen; see its decadence!

The UN vote [on the blockade] was mentioned. See the level of discredit, in spite of the huge propaganda machinery daily harping against this small country. Dante would not have been capable of painting a country such as the Cuba painted by these media, by this hideous imperialist machinery, with these lies about our small and — allow me to say it, although blushing — heroic country, not because of its own merits, but because of the circumstance of having such a mighty power as its neighbor and opponent. If our enemy were a small, powerless adversary, there would be no talk about Cuba in the world.

They have used all these means and, in spite of this, unbelievable things have happened like what took place in the last UN vote. Someone was late and went to the podium to explain that he had not cast his vote, but his position was in favor of the Cuban resolution. Another had pressed the button, but his name did not show on the board among those who voted, and he said: "Listen, I am here to say that I pressed the button and that we support the Cuban resolution." This never happened before; and there was a representative from the United States denying the existence of the blockade on food and medicines.

I have had real fun these days, because I have seen them embarrassed, confused, tangled up and bewildered — whatever you want. What was all their media worth? What was the use of portraying Cuba as pure hell and making who knows how many people believe it? I can bear witness to this. I receive many people visiting Cuba. When they see this is not the hell they expected, they start criticizing us, as if we were to blame for the fact that the rest of the world does not know about all the things that happen in Cuba, all the things the Cuban Revolution has done, and they almost call us morons for not having made this known.

For example, how many million people in the world would have to have it explained that those 157 votes against two were actually 155 plus two that stated their position right there and the reasons why they had not voted? There was a third country that declared the same thing the following day. Its ambassador had not been there, and he asked the organization to record in the minutes that he was absent that day, but wanted to express his support. That makes 158. There were also six countries that had always supported the Cuban resolution but because of the enormous poverty many Third World countries are suffering they were in default, since they had been unable to pay their fees.

Why this support despite all the slander? What happened this year with the notorious Geneva Resolution [on human rights] comes to my mind: the day before the voting at midnight we had 25 votes for us, six more than the empire; that is, votes against the U.S. resolution. By 8:00 a.m. the following morning, just a few hours later, we had one vote less than they did: 20 votes for them and 19 for us. The top leaders of that country — the distinguished secretary of state, the very distinguished vice-president of that country, and even the very illustrious president of the United States — had been desperately working the phone. I will not mention the circumstances; I will not mention any of those countries, because they really wanted to vote for us.

An abstention that became a vote against and five countries that were for us but were asked, urged, practically forced, to abstain caused the result against us. This happened in seven to eight hours, because when they saw they were losing, they did not sleep that night. They cannot imagine the humiliation it is for a leader to be forced to act against his wishes, or even his commitments.

That took place in Geneva, where they were going to get a real thrashing, but the number of participants was smaller, much smaller than in the General Assembly. They have a group of allies there that are unconditionally with them on these issues, mainly because of the slander.

You were discussing the thousands of journalists murdered in these last few years in Latin America and other places and I racked my brains trying to find the name of a Cuban journalist murdered in these 40 years of revolution. I racked my brains trying to make sure that I had not become amnesic, looking for the name of a Cuban journalist tortured by the revolution, the name of a Cuban journalist beaten by the revolution.

There have been some who have dishonored that noble profession and acted not like journalists, but like servants of that mighty empire, like mercenaries, betraying their small country, even though the revolution had given them the opportunity to study a university career such as journalism.

No matter what our mistakes may have been, no one has the right to betray their country, no one has the right to sell out and act like a mercenary for the enemy not only of our people, but the enemy of humankind. They betray their country and betray all humankind!

But not even for being traitors has anyone beaten them, physically eliminated them or committed an act of cruelty against them. If any of these mercenaries gets sick, he goes to a hospital sooner than a minister or a health official in this country. Some traitors have been tried and sentenced when they have committed serious crimes, when they have damaged the country, but not with death, not with beatings or torture; they enjoy the same rights and benefits of all other citizens.

There are those who left the country and today make a living by contributing to the lies and slander of the empire. Even worse, there are some that have never written a page nor read a text on journalism and yet call themselves journalists. It is the empire that grants their certificates. They mix up all sorts of people and call them independent journalists. Independent no less! They are the very embodiment of dependency and mercenary attitudes.

To call them that is as big an offense to such an honorable profession as giving José Martí's name to a U.S. radio station operating from Miami, with an antenna set on a balloon many meters high and whose power, in their anger and desperation, they now want to double from 50,000 watts to 100,000. This is because the talented and brilliant owners of the most impressive technology have not been able to have their television station seen, nor their radio stations heard, except for a few broadcasts at some given times, because our very modest technicians always come up with something to silence them. They broadcast thousands of hours a day, thousands of hours of lies!

Is that democracy, is that freedom of the press? No, it is the press and the mass media at the service of the most grotesquely lying individuals, professionals in lies, slander and betrayal.

They spread their main propaganda from there but they also do it from here. More than a thousand foreign journalists are here right now for the summit. It is similar to what happened when the Pope came and thousands of journalists came to the country. Many of them were honest journalists coming from different places, but many were also sent to witness the fall of the walls of Jericho at the sound of the supposed trumpets. They believed the visit of the Holy Father to our country would mean the fall of the revolution in a few hours. First, they deceived themselves by ignoring the ideological, political and intellectual strength of our people — a mistake they have made very many times — and, second, they were mistaken about the Pope.

I read a cable recently [about] a new biography of Pope John Paul II by a U.S. author; it was an official biography. What is the image they present of him in this biography? That of a lion tamer, something very far from the kindly image we have of this Pope.

The Pope was in this very Aula Magna giving a lecture. There, from that seat [over there]. I listened to the Pope's lecture. According to the program, I did not have to attend, but I wanted to come and listen to him. He is very far from being the person [they] would make you believe — a lion taming Pope.

Although it is a biography that evidently took years to conceive and write, what is the first thing the cable says about the book? That it devotes a chapter to Cuba. Oh, nothing good. It says that the book reveals the private matters, the details of what it calls the hardest test of the Pope's strategy — a military term — in the second decade of his mandate, his trip to Cuba.

The first issue emphasized is that the Pope's visit to Cuba was imposed on Castro. Actually, it was very sad for me to learn that day that, for the first time in my life, something had been imposed on me; that for the first time in the history of this revolution, something had been imposed on our people, our government, our party, our homeland. It was really disgusting, that phrase.

Of course, there were other issues. The cable discusses a letter, real or false, which, according to the author of the book, the Pope sent to Brezhnev to prevent the invasion of Poland. I don't know anything about that matter, nor whether the Pope sent a letter to Brezhnev; if that is the case, there will certainly be copies of it in the archives of the CIA, because it is well known that, when Russia became "democratic," its archives fell into the hands of U.S. intelligence, and so they would know, better than anyone else, the contents of that letter. I don't. The cable only contains a few sentences in quotation marks. The complete version must be in the book. This issue also supports the theory of the Pope as a lion tamer: the Pope, with his letter, prevented the invasion of Poland.

I knew Brezhnev well and other Soviet leaders of his era, too, as well as their methods, styles, edicts and errors. But they were extremely cautious since they were particularly interested in avoiding certain risks in their relations with the West. When Cuba decided to send troops to Angola, to challenge the South African racists' invasion, there were more than a few differences with them and signs of fear.

In my opinion, the Soviets could not invade Poland; I could list many reasons, the most important of which is the high risk that such a foolish action, right in the heart of Europe, could have led to a nuclear world war.

Anyone who is familiar with history and who has an ounce of common sense, can imagine heavy pressure and even strong words from the Soviet Union; but that country, already embarked on the Afghanistan adventure was not in a political situation to simultaneously launch troops against Poland, a courageous people with fighting traditions and tens of millions of inhabitants. That, in addition to the important and decisive political factor, would have overloaded and created chaos within the Soviet military, amidst great world tension.

It is commendable that the Pope would write a letter; it is commendable that he would argue and reason against the remote possibility. But the clumsy eagerness to present him as a lion tamer undoubtedly leads to an overstatement in claiming that with his letter he prevented the invasion of Poland.

The Pope's great influence over political events in the country where he was born is unquestionable, as it is that the Pope's views hold great sway. It could be a major subjective factor, which added to the true and objective reasons for which Poland could not be the target of a Soviet invasion.

Even worse: according to the much talked-about cable, the book recounts a message from the Pope to Bush, trying to persuade him against starting a war with Iraq, to which Bush replied that it was impossible; and several hours before the combat began — so goes the text of the cable — the Pope called President George Bush, and "even though he once more declared his opposition to the use of force, he offered his support."

Thus, the Pope is portrayed supporting that war. Actually, I cannot conceive of this Pope supporting a war. Anyone who knows him, anyone who has listened to him, and who knows that he is very cultured, holds deep convictions, has a knowledge of almost every language, of all philosophies, and all religions, cannot imagine the Pope taking such a stand.

I believe that if the Pope were unable to convince someone that it is better not to embark on a vicious and destructive war, his reaction would be: I am very sorry, it is sad, it is painful, thousands are going to die, tens of thousands of people; hundreds of thousands of children are going to die in this country, from starvation, from lack of medicine — as has happened. It is impossible to accept the idea that the Pope would give his best wishes for victory to the head of an empire which years ago killed more than four million human beings in Vietnam, left an unknown number physically disabled, poisoned land and forests for tens of years and caused, with its brutal and unjust aggression, tens of thousands of Vietnamese of all ages to suffer psychiatric trauma from which they will never recuperate as long as they live.

You do not need to be a member of his church; you do not need to be a believer to be absolutely convinced that this is impossible, that it is untrue.

How can anyone pretend to write an authorized biography of the Pope, depicting him in such a way? Is this really going to help the Catholic church, which, just like other churches, wishes to promote its doctrine, its religion and to expand worldwide?

And as far as the chapter about our country is concerned, how could anyone be so infamous as to respond to all the attention, the consideration, the courtesy and the gestures that we extended to the Pope — sincere, hospitable, respectful and friendly gestures — with such crude lies?

I spoke for hours on the television, clarifying historical events and dispelling prejudices, with the aim of persuading Party members and young people, our heroic nation's fighting revolutionary masses made up of millions of people that, despite the philosophical and political differences, we had to set an example by taking part without posters and slogans, and with utmost respect, in the events involving our illustrious visitor.

We practically gave our country over to the Pope. There was not a single person with a gun or a revolver in the streets. There was not even a traffic accident caused by the mobilizations. It was — according to what many people in the Vatican later said — the best organized visit that the Pope had made. One hundred and ten foreign television channels, thousands of journalists, just to broadcast his visit! All the necessary means and transport, which was practically everything available in the country, facilities and squares chosen by the Pope's representatives were placed at his disposal, without a single exception.

They inspected in detail the chambers and rooms of the Council of State which were of interest to them. They requested the use of the Aula Magna of the University of Havana; Antonio Maceo Square, in Santiago de Cuba; Ignacio Agramonte Square in Camagüey, and finally, Revolution Square, in the capital of the republic. They were given them all. For the mass in Santa Clara they were offered Ernesto Che Guevara Square, which they turned down. A square had to be hurriedly set up on the playing fields of the Villa Clara Faculty of Physical Education.

Cuban Television's main channel was placed at the service of the Pope to broadcast the masses, the homilies and the speeches made in every location. It was a perfect example of our traditional hospitality, decency, culture, the political courage of our people, and quite simply, an undeniable demonstration of our respect for the Pope as an eminent personality, head of a centuries-old religious institution, in the same way as we have known how to express our respect and recognition for all religions which are practiced in our country.

The official invitation to visit Cuba was personally delivered to the Pope on November 19, 1996, when I had an interview with him in the Vatican, where he received me with impeccable friendliness and respect.

Many of those measures adopted to guarantee the brilliance and success of the visit were not asked for by anybody — they were Cuba's initiative.

Is it fair, then, is it decent to present the Pope's visit to Cuba as something that was imposed on us?

The person who worked the most and best, among the Pope's envoys, was Father Tucci, a noble and devoted priest, who has organized the Pope's trips for the past 17 years, and with whom I had several meetings; he is not even mentioned in that cable.

Regardless the intentions of those who cooperated with the writing of this biography, whose author obviously had good access to the Vatican's archives, and held long and intimate conversations with Navarro Valls — whose words he transcribed, manipulated and interpreted in his own way, with an unquestionable hatred of Cuba — how could the Catholic Church benefit from such an unfair image as that which is portrayed, both of the Pope and Cuba?

It is known that the Pope wants to visit Vietnam; if someone is later going to say that the Pope forced the Vietnamese into it, and that one of his emissaries imposed the visit on Vietnam, the chance of the Vietnamese risking a visit from the Pope is going to diminish considerably.

It is known that the Pope would like to visit China. If the Chinese read a book of this sort, with the image of the Pope as a lion tamer, it is going to be very difficult for the Chinese to agree to the Pope's visit. It is completely absurd, and not in the slightest Christian, diplomatic or politic. I am entirely convinced that John Paul II will feel disturbed and embittered by this blatant manipulation of his trip to Cuba, where he received so much attention, such displays of respect, consideration and affection.

I have told you this story as further proof of how the media are used and of how myths about our homeland are invented, something which causes visitors to criticize us for not having been capable of letting the world know the truth, that this country is not Dante's inferno.

I was telling you of the satisfaction and inspiration stimulated by the congress of the Journalist's Union of Cuba. It was a congress that lasted several days longer than was planned. Every day it went on into the early hours of morning, and on the last day, if I am not mistaken, it was almost dawn when they finished. Four and a half days were spent discussing our problems, analyzing them in depth with a critical approach.

Of course, our difficult circumstances were made worse by our failure to make the best possible use of the media resources in our battle against imperialism. Because the fundamental aim of the revolution has been to fight for social and human justice, and to fight against those people in the world who oppose that justice, which is the raison d'être of the revolution.

At the congress, we discussed the enormous possibilities offered by the media to a revolution and to a socialist revolutionary state. There, we were more acutely aware than ever before that the battle was not our battle, that we were the least important players, and that our country's struggle and the struggle of our communicators were turning into a battle for the world. Believe me, it was a great source of encouragement.

It was there that the decision was made to create brigades of journalists, who would report on the work undertaken by our doctors in the most isolated corners of Central American and Caribbean countries. This proved to be of enormous value, because it helped to maintain communication lines between our people and those doctors; between the doctors and their families, and the families with them; it served to uplift the spirit of those people who were doing heroic work in places where they sometimes had to walk three or four days along a swampy path to reach a remote community where there was neither drinking water, nor electricity, and sometimes not even a radio. They set up a communication mechanism between the country and the most distinguished, the most heroic apostles of humanism in our nation today.

Yes, because our country has had many heroic teachers, like the 2,000 who went to the mountains of Nicaragua, where many thousands passed through over several years. I would not be able to tell you the exact number now, but it may well be that between 8,000 and 10,000 teachers passed through there, living in unimaginable conditions, where at times a couple, their large family, the horse and the teacher lived in a single room — they did not live in five-star hotels. They were days away, and even living in physical conditions that were sometimes a threat to their health, because all of them were used to better nutrition standards back in Cuba.

At that time we wanted to boost their food supply, to see how we could send them something to prevent them falling ill due to weakening immune systems. It was not possible, because when we sent them the first packages of food supplies, the first thing they did was to share what we had sent them, whether it was chocolate, powdered milk, anything of that nature, among the children and the family — a very logical reaction. We remember with shame the stupidity of trying to boost their food supplies. It was an impossible task.

That is why, when I say heroes, apostles, I am not just talking about those doctors. Nowadays we do not have teachers in such tasks abroad; nowadays we do not have soldiers confronting racist and fascist troops in South Africa. It is the role that our doctors are playing which is truly impressive, and what they are going to undertake in the near future will be five or six times greater than what they are doing at the moment.

Our country has created an enormous human potential, because paper was not used for gossip magazines, or for advertising. Instead they were invested in training doctors, so that we became the country with the highest per capita number of doctors in the world; we invested in training teachers, so that we would have the highest per capita number of professors and teachers in the world; physical education and sports teachers were trained, who devote themselves to comprehensive education and training, not professional sport, so that we have achieved the highest per capita number of all the countries in the world. Perhaps in the number of researchers and scientific personnel, and other fields, we are also among the top few.

That is how we have invested our very modest resources while enduring a blockade that has already lasted 40 years and which we were able to withstand even when it became more than just a U.S. blockade, that is, when the former Soviet Union joined that blockade. At the moment when [the Soviet Union] disintegrated and disappeared, trade was practically wiped out, until things began to improve slightly; but without a shadow of resemblance to what it used to be.

Almost 10 years of double blockade have passed, without the closure of a single school, a single day-care center, or a single polyclinic; not a single worker has been left without a guaranteed income. Moreover, our country managed to increase the number of doctors by approximately 30,000 during the years of the "special period."

Thirty thousand new doctors graduated during the last decade, and such doctors, such training! This is because we had already been running the programs for years. Twenty-one university faculties, all the hospitals and health care centers turned into training centers. The value of all this is as yet unknown, all that accumulated experience, which can be offered to those countries in urgent need to train specialists. They can have a teacher each or a professor each, because just put a recently graduated doctor in the hands of any of those Cuban specialists who are fulfilling their mission abroad, and he or she will be a specialist in half the time it would take to train in a teaching hospital.

I have referred to this because these are issues relating to our country that are never, or at least very rarely, reported in the news around the world. However, if a mercenary working for the empire is arrested and sentenced to a few years in prison, a much lighter sentence than acts of treason receive in the United States, then it is news for a whole year, every day, in press releases and cables. I am not blaming foreign journalists; in fact, we have recently had more contact with them as a result of certain events, and we have come across very able people and a high proportion of people that we can talk to and who appreciate the truth.

No, they cannot be held responsible, although we have had the misfortune of having received some who were solely on the payroll of the United States, and who worked in close collaboration with the U.S. Interests Section in Havana. There have been a few, not very many, not the majority, not even a small minority, but there have been cases which were particularly outrageous for the role they played in our country, promoting subversive activity, carrying out U.S orders, inciting mercenaries, creating false leaders and figures who were only known through cables and who could not even attract 10 followers in this country.

That is what the empire was most interested in, that is, dividing, destabilizing, artificially creating figures and extolling them by unscrupulous means. I do not blame the journalists, because they, too, have to make a living, they need their salaries. That was why I was asking if there was someone from IAPA here, because you know that cables are sent to headquarters and it is headquarters that decides what gets published. That is the freedom of the press enjoyed, as a rule, by many media intellectuals who have to work for big advertising and news agencies.

Well-known newspapers such as *The New York Times*, when the White House called to prevent the release of information they had on the imminent [1961] Bay of Pigs invasion, they did not print a single word.

Other things happen with the press in the capitalist world that are not ordered by the government. Some members of the press are open, all-out enemies of anything to do with progress; some hold positions linked, above all, to national interests; and some simply indulge in self-censorship. So, some of them side with the worst interests and others side with the government, or the government's positions; while others, out of patriotic or falsely patriotic feelings, do not publish things which, in their opinion, could harm their country. What I mean is that if there is a humiliating defeat in the United Nations they do not publish it, the same as many other news stories; if there is hysteria against Cuba or certain images have been spread, they do not risk saying something positive about Cuba.

By considering us enemies of the U.S. government, practically by instinct, by habit, by tradition they do not publish certain news stories that contradict the blockade or the official policy of the empire. These are reasons why the truth is not known throughout the world.

It is not that they are told, "Listen, don't publish that." They simply abide by a certain line, a common practice. So where is the freedom of the press? Where?

All right, I am not saying that there is absolutely no freedom of the press; every once in a while a journalist writes a few truths. There are journalists who study, do research and other efforts. There are very good U.S. journalists, yes, but they publish only once; the second article is not published because there are pressures that come down from the White House advising them not to touch on this or that in the name of allegedly national interests.

Even the most serious U.S. media are put under pressure to prevent publishing certain articles and materials, and in general, they echo stereotyped clichés about our country. There are never-failing, constant clichés to refer to Cuba, a single adjective. Even when they oppose the monstrous blockade they argue that it has failed, that it has lasted 40 years and not achieved the goal of truly democratic changes, respect for human rights, a multiparty system, etc., etc., etc. There are no ethical or human considerations.

Even when they recommend rectifying something they say — like Mr. Clinton does — that they are trying to destroy the Cuban Revolution. They want to destroy — and I say this without chauvinism — the best and most humane social project of this century. Which Third World country reduced illiteracy to zero and how long did it take?

Which Third World country reached an average ninth-grade educational level in such a short period of time? Which country in the world has a population with the knowledge and political culture of our people, where every youth knows where China, Vietnam or any distant Pacific country are, while the immense majority of U.S. politicians do not know?

What other country has such knowledge of universal history, for instance, and the basic problems anywhere in the world? What happened in Vietnam, what happened in the Sahara, what happened in South Africa? What happened in any Latin American country: in Argentina, in Uruguay, in Chile? What happened in Central America? What happened in the dirty wars? Who armed and trained the biggest torturers and criminals in the world? Who is to blame for that Bay-of-Pigs-type invasion of a sister Central American nation that left 150,000 dead, including about 100,000 missing people?

They are the "apostles" of democracy, justice, human rights: those who came to an agreement with fascist governments at the end of World War II and took Nazi weapons experts back to the United States, where they had the means for manufacturing the most perfect bombs, missiles and all the sophisticated weapons with which they dominate or try to dominate the world today.

What country has taken the largest number of brains? Suffice it to say that over several decades this continent graduated 1.5 million doctors, 750,000 of whom are now abroad, almost all of them in the United States.

In the last 40 years, industrial nations have taken away from Latin American a huge number of professionals — I don't recall the exact figure. I only know that, according to a study the cost of training these professionals was not less than $30 billion and they took them away without paying a dime.

Graduates from U.S. universities do not go to Haiti, Central

America or South America to help develop these countries with their know-how. Through the brain drain they have robbed many of the finest minds in this hemisphere. And today everybody admits that intellect, know-how, and information are key factors for development. You should not believe that they only rob us through high interest rates, public debt, unequal trade and the brutal exploitation of cheap labor in our countries.

Cuba does not suffer from this problem to the same degree. We have achieved high educational levels; in elementary education we have surpassed the United States, the richest county in the world; we are already ahead of them in the infant mortality rate — almost 10 percent lower. A better rate, yes, and evenly distributed in all provinces, too. There was a time when they had an average rate of 10 per 1,000 live births, now it is a bit over seven, this year nobody knows if it is going to be seven or eight, there are still no final figures. This year it is almost certain that we shall have about 6.5 when it seemed impossible to go below seven. This is because of all those doctors, their dedication, because of health care workers and what they do to save lives.

That is why I say that no country has done the work that our people have carried out, more humane, more just. Still, for many millions of people in the world, we are torturers, violators of human rights, totalitarian. Yes, we are totalitarian in as much as we have established total justice and a totally true humane spirit.

Democracy, multiple parties, how many parties do they want and what do they want them for? Because we can show them all they want. We can show them about seven or eight million parties.

I am speaking of a people who can read and write, and of young people who vote at the age of 16, young people who know about politics and who know what they are doing, the children of a country where citizens nominate local district candidates in free, open assemblies; where the party cannot interfere, according to its own regulations, and is also prohibited from doing so by the electoral system; a system promoted by the party itself where almost 50 percent of the National Assembly — the final product of the process — is made up of delegates elected directly at the grassroots level, in the local voting district. This does not happen anywhere else. They had better research this instead of launching empty slogans.

As I recently said in a press conference, we have a formula for those calling themselves dissidents: they should go to the assemblies where candidates are nominated and the polling stations where they are elected, because if the revolution loses its majority, it loses power. All they have to do is win. Let them run in a voting district, at the grassroots level, because voting districts are divided into areas — they can be nominated in one or several of them. Let them go where the candidates are nominated by ordinary people in open assemblies; let them go to elections to be elected. And they do not need anything extra to take power in this country. It is not the party that nominates and writes on a list, in the top positions, the people it wants to see elected after the polls have showed them the voters' inclinations with mathematical accuracy; that is how many are going to be elected, and the party leadership says: "These are going to be the three deputies: numbers one, two and three on our list." Such a thing does not happen in Cuba.

All citizens have the right to nominate, to elect and be elected. All that is needed is merit. It is not because they have money or can pay for all the propaganda the same way that Coca-Cola, or a certain cigarette, or a certain car are advertised, which as you know has a lot of influence in the final outcome. If that were not the case, the world would not spend billions of dollars on commercial advertising every year. The resources spent in just one of these election years would be enough to build all the schools the world needs, and top quality too; and with a small amount of the annual figure, they could offer school meals to all the children who need it, and pay teachers a decent salary.

Would not any sensible person believe that this would be somewhat better than spending a billion dollars on poisonous, stultifying propaganda aimed at filling the heads of billions of poor, humble people with dreams of having a luxury, state-of-the-art car, an exquisite watch manufactured in Switzerland, the most sophisticated clothes from Paris, London or New York, or telling them which razor blade to use, which soft drink to buy or which television set to buy?

Why are a billion dollars spent? Because the one who does not resort to propaganda cannot win. Why does a candidate with solid publicity win? Or why do they withdraw because they only have $18 million, as they themselves say in the United States? Mrs. Dole, for instance, has just withdrawn because she only had $18 million while Bush already had about $70 million. She gave up. Eighteen million is not enough, so I am going home. That is true democracy! Who would dare question it?

Money for publicity, and publicity to drive into people's heads who they have to vote for. And to plant there such a brilliant and transparent political idea, it is also necessary to fix a candidate's hairstyle, follow the strict instructions of image makers, write the speeches he has to deliver and persuade the masses of his tremendous statesmanship and enormous moral virtues to become a great president. Who actually elects in this system? Money and publicity;

these are the main electors.

Such electors do not exist in our totalitarian country. The electors here are the eight million citizens aged 16 and up who go out to vote. In that super-democracy, citizens are so convinced of that trash and that hypocrisy that even if they have not fully intellectualized it, they react by instinct. They hold their right to vote in such high esteem that on election day they go fishing — something unbelievable. Here, where voting is not compulsory, more than 95 percent of eligible voters go to the polling stations and in some cases up to 98 percent, 99 percent, according to the voting district. And people really vote; some even cross out their ballot or write counterrevolutionary remarks. But those who go to vote, and do so honestly, amount to more than 90 percent of the electorate.

You know the way Cubans are. If they are not afraid to openly receive instructions from U.S. officials at the U.S. Interests Section, are they going to be afraid of not casting a vote? Could anyone here be so coerced? No, whoever knows Cubans knows that that is completely out of the question.

Actually, I have a very high opinion of these Ibero-American Summit Conferences. I have high regard for these political summit conferences, but I also have a very high opinion of intellectual summit conferences, and for me that is what you are, especially courageous intellectuals, because all of us have lived through our "special period." You have lived through these years, and so have we, but from these years we are going to draw tremendous strength. We have embraced the most beautiful and magnificent of causes and we know that these causes are defended, consolidated, advanced and made triumphant by ideas and by disseminating ideas and messages. It is by spreading the truth to create the subjective factors that the course of history can be accelerated, since we cannot simply wait for societies to explode, for the system to explode in a world populated by billions of people who do not even know what is going on, who do not even know what to think, what to do, what to expect or even if there is a chance or hope.

Those of us who do believe that there is a chance or hope, based on solid reasons, can convey this hope, can persuade others of this possibility, let us do our job. And this has nothing to do with parties, nor does it mean that we are against parties. The more there are — and truly left-wing parties — the better, because things are not always what they seem.

I was recalling a cable I read recently that said that even the Democratic Party, that is, the party of the Vietnam War, of the Bay of Pigs invasion, the party that created the blockade against Cuba, which was later supported by successive presidents from the same party... I say the same party because both the Republican Party and the Democratic Party are so exactly alike that they have established a true one-party system, or better still, the most perfect single-party system in the world, through this fabulous mechanism of having two parties resembling each other like two peas in a pod.

Those parties are twins, identical twins, the kind of twins that are born from one egg that divides into two parts, so that they resemble each other so much that if they lived in the same house even their spouses could not tell them apart. The U.S. Democratic Party was strongly mentioned at a recent congress of the Socialist International as a possible candidate for membership; yes, the party of the Torricelli and Helms-Burton Acts, that was behind the genocidal blockade against Cuba and that still sustains it, even though many of its members save the honor of the party by opposing such a horrendous crime. Leaving aside brutal genocidal wars, such as the one that has just taken place in Europe, and the new strategic concepts of NATO, this movement is supposed to represent a major part of the world's left-wing forces in their unstoppable advance to the future, to progress, to justice, to democracy, to freedom. They have certainly gone far along that confusing third way!

We prefer our socialism with all its imperfections; we prefer the totalitarianism of truth, justice, sincerity, authenticity; the totalitarianism of truly humanitarian feelings; the totalitarianism of the type of multiparty system we practice.

We prefer the totalitarianism of eight million parties, eight million united parties, because they nominate and they elect, because they draw guidelines, because they adopt and support policies, and because they discuss them from the grassroots to the highest state institutions. It is better than 80 parties, and it is better than that miracle of two parties in one tyrannizing U.S. society, a luminous example, a beacon and guide to the world.

It would be better to be blind so as not to see that light ever, and to walk alone, not even with a dog to guide us, because our own feet, our own instincts, would lead us through the correct path.

Let us shed light, because the possibilities of shedding light are there; the people are not blind. Some of the aforementioned things may be used to stultify them and are stultifying them. What is needed is an antidote against stultification, which is worse than AIDS. A remedy against stultification! A vaccine against stultification! And you have that vaccine, it is the truth aimed at people's minds and hearts.

The person standing before you is not in this hall for the first time; he was a student in this university more than 50 years ago, one who could have been taken for a lunatic, a dreamer, a utopian. And I could say they were right if they took me for a lunatic, because thinking as I did in that society, in the world I lived in and in that university with more than 15,000 students, where McCarthyism and the media, with very few exceptions, molded minds into a hatred of socialism, a submissive and servile admiration for the greatness of the empire that "had given us our independence," the same our forefathers had conquered with so much blood.

Although students were always rebellious, combative and idealistic, the number of openly anti-imperialist university students amounted to less than 50. These were the sad times when the minds of a whole people were blocked and deceived by the mass media in the hands of the bourgeoisie and the landowners allied to imperialism, serving imperialism, unconditional lackeys of imperialism.

Isn't it true that most current U.S. society is vaccinated with the most efficient vaccine in the world against everything that smells of socialism? Their minds have been snatched away and turned into receivers of ideas instilled in them in the same way as the preference for a soft drink or a cigarette; their heads are full of absurd biases and lies about the world.

The economic, social and political system that plunders the world is the one we denounce, the one we challenge, the one we deny the slightest right to consider itself democratic, fair and humanitarian. It is all a huge lie.

Who can persuade others in this world? Communicators, those who transmit messages, and the greater the effectiveness, grace, art, transparency and courage with which they transmit them, with no concessions, the more people they will attract, the more minds they will free from lies.

Of course, we should not be alarmed or discouraged. That system would not be safe even if none of you wrote a word for true and vital change.

When they speak of Cuba, they frequently speak of change. They try to ignore that the greatest change in a long time, the most radical change, is that with which Cuba has been able not only to exist but to resist. They speak of change, that is the fashionable word, but what is at stake or, at least, what is very urgently in need of change is that despicable existing world order. When it changes, all the countries in the world will have changed, even U.S. society itself.

Anyone with the slightest knowledge of arithmetic — not to mention mathematics — knows that no one will be able to save that society from a crisis worse than the 1929 crash, much worse, since 50 percent of the people in that country now have their savings invested in stocks, while in 1929 the figure was only five percent.

The world will change; that is unavoidable. But our duty is to help it change, the sooner the better, without waiting for the crisis to act as a big bang that is still propelling stars to infinity. We should expect not a big bang, but a big change and a big revolution. I say this because I believe it and because it is inescapable.

The doctors I have been telling you about of whom over 1,000 are already working [in Central and South America], and who in the not-so-distant future will amount to several thousand, reflect that human capital capable, that is, the people willing to go to places where, as a rule, the doctors from industrial nations would not go.

It is very unlikely that those having nice houses, three cars, four TV sets and all the domestic gadgets produced by their industries and who even dress in the latest fashion by the latest male or female couturier in Paris, New York or California would leave their families and go for an indefinite period — one year, a year and a half or two years — to places where there are snakes, mosquitoes and heat, where an incredible amount of devotion and sacrifice are required.

Those from rich countries would not do it even for $100,000, because they would rather have $50,000 or $60,000 and stay where they are. They have not been reared in other concepts and other ideals. The most they do — those who are generous or philanthropic — is organize a small team and go to a country for a week. That is not bad, it is good: disseminating techniques, taking care of difficult cases. They do not go beyond that, except in some admirable cases.

They have infinite financial capital and almost zero human capital. We are doing things with zero financial capital and, I am not going to say infinite, but substantial human capital created throughout these 40 years. I want to ask you if a Third World country divided into 1,000 pieces, in constant and eternal instability, with no program or anything like it could have done this.

These are the facts that feed our conviction, our determination, our hope; these are the arguments we can use in the struggle. And I am not asking you to defend us; I am asking for a high awareness of the facts of the world today, the denunciation of the horrors of the system we are suffering, which can even lead to the obliteration of the human species.

This abominable system is not only driving humankind to its physical annihilation, but is spiritually destroying it, too, turning human beings into selfish individuals, blindly competing with each other, enemies of all the rest; turning the citizens of every country into liars and greedy, selfish and false people.

Can a people be educated by politicians who only feel what they do not say and say what they do not feel? For instance, President Clinton himself — with all due respect — has a discourse for New York, another one for Florida, another one for the state of Washington; a discourse for Hispanics, another one for Asians and still another one for African Americans; a discourse for every one of them; a discourse for every country he visits. Sometimes a president makes mistakes; this is what happened to Reagan, who spoke to Brazilians as if he was in Bolivia. I don't know if it was a lapsus linguae or a cultural blunder; actually both countries are unmistakable.

But they are not to blame, they did not learn it in school, they do not usually receive a sound political training. It would be more accurate to say that the system prevents it. If the only concept they are aware of is competition and the individual struggle between human beings, if they only believe in the power of their weapons and their wealth, how can they possibly be educated with a humanist concept of tomorrow's world?

I talk, I discuss things with a lot of politicians, of different standing, and not only from the United States, among whom I have seen, without a doubt, highly trained and serious people; but at times I am appalled. It is like this: Three assistants on one side and three on the other, and whatever the topic, this one passes a piece of paper, the other passes another. It is tragic. Worse still, it is a lack of courtesy, because if you have to wait for all the sheets of paper to be passed around and try to guess what the topic was that brought this about, what the crucial point was which triggered this conditioned reflex, how you can help your distinguished guest with information, then the line of the conversation is lost and the impression is one of rudeness.

I do not wish to specify countries, because whatever the country, we have many friends; but I have seen prominent people from countries which boast about being among the best informed in the world, or countries which have access to the most advanced information media, and yet their citizens are completely disinformed, they know nothing about the world, and some even have university degrees. They cannot read, they cannot study.

We often send documents to important people in the hope that their assistants will read them; we give them to the assistants as well. We can hardly ever be sure that they have had time to read an important piece of information in line with their political interests; but what is worse, often not even the assistants read them.

I am telling you about experiences that we have had to live through. They do not have enough time to study, they cannot read, swept up in a whirlpool of activities which often boils down to nothing more than spending their entire time, every free day, going around from house to house, knocking on the voters' doors. Any sense of national interest? Very little! The speeches made by each of the representatives from some of these countries, and the attitudes they display are about nothing other than the defense of the interests of the ethnic group, or the economic group, or the social group based in their electoral district.

We have always told our deputies that they must defend the interests of the district that elected them but that they must always defend, above all else, the nation's best interests, so that it is not a question of "I am concerned with this place, and nothing else matters to me."

Today, on the eve of the [Ibero-American] Summit, we are saying that what we are least concerned about is our own interests, and we have discussed the documents based on our concern for the interests of others; and more than that, for the collective interests of our region, of Latin America and the Caribbean. There is no doubt that globalization exists, the world is inevitably moving in that direction. What is it going to be like? That will very much depend on how clear we are now and what we are capable of achieving today.

What can we offer you? We can strongly urge you not to be discouraged by anything or anybody; we can strongly urge you not to be intimidated by the overwhelming power of the bosses in the press agencies and the media, that nowadays are not just national, but are often transnational, and which threaten integrity; and above all, they threaten the culture of every country in the world, as a major instrument of domination.

13

Third World Must Unite or Die

Opening of the South Summit, Havana

Never before has humanity had such formidable scientific and technologic potential, such extraordinary capacity to produce riches and well-being, but never before have disparity and inequity been so profound in the world.

Technological wonders that have been shrinking the planet in terms of communications and distances coexist today with the increasingly wider gap separating wealth and poverty, development and underdevelopment.

Globalization is an objective reality underlining the fact that we are all passengers on the same vessel — this planet where we all live. But passengers on this vessel are traveling in very different conditions.

A trifling minority is traveling in luxurious cabins furnished with the internet, cell phones and access to global communication networks. They enjoy a nutritional, abundant and balanced diet as well as clean water supplies. They have access to sophisticated medical care and culture.

The overwhelming and suffering majority is traveling in conditions that resemble the terrible slave trade from Africa to America in our colonial past. That is, 85 percent of the passengers on this ship are crowded together in its dirty hold, suffering hunger, disease and helplessness.

Obviously, this vessel is carrying too much injustice to remain afloat, pursuing such an irrational and senseless route that it cannot

Fidel Castro gave this speech at the opening session of the South Summit, convened by the Group of 77, Havana, April 12, 2000.

call on a safe port. This vessel seems destined to crash into an iceberg. If that happened, we would all sink with it.

The heads of state and government meeting here, who represent the overwhelming and suffering majority, have not only the right but the obligation to take the helm and correct that catastrophic course. It is our duty to take our rightful place at the helm and ensure that all passengers can travel in conditions of solidarity, equity and justice.

For two decades, the Third World has been repeatedly listening to only one simplistic discourse, while one single policy has prevailed. We have been told that deregulated markets, maximum privatization and the state's withdrawal from economic activity were the infallible principles conducive to economic and social development.

In the last two decades, along this line the developed countries, particularly the United States, the big transnationals who benefit from such policies and the International Monetary Fund have designed the world economic order most hostile to our countries' progress and the least sustainable, in terms of the preservation of society and the environment.

Globalization has been held tight by the patterns of neoliberalism; thus, it is not development that becomes global but poverty; it is not respect for the national sovereignty of our states but the violation of that respect; it is not solidarity amongst our peoples but *sauve-qui-peut* in the unequal competition prevailing in the marketplace. Two decades of so-called neoliberal structural adjustment have left us economic failure and social disaster. It is the duty of responsible politicians to face up to this predicament by taking the indispensable decisions conducive to rescue the Third World from a blind alley.

Economic failure is evident. Under the neoliberal policies, the world economy experienced a global growth between 1975 and 1998 which hardly amounted to half of that attained between 1945 and 1975 with Keynesian market deregulation policies and the state's active participation in the economy.

In Latin America, where neoliberalism has been applied with strict adherence to doctrine, economic growth in the neoliberal stage has not been higher than that attained under the previous state development policies. After World War II, Latin America had no debt, but today we owe almost one trillion dollars. This is the region with the highest per capita debt in the world and also the greatest income difference between the rich and the poor. There are more poor, unemployed and hungry people in Latin America now than at any other time in its history.

Under neoliberalism the world economy has not been growing faster in real terms; however, there is more instability, speculation, external debt and unequal exchange. Likewise, there is a greater tendency to financial crises occurring more often while poverty, inequality and the gap between the wealthy North and the dispossessed South continues to widen.

Crises, instability, turmoil and uncertainty have been the most common words used in the last two years to describe the world economic order. The deregulation that comes with neoliberalism and the liberalization of the capital account have a deeply negative impact on a world economy where speculation booms in hard currency and derivative markets and mostly speculative daily transactions amount to no less than $3 trillion.

Our countries are urged to be more transparent with their information and more effective with bank supervision, but financial institutions like the hedge funds fail to release information on their activities and are absolutely unregulated, conducting operations that exceed all the reserves kept in the banks of the South countries.

In an atmosphere of unrestrained speculation, the movement of short-term capital makes the South countries vulnerable to any external contingency. The Third World is forced to immobilize financial resources and grow indebted to keep hard currency reserves in the hope that they can be used to resist the attack of speculators. Over 20 percent of the capital revenues obtained in the last few years were immobilized as reserves, but they were not enough to resist such attacks as proven by the recent financial crisis in Southeast Asia.

Presently $727 billion from the world central banks' reserves are in the United States. This leads to the paradox that with their reserves the poor countries are offering cheap long-term financing to the wealthiest and most powerful country in the world while such reserves could be better invested in economic and social development.

If Cuba has successfully carried out education, health care, culture, science, sports and other programs, which nobody in the world would question, despite four decades of economic blockade, and revalued its currency seven times in the last five years in relation to the US dollar, it has been thanks to its privileged position as a non-member of the International Monetary Fund.

A financial system that keeps forcibly immobilized such enormous resources, badly needed by the countries to protect themselves from the instability caused by that very system that makes the poor finance the wealthy, should be removed.

The International Monetary Fund is the emblematic organization of the existing monetary system and the United States enjoys veto power over its decisions. As far as the latest financial crisis is concerned, the IMF showed a lack of foresight and a clumsy handling of the situation.

It imposed its conditioning clauses that paralyzed the governments' social development policies thus creating serious domestic hazards and preventing access to the necessary resources when they were most needed. It is high time for the Third World to strongly demand the removal of an institution that neither provides stability to the world economy nor works to deliver preventive funds to the debtors to avoid their liquidity crises; it rather protects and rescues the creditors.

Where are the rationale and the ethic of an international monetary order that allows a few technocrats, whose positions depend on U.S. support, to design in Washington identical economic adjustment programs for implementation in a wide variety of countries to cope with specific Third World problems?

Who takes responsibility when the adjustment programs bring about social chaos, thus paralyzing and destabilizing nations with large human and natural resources, as was the case in Indonesia and Ecuador?

It is of crucial importance for the Third World to work for the removal of that sinister institution, and the philosophy it sustains, to replace it with an international finance regulating body that would operate on a democratic basis and where no one has a right of veto. An institution that would not defend only the wealthy creditors and impose interfering conditions, but would allow the regulation of financial markets to arrest unrestrained speculation.

A viable way to do this would be to establish not a 0.1 percent tax on speculative financial transactions as Mr. Tobin brilliantly proposed, but rather a minimum one percent which would permit the creation of a large indispensable fund — in excess of one trillion dollars every year — to promote a real, sustainable and comprehensible development in the Third World.

The underdeveloped nations' external debt is amazing not only because it is terribly high but also due to its outrageous mechanism of subjugation and exploitation, and the absurd formula offered by the developed countries to cope with it. That debt already exceeds $2.5 trillion and in the present decade it has been increasing more dangerously than in the 1970s. A large part of that new debt can easily change hands in the secondary markets; it is more dispersed now and more difficult to reschedule.

Once again I should repeat what we have been saying since 1985: the debt has already been paid if note is taken of the way it was contracted, the swift and arbitrary increase of the interest rates on the U.S. dollar in the previous decade and the decrease of the basic commodity prices, a fundamental source of revenue for developing countries. The debt continues to feed on itself in a vicious circle where money is borrowed to pay its interests.

Today, it is clearer than ever that the debt is not an economic but a political issue; therefore, it demands a political solution. It is impossible to continue overlooking the fact that the solution to this problem must basically come from those with resources and power, that is, the wealthy countries.

The so-called Heavily Indebted Poor Countries Debt Reduction Initiative exhibits a long name but poor results. It can only be described as a ridiculous attempt at alleviating 8.3 percent of the South countries' total debt; but almost four years after its implementation only four countries among the poorest 33 have completed the process simply to reach the negligible figure of $2.7 billion, which is 33 percent of what the United States spends on cosmetics every year.

Today, the external debt is one of the greatest obstacles to development and a bomb ready to blow up the foundations of the world economy at any time during an economic crisis.

The resources needed for a solution that goes to the root of this problem are not large when compared to the wealth and the expenses of the creditor countries. Just to mention three examples: Every year $800 billion are used to finance weapons and troops, even after the Cold War is over, while no less than $400 billion go into narcotics and an additional one billion into commercial advertising, which is as alienating as narcotics.

As we have said before, sincerely and realistically speaking, the Third World countries external debt is unpayable and uncollectable.

In the hands of the rich countries, world trade is already an instrument of domination, which under neoliberal globalization will become an increasingly useful element to perpetuate and sharpen inequalities as well as a theater for strong disputes among developed countries for control over the present and future markets.

The neoliberal discourse recommends commercial liberalization as the best and only formula for efficiency and development. Accordingly, all nations should remove protection instruments from their domestic markets while the difference in development between countries, no matter how big, would not justify separation from the only way offered without any possible alternative. After hard negotiations in the WTO, the poorest countries have been conceded a narrow time difference for full access to that nefarious system.

While neoliberalism keeps repeating its discourse on the opportunities created by trade openings, the underdeveloped countries' participation in world exports was lower in 1998 than in 1953, that is, 45 years ago. With an area of 3.2 million square miles, a population of 168 million and $51.1 billion in exports during 1998, Brazil is exporting less than the Netherlands with an area of 12,978 square miles, a population of 15.7 million and exports of $198.7 billion that same year. Trade liberalization has essentially consisted in the unilateral removal of protection instruments by the South. Meanwhile, the developed nations have failed to do the same to allow the Third World exports to enter their markets.

The wealthy nations have fostered liberalization in strategic sectors associated to advanced technology where they enjoy enormous advantages that the deregulated markets tend to augment. These are the classic cases of services, information technology, biotechnology and telecommunications.

On the other hand, agriculture and textiles, two particularly significant sectors for our countries, have not even been able to remove the restrictions agreed upon during the Uruguay Round because they are not of interest to developed countries.

In the OECD, the club of the wealthiest, the average tariff applied to manufactured exports from underdeveloped countries is four times higher than that applied to the club member countries. A real wall of non-tariff barriers is thus raised that leaves out the South countries.

Meanwhile, in international trade a hypocritical ultraliberal discourse has gained ground that matches the selective protectionism imposed by the North countries.

The basic commodities are still the weakest link in world trade. In the case of 67 South countries such commodities account for no less than 50 percent of their export revenues.

The neoliberal wave has wiped out the defense schemes contained in the terms of reference for basic commodities. The supreme dictum of the marketplace could not tolerate any distortion, therefore the Basic Commodities Agreements and other defense formulas designed to confront unequal exchange were abandoned. It is for this reason that today the purchasing power of such commodities as sugar, cocoa, coffee and others is 20 percent of what it used to be in 1960; consequently, they do not even cover the production costs.

A special and differentiated treatment of poor countries has been considered not as an elementary act of justice and a necessity that cannot be ignored but as a temporary act of charity. Actually, such differential treatment would not only recognize the enormous differences in development that prevent the use of the same yardstick for the rich and the poor but also a historically colonial past that demands compensation.

The failed [WTO] Seattle meeting showed the tension caused by and the opposition to neoliberal policies in growing sectors of the public opinion, in both South and North countries. The United States presented the Round of Trade Negotiations that should begin in Seattle as a higher step in trade liberalization regardless, or perhaps forgetful, of its own aggressive and discriminatory Foreign Trade Act still in force. That act includes provisions like the "Super-301," a real display of discrimination and threats to apply sanctions to other countries for reasons that range from the assumed opposition of barriers to U.S. products to the arbitrary, deliberate and often cynical qualification that that government decides to give others on the subject of human rights.

In Seattle there was a revolt against neoliberalism. Its most recent precedent had been the refusal to accept the imposition of a Multi-lateral Agreement on Investments. This shows that the aggressive market fundamentalism, which has caused great damage to our countries, has found a strong and deserved world rejection.

In addition to the above-mentioned economic calamities, on occasion the high oil prices significantly contribute to the worsening of conditions in the South countries, which are net importers of that vital resource. The Third World produces about 80 percent of the oil traded worldwide, and 80 percent of that amount is exported to the developed countries.

The wealthy nations can afford to pay any price for the energy they waste to sustain luxurious consumption levels and destroy the environment. The U.S. consumption is 8.1 tons oil equivalent per capita while the Third World consumes an average of 0.8 tons, and the poorest among them only 0.3. When the prices jump abruptly from $12 to $30 a barrel, or more, it has a devastating effect on the Third World nations. This is in addition to the external debt, the negative impact of the low prices of their basic commodities, the financial crises and the unequal terms of reference, which weigh heavily on them. Now, we perceive a similarly devastating situation emerging again among sister South nations.

Petroleum is a universally needed vital commodity, which actually escapes the law of the market. One way or another, the big transnationals or the Third World oil exporting countries that joined together to defend their interests were always able to determine its price.

The low prices mostly benefit the rich countries that waste large amounts of fuel, restrain the search for and the exploitation of new deposits as well as the development of technologies that reduce consumption and protect the environment; and they affect the Third World exporters. On the other hand, high prices benefit the exporters and can be easily handled by the rich but they are harmful and destructive to the economies of a large part of our world.

This is a good example to show that a differential treatment to countries in different stages of development should be an indispensable principle of justice in world trade. It is absolutely unfair that a poor Third World country like Mozambique with $84 per capita GDP needs to pay for such a vital commodity the same price as Switzerland with $43,400 per capita. This is a 516 times higher per capita GDP than that of Mozambique!

The San José Pact, formed 20 years ago by Venezuela and Mexico with a group of small oil-importing countries in the region, set a good precedent of what can and should be done, bearing in mind the particular conditions of every Third World nation in similar circumstances, although avoiding this time any conditions associated with the differential treatment they might receive.

Some countries are not in a position to pay more than $10 a barrel, others no more than $15, and none more than $20. However, the world of the rich countries, prone as it is to big spending and consumerism, can pay over $30 a barrel causing hardly any damage. As they consume 80 percent of the Third World countries' exports, this can easily compensate a price lower than $20 for the rest of the nations.

This could be a concrete and effective way to turn South-South cooperation into a powerful instrument of Third World development. To do otherwise would invite self-destruction.

In a global world where knowledge is the key to development, the technological gap between the North and the South tends to widen with the increasing privatization of scientific research and its results.

The developed countries with 15 percent of the world's population presently concentrate 88 percent of internet users. In the United States alone there are more computers than in the rest of the world put together. These countries control 97 percent of the patents the world over and receive over 90 percent of the international license rights, while for many South countries the exercise of the right to intellectual property is nonexistent. In private research, the lucrative element takes precedence over necessity; the intellectual property rights leave knowledge out of reach for underdeveloped countries and the legislation on patents does not recognize know-how transfer or the traditional property systems, which are so important in the South.

Private research focuses on the needs of the wealthy consumers. Vaccines have become the most efficient technology to keep health-care expenses low since they can prevent diseases with one dosage. However, as they yield low profits they are put aside in favor of medications that require repeated dosages and yield higher benefits.

The new medications, the best seeds and, in general, the best technologies have become commodities whose prices only the rich countries can afford.

The murky social results of this neoliberal race to catastrophe are in sight. In over 100 countries the per capita income is lower than 15 years ago. At the moment, 1.6 billion people are worse off than they were at the beginning of the 1980s. Over 820 million people are under-nourished and 790 million of them live in the Third World. It is estimated that 507 million people living in the South today will not live to see their 40th birthday.

In the Third World countries represented here, two out of every five children suffer from growth retardation and one out of every three is underweight; 30,000 who could be saved are dying every day; two million girls are forced into prostitution; 130 million children do not have access to elementary education and 250 million minors under 15 are bound to work for a living.

The world economic order works for 20 percent of the population but it leaves out, demeans and degrades the remaining 80 percent. We simply cannot accept to enter the next century as the backward, poor and exploited rearguard; the victim of racism and xenophobia, prevented from accessing knowledge and suffering the alienation of our cultures due to the foreign consumer-oriented message globalized by the media.

As for the Group of 77, this is not the time for begging from the developed countries or for submission, defeatism or internecine divisions. This is the time to rescue our fighting spirit, our unity and cohesion in defending our demands.

Fifty years ago we were promised that one day there would no longer be a gap between developed and underdeveloped countries. We were promised bread and justice; but today we have less and less bread and more injustice.

The world can be globalized under the rule of neoliberalism, but it is impossible to rule over billions of people who are hungry for bread and justice.

The pictures of mothers and children under the scourge of droughts and other catastrophes in whole regions of Africa remind us of the concentration camps in Nazi Germany; they bring back memories of stacks of corpses or of moribund men, women and children. Another Nuremberg is required to put on trial the economic order imposed on us, the same that is killing of hunger and preventable or curable diseases more men, women and children every three years than all those killed during the six years of World War II.

We should discuss here what is to be done about that.

In Cuba we usually say: "Homeland or Death!" At this summit of the Third World countries we would have to say: "We either unite and establish close cooperation, or we die!"

14

Abolish the IMF

Closing of the South Summit, Havana

Perhaps after the generous resolution you have just adopted regarding the U.S. economic war against Cuba, without our having requested it, it would be better to say: dear brothers and sisters.

I have been truly impressed by the speeches we have heard here today. Over the course of many hours, I took note of the main ideas expressed by every head of state or government, vice-presidents and other high officials who took the floor.

I have attended many summit meetings, but never before have I seen such a coincidence of opinion among Third World leaders. This shows two things:

Firstly: talent, clear thinking, the ability to elaborate and communicate ideas, and the experience accumulated by the leaders of our countries throughout 40 years, since the inception of the Non-aligned Nations Movement, and later the Group of 77, as many of the peoples represented here achieved independence and we supported each other as free states or as liberation movements.

Secondly: the severity of the crises facing our countries in their efforts to achieve development, and the growing inequality and discrimination they suffer.

The participants here have denounced, one by one, the injustices and calamities that plague our nations and which are a constant source

---

Fidel Castro gave this speech to the closing session of the South Summit in Havana, April 14, 2000.

of concern to us all. Every single speaker alluded to the debt tragedy that limits our resources for economic and social development in a thousand different ways.

There was practically unanimous agreement on the view that the benefits of globalization extend to only 20 percent of the world's population, at the expense of the other 80 percent, while the gap between the wealthy countries and the marginalized world grows increasingly wider.

There was also a unanimous approach to the need for a transformation of both the United Nations and the international financial system.

One way or another, every delegation expressed the view that unequal and unfair trade is decimating the Third World's export revenues through tariff and non-tariff barriers that deprive it of the minimum amount required to pay off debts and achieve sustainable economic and social development.

Equally unanimous was the complaint that scientific and technical development, currently monopolized by the privileged club of wealthy countries, remains beyond our reach; it is the wealthy countries that control the research centers, hold almost 100 percent of patents, and increasingly hinder our access to know-how and technology. Quite a few leaders of the South took it upon themselves to remind us of something that is barely mentioned in the neoliberal manuals on economics: the shameless theft of the most highly qualified minds of the Third World. The North countries are appropriating them because the South cannot offer enough research centers, and much less the high salaries that draw these minds to the consumer societies, which did not spend a penny on training them. In addition, many of the outstanding young people from the Third World studying at universities in the former colonial powers or other wealthy countries do not return home after graduation.

Many of our world leaders used truly overwhelming figures and statistics to reflect the sum total of accumulated financial obligations and the brutal mockery at dozens of the poorest countries, of which only four have been targeted for a slight relief. There is a clearly resounding clamor for the Third World's debt to be considerably reduced if it cannot be completely cancelled, which is what would be most fair and equitable because the peoples have paid it off many times over in the course of centuries past and present.

Many of our colleagues have addressed the need to establish fiscal obligations on various activities in order to finance development.

Cuba has sustained, and steadfastly insists, that a one percent tax on all speculative operations would suffice to finance the development of the Third World. Pay no attention to those who claim that it would be impossible. The technical resources and know-how currently available would make it perfectly possible.

When one hears the participants at this summit describe the billions of people who receive less than two dollars, less than one dollar or only a few cents with which to survive, one might come to believe that our planet is devoid of even the slightest sense of humanity. Nobody could have imagined that after the revolution for liberty, equality and fraternity over 200 years ago, the recently concluded century of accelerated industrialization and the great breakthroughs in communications, science and the productivity of human labor we would be discussing the hundreds of millions of people who are going hungry, malnourished, illiterate, unemployed and suffering from disease, in addition to the colossal numbers of children who are undersized or underweight for their age, who have no access to schools or medical care, or who are forced to work at grueling and low-paying jobs, not to mention infant mortality rates that are sometimes over 20 times higher than in the wealthy nations. These are the permanent human rights reserved for us. Fixed in our memories, as a symbol of our era, is the figure of 36 million people in the world infected with AIDS, of which 26 million live in the African continent, as indicated by the secretary general of the United Nations; medical treatment for them would require $10,000 per person per year. And, in the next 12 months, another six million newly infected people will engross this figure.

Why does all of this happen? How much longer will it last?

One way or another, practically everyone here expressed their expectations about this summit.

Never before have I seen such awareness. Let us hope that we are as aware of our combined strength as we are of the pettiness and the injustices we suffer.

Perhaps in the future people will speak in terms of before and after the first South Summit. It is up to us to make it happen.

People used to talk about apartheid in Africa. Today, we can talk about apartheid throughout the world where more than four billion people are deprived of the most basic rights of human beings: the right to life, to health, to education, to clean water, to food, to housing, to employment, to hope for their future and that of their children. At the rate we are going, we will soon be deprived even of the air we breathe, increasingly poisoned by the wasteful consumer societies that pollute the elements essential for life and destroy human habitat. Natural disasters like those that have affected Central America, Venezuela, Mozambique and many other countries — almost all of them in the Third World and all in the course of barely 18 months — were completely unprecedented in the 20th century. They took the lives of thousands of people. These are the consequences of climatic changes and the destruction of nature; the blame cannot be laid upon those of us gathered here to fight not only for universal standards of justice but also for the preservation of life on the planet.

The wealthy world pretends to ignore that slavery, colonialism and the brutal exploitation and plunder to which our countries were subjected for centuries are the causes of underdevelopment and poverty. They look upon us as inferior nations. They attribute the poverty we suffer to the inability of African, Asian, Caribbean and Latin American peoples, that is, of dark and yellow skin, indigenous and mixed-race peoples to achieve any degree of development or even to govern ourselves. They speak of our flaws as if it were not they themselves who impregnated our pure and noble ancestral peoples with the vices of the colonizers or the exploiters.

They also pretend to ignore that when Europe was populated by those whom the Roman empire called barbarians, there were civilizations in China, India, the Far East, the Middle East and north and central Africa that had created what are still known today as the Wonders of the World and that had developed written languages before the Greeks learned to read and Homer wrote *The Iliad*. In our own hemisphere, the Mayans and pre-Incan civilizations had attained knowledge that still today continues to astound the world. I am firmly convinced that the current economic order imposed by the wealthy countries is not only cruel, unjust, inhuman and contrary to the inevitable course of history but also inherently racist. It reflects racist conceptions like those that once inspired the Nazi holocaust and concentration camps of Europe, mirrored today in the so-called refugee camps of the Third World, which actually serve to concentrate the effects of poverty, hunger and violence. These are the same racist conceptions that inspired the monstrous system of apartheid in Africa.

At this summit, our reflections were aimed at building unity, accumulating forces, strategies, tactics and the means to coordinate and guide our efforts to ensure that our vital economic rights are recognized. But this summit also reflects our obligation to fight for our dignity, our culture and our right to be treated as equals.

In the same way that, in the not-so-distant past, we defeated colonialism and attained the status of independent countries, and much more recently crushed the heinous and fascist apartheid system through the common efforts of the Third World in support of the heroic South African fighters, we can show that we are not inferior to anyone when it comes to fighting capacity, bravery, talent and virtue.

We are fighting for the most sacred rights of the poor countries; but we are also fighting for the salvation of a First World incapable of preserving the existence of the human species, of governing itself in the midst of contradictions and self-serving interests and much less of governing the world whose leadership must be democratically shared.

This is only way that we can prevent the ship, of which I spoke in my welcoming address, from colliding with the iceberg that could sink us all. This is only way that we can look forward to life and not death.

Books on Latin America from Ocean Press

CHE GUEVARA READER
Writings on Guerrilla Strategy, Politics and Revolution
Edited by David Deutschmann
The most complete selection of Guevara's writings, letters and speeches available in English. As the most authoritative collection to date of the work of Guevara, this book is an unprecedented source of primary material on Cuba and Latin America in the 1950s and 1960s.
ISBN 1-875284-93-1

JOSE MARTI READER
Writings on the Americas
An outstanding new anthology of the writings, letters and poetry of one of the most brilliant Latin American leaders of the 19th century.
ISBN 1-875284-12-5

SALVADOR ALLENDE READER
Chile's Voice of Democracy
Edited with an introduction by James D. Cockcroft
This new book makes available for the first time in English Allende's voice and vision of a more democratic, peaceful and just world.
ISBN 1-876175-24-9

LATIN AMERICA: FROM COLONIZATION TO GLOBALIZATION
Noam Chomsky in conversation with Heinz Dieterich
An indispensable book for those interested in Latin America and the politics and history of the region.
ISBN 1-876175-13-3

CUBA – TALKING ABOUT REVOLUTION
Conversations with Juan Antonio Blanco by Medea Benjamin
One of Cuba's outstanding intellectuals discusses Cuba today, featuring an essay, "Cuba: 'socialist museum' or social laboratory?"
ISBN 1-875284-97-7

CUBA AND THE UNITED STATES
A Chronological History
By Jane Franklin
This chronology relates in detail the developments involving the two neighboring countries from the 1959 revolution through 1995.
ISBN 1-875284-92-3

Also from Ocean Press

FIDEL CASTRO READER
The voice of one of the 20th century's most controversial political
figures — as well as one of the world's greatest orators — is captured
in this new selection of Castro's key speeches over 40 years.
ISBN 1-876175-11-7

MY EARLY YEARS
By Fidel Castro
In the twilight of his life, Fidel Castro reflects on his childhood, youth
and student days, describing his family background and the religious
and moral influences that led to his early involvement in politics.
Introductory essay by Gabriel García Márquez
ISBN 1-876175-07-9   *Also available in Spanish (1-876175-16-8)*

CUBAN REVOLUTION READER
A Documentary History
Edited by Julio García Luis
An outstanding anthology presenting a comprehensive overview of
Cuban history and documenting the past four decades, highlighting 40
key moments in the Cuban Revolution up to the present day.
ISBN 1-876175-10-9   *Also available in Spanish (ISBN 1-876175-28-1)*

CHE — A MEMOIR BY FIDEL CASTRO
Preface by Jesús Montané
For the first time Fidel Castro writes with candor and affection of his
relationship with Ernesto Che Guevara, documenting his extraordinary bond with Cuba from the revolution's early days to the final
guerrilla expeditions to Africa and Bolivia.
ISBN 1-875284-15-X

WASHINGTON ON TRIAL
Cuba's $181 billion claim against the U.S. government for war crimes
Introduced by Michael Ratner and David Deutschmann
ISBN 1-876175-23-0

Ocean Press, GPO Box 3279, Melbourne 3001, Australia
● Fax: 61-3-9329 5040 ● E-mail: edit@oceanpress.com.au

Ocean Press, PO Box 834, Hoboken, NJ 07030, USA
● Fax: 1-201-617 0203

Website: www.oceanpress.com.au